RATS' TALES

The Staffordshire Regiment at War in the Gulf

This book is dedicated to the memory of Shaun Taylor, Carl Moult and Dean Oliver.

RATS' TALES

The Staffordshire Regiment at War in the Gulf

NICHOLAS BENSON

BRASSEY'S
LONDON * NEW YORK

UK editorial offices: Brassey's, 165 Great Dover Street, London SE1 4YA
orders: Marston Book Services, P.O. Box 87, Oxford OX2 0DT

USA orders: Macmillan Publishing Company, Front and Brown Streets, Riverside, NJ 08075

Distributed in North America to booksellers and wholesalers by the Macmillan Publishing Company, NY 10022

First English edition 1993

Library of Congress Cataloging in Publication Data
Available

British Library Cataloguing in Publication Data
A catalogue record for this book is available from the British Library

ISBN 1–85753–060–8 Hardcover

Printed in Great Britain by BPCC Wheatons Ltd, Exeter

Contents

Foreword by HRH Duke of York

I became the Colonel in Chief of the Staffordshire Regiment in 1989. It was at the summer ball the next year that I first heard of the idea that the Regiment might go to the Gulf because of the performance the Brigade had shown at BATUS. When the order came that the 7th Armoured Brigade was to deploy to the Gulf I had an opportunity to visit the Regiment during their preparations. The thing that struck me most was the determination and certainty that there was a job to be done if, after every avenue had been explored and had failed, they were called upon to fight.

The sad fact was, we had to go to war, and we were called upon to do the job we had been deployed to do. The conduct and professionalism of the Regiment throughout the deployment was exemplary. The gallantry and courage shown by everyone has also been recognised in the various awards to the Regiment.

This book is a regimental history in a complete sense because it takes as its sources soldiers from throughout the Regiment and their experiences during the campaign. It provides an excellent insight into the attitudes and skills of the highly trained and professional soldiers in the Army. The descriptions of how inhospitable the weather can be in the desert, and how large scale encounters with an enemy are fought on the modern less dense battlefield in complex combat vehicles, makes fascinating reading.

It may be that the Gulf War, as we know it, will be the last campaign fought by the Staffordshire Regiment in its own name; it is a glorious ending and a stepping stone to the future. I will conclude this foreword by expressing my pride in the achievements of the Regiment throughout its history and in its contribution to a decisive and brilliantly executed victory in the desert.

Andrew

Tribute by General Sir Norman Schwarzkopf KCB

Dear Soldiers and Families of the Staffordshire Regiment,

It is indeed a privilege to have this opportunity to express my appreciation for your superb service during the liberation of Kuwait.

Your many months training in the harsh environment of the Saudi Arabian Desert fully prepared you for the monumental task we faced. The American Soldiers and Marines who trained and conducted operations at your side will never forget your comradeship and professionalism.

Those of us who served will be forever grateful to the families we left behind. We would not have been as successful as we were without your continuous support. The letters and parcels we received were constant reminders of your love and faith.

I wish each of you my very best wishes in all future endeavors. I am deeply grateful and proud to have served with you.

Sincerely,

H. Norman Schwarzkopf
General, U.S. Army
Commander in Chief

Acknowledgements

This book was not prepared on a large budget, and I am particularly grateful to Roger Rudman of Midland Dictating Equipment who lent me transcribing machines over a long period for a nominal sum. Similar thanks must also go to Grahame Foster of Fosters, Lichfield, who hired me a computer at short notice and again for a very small sum. All the staff at Brassey's (UK) have been most helpful, but special thanks are due to Jenny Shaw who placed her faith in me from the outset and who has been available throughout when I have needed advice.

I would like to thank the following individuals for supplying photographs: Private Ian Burns (1st Battalion photographer), Major John Rochelle, WO II Nigel Whitehouse, WO I R.S.M. Huyton, Robert and Vicky Lane, and LSGT Dillon.

I have been greatly assisted in the writing of this book by the members of two families. From my own family I am indebted to my sister Hilary, who was my research assistant during the initial stages and who conducted most of the interviews with the soldiers' families and the personnel who remained in Fallingbostel during the War. I could not have gathered so much material in such a short space of time without her, and her subsequent advice and comments have been extremely helpful. My father, Tony, undertook the time-consuming tasks of proof-reading the manuscript chapter by chapter as it was written, and casting a critical civilian eye over it. His comments were invaluable. I must also give a special thank you to my wife, Liz, who tolerated my late night sessions at the keyboard and my endless discussions about the book with her usual good humour and forbearance.

The other family of which I am proud to be a member is the Regimental family. The book could not have been written without their support. In particular, I would like to thank the Colonel of the Regiment, Major-General Ian Freer, who backed me from the outset, Captain Nick Foster, without whose encouragement during the very early days I would probably not have continued, and Major Mac MacLean and all the staff at Regimental Headquarters who put up with me during the summer and fed me endless cups of coffee. Special thanks go to Major Jim Tanner, who spent a considerable amount of his spare time drawing the excellent maps which appear in the book. Major (now Lieutenant Colonel) Simon Knapper deserves a mention for suggesting the title; the double pun will be appreciated by military readers. Everyone I interviewed was most accommodating, but none more so than the families of Carl Moult and Shaun Taylor. They spoke to me at a time when their losses were still very recent, and I am most grateful for their candour and hospitality. Finally, I must thank all the soldiers and their families who allowed themselves to be interviewed for this book. It is their story and it would not have been possible without their cooperation.

Introduction

When, in the summer of 1990, Saddam Hussein first started to make belligerent overtones towards Kuwait, few Britons could have thought that his posturing would eventually result in the largest deployment of British military forces since the Korean War. Few people could accurately place Kuwait on a map of the Middle East, and even fewer could have explained the political, social and economic circumstances which were to lead to the invasion of Kuwait by Iraqi forces. I had just retired from the Army after ten years of service with the Staffords, and I had few regrets about leaving as I prepared to spend the next two years as a student.

As the events of the summer unfolded, it became increasingly obvious that the British would join the Americans and their other allies in sending some military presence to Saudi Arabia to counter the threat of continued Iraqi expansionism in the Middle East. Many of my serving colleagues presumed that a small, lightly equipped force capable of rapid deployment would be chosen: most bets were being placed on the Royal Marines or the Parachute Regiment.

But as the situation developed, the option of sending an armoured contingent was more and more widely discussed. The only British armoured formations were based in Germany, and 7 Armoured Brigade, of which the Staffords formed the infantry element, was the obvious choice. They were fully equipped with the latest armoured fighting vehicles; Challenger tanks in the tank regiments and Warriors in the Staffords.

No soldier would be surprised to hear that the Staffords were jubilant when it was confirmed that they had been selected to go. This was the purpose for which every professional soldier serves. For my part, I was very disappointed that I had decided to leave the Army just a couple of months previously, but I had made my bed and could do nothing more than follow the events of the next six months with massive interest.

With the succesful conclusion of the campaign and the return of the Staffords, I took every opportunity to meet up with old friends and spend hours avidly listening to their tales, asking questions about every aspect of their particular war. It was clear to me that, as a battle group, they had probably seen more action than any other British infantry, and had been in the vanguard of the advance of the British 1st Armoured Division. The stories they told were what I had expected to hear, but didn't reflect what the British public had learned from the intense international media coverage. The television sets and newspapers were full of pictures and stories about the high-technology aspects of this war – Smart bombs, Cruise missiles, Stealth bombers – but there was relatively little accurate reporting of what it was like for the men at the sharp end who ultimately had to get out of their vehicles and confront the enemy face to face.

With a long summer vacation looming, an idea began to form that I could somehow record these stories and experiences while they were still fresh in the minds of the men who had been so involved. It would give me the perfect excuse for discussing the war at some length, thus satisfying my appetite for the vicarious experience. It would also be an opportunity to convey to the reader something of the style and procedures of a modern, 'unglamourous', infantry line regiment. There was no thought to profit from the experiences of my colleagues and the royalties from the sale of this book will go to Regimental charities to help soldiers in financial need.

With my exams on the horizon, I sketched out a synopsis based on what I had heard so far and then discussed the idea with the Commanding Officer of the 1st Battalion and the Colonel of the Regiment. They were extremely supportive, and with their backing I visited the Staffords in Fallingbostel in June 1991 with a research assistant, and spent two weeks interviewing anyone and everyone who was willing to talk to me, day and night. Back in England, I spent another ten days interviewing relatives of these soldiers and others who had since been posted back to England. I also spoke to the senior commanders, Brigadier Patrick Cordingley and General Sir Peter de la Billière. By the end of June I had over 150 hours of taped interviews and boxes full of other material: maps, diaries, letters, and photographs which I had been given or lent.

The book was written between July and October 1991, and was a time-consuming but fascinating task. From the outset I had seen the book as being a montage of the Staffords' role in the campaign, made up of a collection of snapshots represented by the extracts from the soldiers' interviews and other material. I had never doubted that the whole would be more interesting if, as far as possible, the tale was told in the soldiers' own words, and I hope this is what I have achieved. As a commentator, I have attempted to be as objective as possible and have intended from the outset that the book will portray the Battalion, 'warts and all'. It is not a eulogy and it does not paint the Battalion as whiter than white. But having spent so much time concentrating on these men, I feel it does accurately depict them and the experiences they underwent.

When I started work on this project, Options For Change, the Government's defence review, had been suspended because of the Gulf War. When it was resurrected in the summer of 1991 few people imagined that the Staffords would suffer the cruel fate of being selected for amalgamation. When this was in fact announced, a massive campaign got underway in an attempt to try to save the Regiment. Unfortunately this appears to have failed, so Operation GRANBY will probably be the last large scale operation in which the Staffordshire Regiment will have served. The name of the Regiment will live on, and its battle honours will adorn the colours of the amalgamated Staffordshire and Cheshire Regiment. Future historians will no doubt write a more detailed epitaph for the Staffords, but as a swansong, their performance in the Gulf has upheld the proud traditions of a brave and glorious Regiment.

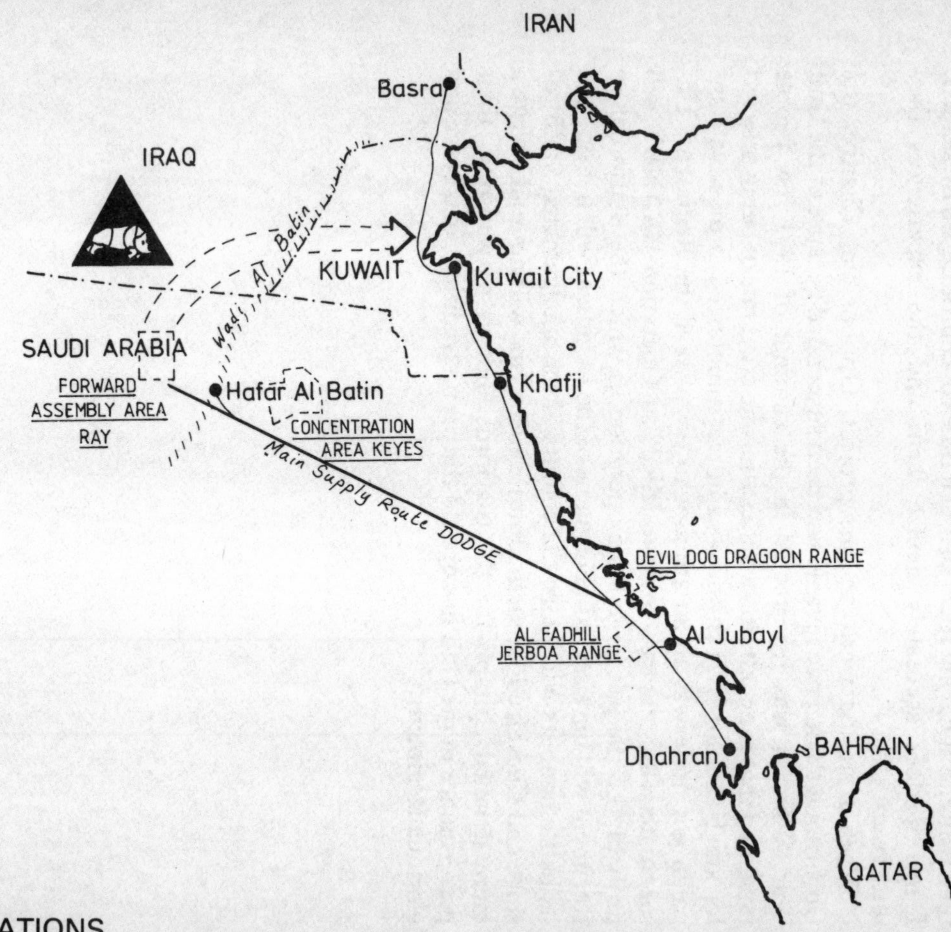

THE THEATRE OF OPERATIONS
SHOWING THE ROUTE OF THE 1ST
ARMOURED DIVISION

ORDER OF BATTLE

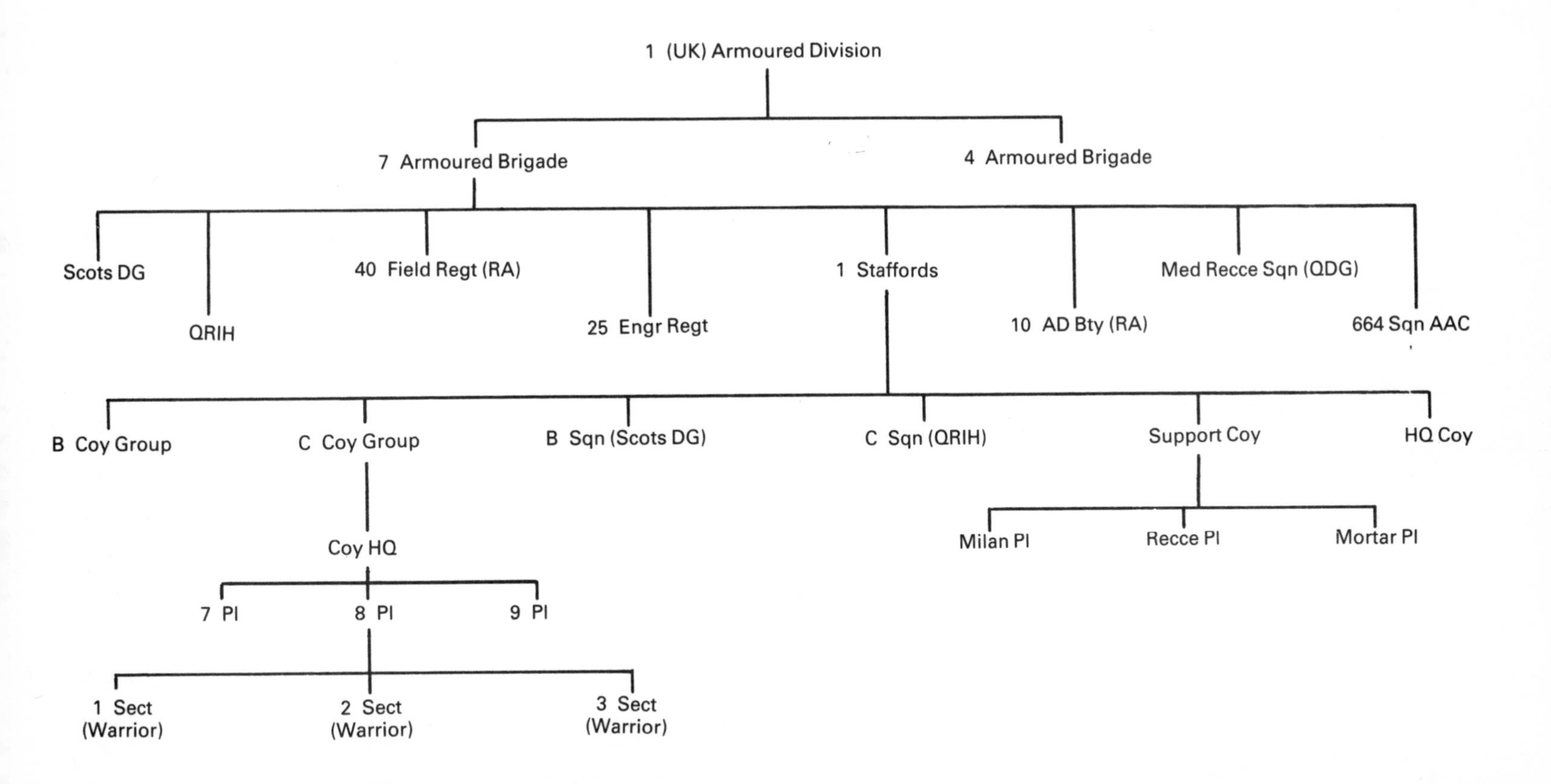

1

Peacetime Training

'We just trained bloody hard and we trained for war.'

'When we went into the attack that night we knew things were going well overall, but we didn't appreciate then that it was to become a total rout of the Iraqi Army. We firmly believed that we were up against a strong, defended position, and we could take heavy casualties.

'It wasn't a pre-planned attack. We knew that there was a communications site in that area and we knew that our battle group had been tasked to clear it. As we advanced into the area, the tanks of the Scots DG began to pick up the extent of the position on their TOGS [night sights]. As they advanced they were able to pick out the radio mast, and we knew that there were going to be bunkers and other positions around it. The whole area was quite clearly still occupied and therefore we went into a quick attack on it.

'The Iraqis must have known we were out there but no artillery was called down on us. It was a particularly unpleasant night; it was raining quite heavily, visibility was so poor that you couldn't see something the size of a Warrior at 15 metres with the naked eye. It was absolutely black. When we lined up on the start line the company could see nothing. I had climbed into a tank to look at the position through TOGS, and after that at least I knew the tanks in front of me could see where we were going. Normally our artillery would prepare the target and illuminate it, but we didn't want to reveal ourselves.

'The attack itself was brilliant, quite brilliant. All the drills worked even though it was pitch black, pouring with rain. There was a main command site and then off to the right hand side an area of bunkers and trenches. I'd given 1 Platoon the command site itself and 3 Platoon the bunker location. I held 2 Platoon in reserve at the start. I literally had to describe it to them, and allocate objectives, over the radio.

'Thirty seconds before H Hour the tanks opened fire, destroying the vehicles and generator. The funny thing I remember about the generator was that even though it had been hit and was on fire it was still chugging away under its smouldering cam net. Once the vehicles started burning we had a reference point to aim for. The run-in worked very well. The tanks led us to exactly the right places and in the last 300 metres, the Warriors broke forward of the protective screen of tanks, and opened up with their chain guns. We debussed the men on site. I followed the troop commander's tank in, in the middle of the two forward platoons.

'1 Platoon had nothing on the first position but there was stuff they could see in depth, so we then moved 2 Platoon in to take on the depth position. We had this constant debussing and re-embussing. I re-embussed 1 Platoon and then put them in to the right where they took on the command bunker and cleared that. Then we re-embussed 3 Platoon from their first position and put them in down the centre. All the time there was this incredible noise of firing; cannon fire and small arms and tracer was bouncing everywhere. It seemed impossible that none of the Company had been hit yet. By the time 3 Platoon came in with their tank we had another tank and one of the Milan wagons grouped together with some Warriors, putting fire support onto that position as the platoon ran in. It was during that attack that 3 Platoon suffered the Company's only casualties of the entire operation who were wounded by grenade fragments. That's how it worked. And it did work extremely well.

'As somebody identified another enemy position what we would then do was say, right, put fire down on it now, put tracer on it now. Then you'd see tracer go off in the dark, and you'd see where it was striking and roughly where they were firing from. Then you'd confirm that it was them who had just fired and say right, was anyone taking rounds, did anyone take that tracer? Once we'd confirmed that we were not doing a blue on blue we then went in. Obviously some of the assaults were fairly tight. It was a massive concern for me. The potential at night of running one platoon into the back of another one in a live assault is enormous.

'And of course, there were Warriors and tanks and Milan vehicles milling around; but there was also enemy armour, and there was a constant concern that you were going to engage one of your own vehicles. We kept the Warriors grouped fairly centrally. Milan had total free-fire, they could fire at anything they identified as a target, and the tanks could as well. The tanks were concerned about using too much main armament ammunition in this first encounter; they were saving it for what was believed to be the main threat: the Republican Guard T72s. In some cases, the tanks were identifying soft skinned vehicles by putting tracer down on them, and the soldiers were engaging them with the Rarden cannon or small arms.

'I am very proud of what the Company achieved that night. It was the first armoured infantry attack of the war, and it worked.'

This was how Major Simon Knapper described the assault by A Company and the tanks of the Royal Scots Dragoon Guards upon objective Copper during the night of 25 February 1991, the first major British engagement of the war.

It was G+1, 36 hours since elements of VII (US) Corps had breached the Iraqi berm and minefields and secured a bridgehead for 7 Armoured Brigade, the original Desert Rats, to break out through. Their task was to close with and destroy the Iraqi tactical reserve formations along their route, which struck deep into southern Iraq before swinging east towards Kuwait. The British 1st Armoured Division was to be led by 7 Armoured Brigade and the Staffords provided the infantry element of this formation, complementing the Challenger tanks of both the Queens Royal Irish Hussars and the Royal Scots Dragoon Guards. Not only was the action on objective Copper the first British assault on dug-in Iraqi troops during the war, it was also the first ever armoured infantry assault carried out by the British Army.

To be able to appreciate the role and capabilities of the Staffords in the Gulf War, it is helpful to understand the tactical and technical foundation of the armoured infantry battalion. Before the delivery of the Warrior fighting vehicle to selected infantry battalions only three years earlier, the infantry were very much the poor relations on the battlefield, trundling around in the FV432 armoured personnel carrier, which is little more than a battlefield taxi. Its armour gives the fighting soldier a degree of protection from small arms fire and shrapnel but, unlike the Warrior with its 30 millimetre calibre Rarden cannon and coaxially mounted chain gun, it has no effective integral weapons system capable of giving intimate support to its troops as they debus to close with the enemy on the ground. Warrior also boasts much improved armour, which had been further enhanced by the addition of Chobham armour plates to the hull during the build-up phase of Operation DESERT SABRE.

The advent of Warrior revolutionised tactical thought among the infantry and the other 'teeth arms' which work so closely with them. No longer were the infantry simply 'mechanised' which suggested a degree of mobility and little more; they were now to be known as 'armoured infantry'. Implicit in that phrase was the increased protection and firepower Warrior gave to a battalion. It was no longer essential for soldiers to debus from their vehicles out of sight or range of enemy weapons. Warrior accorded a hitherto unavailable aggressive option to infantry commanders, allowing them, if the circumstances dictated, to drive to the very edge of the leading enemy trenches before debussing their troops. The vehicle's firepower was available to give dedicated and intimate support to its occupants when they were on the ground.

For the Staffords, the opportunity to test these concepts and further develop skills already acquired in Germany came with their deployment to the prairies of Canada in the summer of 1990 to take part in the 'Medicine Man' series of exercises. They trained there unaware of the impending invasion of Kuwait by the Iraqi forces, or of their own consequent role in the liberation of the small Arab state. Many soldiers and officers would scarcely have been able to point out Kuwait on a map of the Middle East during this hot summer training period.

Participation in Exercise Medicine Man is a common event in the training cycle of any British tank regiment or infantry battalion based in Germany as part of the British Army of the Rhine (BAOR). The training area is established in the province of Alberta in western Canada and is centred on the Canadian forces base of Suffield, which lies some

250 kilometres south-east of Calgary. It is known to all who have been there as BATUS (British Army Training Unit Suffield).

The area has been used since 1972 by the British and Canadian Armies to train armoured formations of battle group size; that is anything up to 1,000 men, 130 armoured vehicles, and a large fleet of wheeled support vehicles. In addition the battle group receives support from Army Air Corps Gazelle helicopters, Royal Artillery M109 howitzers, armoured and field engineer troops with their plant and supporting vehicles, and the indispensable repair and recovery services of the Royal Electrical and Mechanical Engineers. The Medicine Man exercises are controlled by a permanent team of British Army officers and soldiers based at Suffield, and run from May to October each year. Outside these dates the severe winter weather precludes any worthwhile training. Each exercise lasts for approximately four weeks, and so seven battle groups can be exercised each year.

The advantage of undertaking such a costly and lengthy move from Germany is the ability to train with relatively little restriction on the movement of armour across country. In Germany it is no longer environmentally nor politically acceptable to exercise large formations across the agricultural North German Plain in the manner of the 1970s and early 1980s. To these considerations must be added the huge amounts paid out in compensation to landowners, which proved to be a more effective limitation on movement than any obstacle on the ground; so although limited exercises are still carried out in Germany, BATUS is the option favoured by most commanders.

Another crucial advantage offered by BATUS is the ability to exercise with live ammunition. The training area is both unpopulated and vast, which means the troops can fire all their weapons with live ammunition within a realistic tactical scenario. Whilst the emphasis is very much on developing the confidence and awareness of responsibility of the individual soldier in the use of his weapon, be it the SA 80 rifle or the spectacular Giant Viper minefield breacher, a detailed set of safety rules is observed in order to prevent accidents.

An armoured infantry battalion based in Germany is approximately 750 men strong. Its basic fighting units are the three rifle companies, each of which consists of a company headquarters and three rifle platoons. A platoon is approximately 34 men strong and is commanded by a subaltern (lieutenant or second lieutenant) with an experienced sergeant as his second-in-command. The platoon operates from four Warriors, one for each section of 10 men and one for the platoon headquarters. Working in support of the rifle companies are three specialist platoons: Reconnaissance, Mortars and Anti-Tank (the latter normally referred to as the Milan Platoon, after the weapon system it employs). These are deployed and grouped by the Commanding Officer according to the operational requirements and perceived enemy threat. Logistic back-up at battalion level is provided by the Quartermaster's department, who supply everything from vehicle spares to clothing, ammunition and water. The essential items in wartime are fuel, ammunition, water and rations, and are always referred to as combat supplies. The Motor Transport (MT) department provides all the wheeled transport for the movement of supplies: the eight tonne Bedford lorry is the primary vehicle used for this purpose. There are many other smaller departments within the battalion operating in supporting roles; even the bandsmen have a vital wartime role as medics, for which they are fully trained.

Modern concepts of armoured warfare emphasise the need for mixed groupings of tanks, infantry and other supporting arms to fight together, each benefitting from the other's particular strength or skill. It is a symbiotic blend, and it would be unthinkable for an infantry battalion to operate in isolation when set against an armoured enemy. Similarly, a tank regiment without integral infantry support may be an effective force when advancing against enemy armour, but it cannot deal effectively with dismounted enemy infantry. These requirements have lead to the development of the battle group, which is the formation adopted on operations.

The structure of a battle group in war is dictated by the prevailing operational requirements, and is infinitely flexible. It is always based on the headquarters of either an infantry battalion or a tank regiment, which commands a core element of tank squadrons and infantry companies supported by detachments of various other teeth arms and logistic supporting units. These will normally include artillery forward observation officers (FOOs) to direct supporting artillery fire, and field and armoured engineers to clear routes, breach minefields and other obstacles, and assist with the laying of defensive minefields when necessary.

During Operation DESERT SABRE, the fighting nucleus of the Staffords Battle Group was formed around B and C Companies of the Staffords, B Squadron of the Scots Dragoon Guards and C Squadron of the Queens Royal Irish Hussars. This blend of tanks and infantry was under the operational control of the Commanding Officer of the Staffords. A Company of the Staffords was attached to the Scots

Dragoon Guards Battle Group and controlled by their Commanding Officer to provide his tank regiment with an infantry element.

In BATUS the battle groups are formed before departure for Canada, and so in June 1990 1 Staffords Battle Group on Exercise Medicine Man 2 consisted of B and C Companies with two squadrons of tanks from the Scots Dragoon Guards. A Company took part in Exercise Medicine Man 3 in July 1991 as the infantry element of the Scots Dragoon Guards Battle Group. The Commanding Officer of the Staffords, Lieutenant Colonel Charles Rogers, thought this was significant:

'During the summer the whole [Staffords] Battle Group got itself together and trained together. This was useful in that we all knew each other. During Operation GRANBY, one of the squadrons which was in BATUS with me subsequently came with me during the ground offensive. The battery commander [Royal Artillery] was also with us in BATUS and so were some of the sappers. So we were all individually and collectively extremely well trained and that was probably a significant factor in the choice of 7 Brigade to go.

'I'm quite a fan of BATUS. For the desert environment we found ourselves in, BATUS was actually extremely useful; bare-arsed and featureless which caused considerable map-reading problems. The fact that we had live-fired all our weapons in a reasonably realistic environment with the people with whom we eventually went to the Gulf, I think made a lot of difference.'

Although the emphasis at BATUS is on training at the tactical level of command, the exercises are tailored to suit the particular role of the battle group within the formation in which it operates in war time. The Staffords were part of 7 Armoured Brigade, which in peacetime is based around the towns of Fallingbostel and Soltau, lying almost equidistantly between Hamburg and Hanover in Germany. The Brigade is 'armour heavy': there are two tank regiments, which in 1990 were the Royal Scots Dragoon Guards and the Queens Royal Irish Hussars, to one infantry battalion. These major units are all based in Fallingbostel with their supporting REME unit, 7 Armoured Workshop. The Brigade Headquarters and Signal Squadron operate from their barracks in Soltau, and artillery and engineer support comes from the nearby garrison towns of Hohne, Nienberg and Munsterlager.

All these towns lie adjacent or close to the massive Bergen-Hohne NATO Ranges complex, which has facilities for firing all the weapons found in a battle group. The Soltau-Luneburg dry training area to the north-west of the ranges is available for limited armoured exercises using blank ammunition, and it is here that battle groups undergo a work-up exercise before deploying to Canada on Exercise Medicine Man.

The Commander of 7 Armoured Brigade was Brigadier Patrick

Cordingley, a man with a great deal of experience in armoured operations, having served in Germany as a cavalry officer with the British Army for much of his career. He had got to know the Staffords quite well during his term as their brigade commander:

'I was always extremely fond of the Staffords. One of the things that caused this was the fact that they were unruly, and being an infantry battalion, and being the way they are, it was inevitable that every Monday morning there would be a major or minor crisis. Of course, the lovely thing about a county regiment was that you would then send for the Commanding Officer, and you'd give him the most frightful bollocking, and he would immediately defend his soldiers, so you'd got a sort of impasse. If they had had a fight, yet another one, in Fallingbostel, you'd get the Commanding Officer up and he would explain why they should have had a fight!

'There was one incident where a fairly large amount of damage had been caused to one of the accommodation blocks. So you'd get the Commanding Officer up again and say, this has got to cease, and he'd reply, but you can't prove it was Staffords, we had lots of people wandering round, we had hockey teams here over the weekend. So you'd then say, right, if there's another problem I'm going to . . . and you can't think how to punish a battalion. And of course you can't effectively. And actually, secretly, do you really mind? And the answer is, of course you don't, deep down inside, and you respect the Commanding Officer much more for backing up his boys. I did actually threaten to put them all into tents on the Soltau-Luneburg training area for a length of time though.'

Following the rapprochement of East and West Germany, the wartime role of 7 Armoured Brigade along with that of the remainder of BAOR was under review during the summer of 1990. Details of their role prior to this are classified for obvious reasons, but it was well known that the Brigade was trained to operate as a highly mobile force well up in the forefront of allied operations in Central Europe. The re-equipping of the British Army with the Challenger tank and Warrior was programmed, so the Brigade was the first unit of that size to be fully equipped and trained on the new vehicles. As such, it was the obvious choice to go to the Gulf if the political decision was to send a brigade strength contingent.

The only question which could have been raised was that of operational effectiveness. The Staffords and the Scots Dragoon Guards were thoroughly familiar with their vehicles and their role, having been based in Germany for some years, but the Queens Royal Irish Hussars had only arrived in Fallingbostel from England in March and were therefore on a very steep learning curve. As Captain Charles Alexander, Second-in-Command of C Squadron of the Irish Hussars explained:

'We were not due to be operationally effective until 1991. Having been away for two years in England doing a very different job, the physical difficulties of taking over such a quantity of equipment, retraining everybody, and doing the courses that people would have done had we been based in Germany, meant we had a lot of catching up to do. Also we had to get in the necessary amount of range work and work on the Soltau training area. You have got to spend a year to do it all, and this is what we had been given. It was quite amusing, because a few days after the war had ended was the day that we were due to become operational as a regiment in Germany. So we had actually done all the build-up training and the campaign itself and only then, had we been in Germany, would we have been pronounced operational.'

For most soldiers, BATUS is an enjoyable if exhausting training period. At the end of each exercise there is the opportunity for most members of the battle group to get away for R&R; either adventure training in the nearby Rocky Mountains or just relaxing in Calgary or Medicine Hat, the nearest towns of any size. The actual training area is of a scale not seen in Europe, and impressed Private Simon Jones of B Company:

'It's very open, a bit of grass here and there, a couple of hills and just massive. The accommodation in Camp Crowfoot [the base camp] is very basic. You have a big room with perhaps 40 bunk beds in it. There are showers and toilets, but nothing in the rooms except the beds. There is nowhere to put your kit, the odd locker but that's it. It has a good cookhouse which does excellent food, but we spend most of the time out on the training area on compo rations. Those who arrive two weeks early with the advance party get a better time, but they do more work taking the vehicles over and doing whatever jobs are necessary, unloading all the stores and that sort of thing. It's a bit harder on the people who arrive later with the main body, because they've got jet lag and they go practically straight out onto the training area.

'The weather you get depends on when you go. When we went it was very warm one day and then the next day it would be raining all the time. We stop every few days for administration and to sort out the vehicles and then it always rained, but when we were working it was always really hot so you couldn't win either way.'

Not everyone enjoyed BATUS. Private Stuart Burton of C Company thought it was:

'Pretty boring really. All I saw was hills, getting out on top of one hill, going over to another and getting back in the wagon.'

The vehicles used by the battle groups exercising in BATUS are based permanently at the training area. Each battle group sends an advance party to take over the vehicle fleet and carry out routine maintenance in order to get them up to scratch for the exercise. The major disadvantage of this system from 7 Brigade's point of view is that the fleet consists of F432s for the infantry, and Chieftain tanks for the armoured regiments, whereas in Germany they are equipped with Warrior and Challenger. This incompatibility will be resolved when all BAOR units are fully equipped; then additional vehicles will go to

BATUS, but for operational reasons the priority of vehicle allocation was in favour of units over training establishments.

Two significant problems are associated with this inconsistency. Warrior and Challenger drivers have to learn, or in many cases, relearn, how to drive the older vehicles. This is not simply a case of passing a driving test; the driver is responsible for all the basic servicing and daily maintenance carried out on the vehicle, and therefore needs to be familiar with the relevant routines, the tools and equipment necessary for the task.

From a tactical point of view, commanders are faced with a dilemma. The change in armoured tactics brought about by the introduction of Warrior has already been discussed, and commanders have the challenge of trying to apply these tactics whilst operating from vehicles which are slower, less well armed and less well protected. Major Simon Knapper commanding A Company took a pragmatic approach:

'Our preparation started at BATUS. I always believe that you train for war, you don't train for the next exercise, and BATUS itself was training for war. We used the 432s as Warriors. We always worked as armoured infantry. I've always been a great believer that it doesn't matter what a soldier jumps out of, whether it's a Land Rover, a Warrior, a 432, or an aeroplane; if he's a good soldier you can throw him out of anything you like. We looked on that as a sort of philosophy, and we just trained bloody hard and we trained for war. Not for exercise or peace or anything like that – we just trained for war.'

The practical problems of maintaining the petrol-driven 432s devolved upon the Battalion's own REME mechanics, who serve with the Battalion as part of the Light Aid Detachment (LAD), when they were beyond the capability of the driver. Lance Corporal Neil Peacock was a vehicle mechanic with B Company's fitter section:

'From our point of view, BATUS was all extremely hard work. It went very well because although we were constantly working, we kept all the vehicles on the road at all times; and from this point of view the Battle Group was apparently the best for seven years, which was excellent. One thing I will say about the Staffords is that the boys really will muck in. They get involved with the vehicles a lot.

'We coped relatively well with the fact that it was a 432 fleet. You see, all our training was done on 432s, and most of the mechanics have come from units that only have 432s. We had to train up on the Mark I version, being petrol engined, whereas we have been used to diesel engined vehicles. Once we had taken all the vehicles over, we spent a week or so getting to know them before we deployed onto the area. And we had done some additional training in Fallingbostel before we went out, so we had almost reconverted back to the 432.

'It was no problem at all moving back to Warrior for the Gulf, because we have done a lot of exercises with Warrior and the fitter section is very conversant with it now. Warrior is an easier vehicle mechanically to work on; you can lift a power pack out and have a replacement pack in within an hour. It is a much more complex vehicle electrically, and so it's more of an electrician's job really, but being new you don't get an awful lot of problems with it anyway.'

Exercise Medicine Man is actually a series of exercises linked together to allow the battle group to progress from low-level section and platoon training up to company/squadron group and eventually battle group exercises. Before the battle group comes together, the support platoons (anti-tank, mortars and reconnaissance) have the opportunity to hone their individual skills. Sergeant Gino Pulizzi, Platoon Sergeant of 5 Platoon, found the low-level training the most valuable:

'I think BATUS is good for section and platoon level training. When it comes up to company and squadron attacks we spent a lot of time in the back of the vehicles, and I don't think there was a lot of training value for the blokes. They were just cooped up not knowing what was going on outside half the time. As a platoon sergeant the training was very valuable. You are administering your platoon in the field for a long time, issuing ammunition, the lot; you're doing everything that you should do.

'The training we did in BATUS was quite different from the training we did in the Gulf. The enemy tactic in BATUS was to site positions in individual trenches, but in the Gulf we trained against long zig-zag trench systems based on the Soviet doctrine which it was believed the Iraqis would adopt. In the actual war when we deployed we found that a lot of them were similar to those in BATUS, well dug-in bunkers and only a few trench systems.'

The Milan Mobile Section had the chance to work closely with the Reconnaissance Platoon and develop their tactics, particularly those related to movement cross country. Being equipped with the fast but lightly armoured Scimitar, the Recce Platoon have never had an integral anti-armour capability. In the past they have had to rely on the protection of tanks to cover this shortcoming. The arrival in service of the Milan Compact Turret on Spartan (MCT/S) in 1988 meant that infantry battalions now had a dedicated anti-tank weapon which could be fired while the operator remained beneath the protection of the vehicle's armour.

Milan is the standard infantry medium range anti-tank weapon. A French-designed, wire guided missile, the warhead has recently been improved to increase its effectiveness against modern armour. With a range of nearly 2000 metres, it is normally fired by a crew of two from a manportable firing post which can be mounted on the ground or in a trench. In MCT/S a turret with two missile ramps has been fitted onto the top of the Spartan armoured vehicle, and the operator stands inside the vehicle firing and controlling the missile from an assembly which bears some similarity to a submarine periscope. Both the standard Milan and the MCT/S benefit from a thermal imaging sight called MIRA, which enables targets to be engaged at night and in other conditions of poor visibility by picking up the heat signature which all vehicles emit. In the Staffords, the Milan Platoon consisted of four 'ground role' sections each with five firing posts and one 'mobile' section equipped with four MCT/S. Corporal Darren Fern commanded MCT/S callsign 41D:

'We were changing the tactics slowly out there. Captain Wootton [Recce Platoon Commander] was trying deploying one MCT/S alone with two Scimitars. This was something we always argued about; we are supposed to operate in pairs to give each other mutual support, but as it happened in the Gulf operating individually proved to be better, using the Scimitars to back us up. They often operated on four different routes in training for the advance to contact, and this meant we couldn't keep two cars together and at the same time give any part of the platoon protection straight away.

'BATUS was excellent training looking back at what we did out in the Gulf. Working closely with the Recce Platoon obviously made us a better team in the Gulf. We already knew how each other reacted, and so when we deployed to the Gulf we knew how each callsign or each individual would react to any particular problem, which was good.'

Major Jim Tanner, who was to serve as Battalion Second-in-Command in Saudi Arabia, was B Company Commander during Exercise Medicine Man. It was something of a revelation for him:

'In BATUS we got on famously with the Scots Dragoon Guards. They took A Company with them on Med Man 3 and, I must admit, the training was marvellous. We were practising drills. I think that's the thing that I began to understand. We were manoeuvring, but because it's at unit level the CO, who knows pretty well what's going on, can just about order the companies to manoeuvre their platoons and troops; you practise manoeuvre two levels down, you practise drills one level down, is the thing we are beginning to understand.

'So we were practising drills and we got bloody good at it, and you thought to yourself, well in war I don't think we'd really do this. We wouldn't line up in a bit of dead ground, have a good look at where the enemy is and go for it, because we'd get shot to pieces. But that's precisely what we did in the Gulf. We had to move fast and, because the enemy in its attempts to stop us was not pulling out the stops, of course we got away with it. We have not learnt any new lessons from that type of warfare, because it was not an intense engagement. I don't deny that the infantryman and the cavalryman in his tank didn't at stages have a bloody battle. I don't deny that at all. But as far as the bigger picture goes, we learnt nothing new because it was just what we had practised at BATUS. BATUS was the perfect training ground for it.'

Two of the company commanders were at a disadvantage, in that they had taken command of their companies after the companies had returned from BATUS, and so did not have the benefit of this intense training period which those who had been found so valuable. For Major Chris Joynson, commanding B Company, this was exacerbated by the fact that he had never worked as mechanised or armoured infantry before:

'My main concern was that I was going over to the Gulf, possibly to fight a war, and I didn't know anything about the vehicle that I was going to fight in. We just painted the vehicles and sent them on their way. There wasn't any opportunity for me to do any training in the vehicles prior to getting them to Saudi Arabia. The Company of course had just come back from BATUS, so they had got up to speed with armoured infantry tactics. The officers were a help. I had Captain Dave Russell-Parsons from the Grenadier Guards with me, who had BATUS experience, and my watchkeeper was Lieutenant Nick Todd, who had been to BATUS with the Company. They were based in Company Headquarters and gave me any advice I needed. We used to talk things out on a sand drawing and then when we went off to do a training exercise with the tanks we put it into practice. Two of my platoon commanders had been to Canada, but it is a difficult balance to find between on the one hand having to command them and yet on the other wanting to be able to draw on their experience. I think they were probably a bit sceptical at first, because here I was coming into something I knew nothing about and they were quite aware of that, so I probably got a mixed reception in many respects, but I just had to work through that.'

On the Battalion's return from BATUS, preparations began for a major shift of emphasis in training. They were due to undertake an emergency tour of Northern Ireland, based in West Belfast, for six months starting in December 1990. This is quite a normal undertaking for infantry battalions serving in Germany, and is generally welcomed by the soldiers as a complete break from the vehicle based ethos of armoured warfare and a return to basic foot soldiering, albeit in an urban environment, pitted against a terrorist enemy. The maintenance of an armoured vehicle fleet in peacetime tends to dominate training time in camp and, as Corporal Darren Fern explains, not everyone enjoys this aspect of life:

'The routine in camp was that we were nearly always down at the vehicle sheds because we were so heavily involved in maintenance. After BATUS we had to prepare these wagons for long term storage while we were away in Northern Ireland. They were in a fairly poor state anyway because of all the exercises we had done, kit had gone missing or been moved from one vehicle to another, so a lot of people were working on them. Some lads enjoy it, they are happy getting up to their armpits in grease rather than working on training lessons. But there are the others who don't want to be down at the sheds. It goes either way; I would say it's about 50-50 between those who are happy to be down here and those who would prefer to be training. For those who aren't interested, it's not good for their morale being down here all the time.

'The attitude changed completely when we knew the vehicles were going to be deployed operationally to the Gulf. They were worked on intensively by all the sections, because they wanted to prepare them to their individual requirements. Everyone certainly put in far more effort because they wanted to make sure that nothing would fail them on the day. They didn't want to break down and be left behind, in case somebody picked them off. That was worrying them. They wanted a vehicle that got them from A to B and never broke down.'

As well as the moth-balling of the vehicles, deployment to Northern Ireland also meant a radical change in the structure of the battalion where, for example, anti-tank platoons are redundant and the soldiers have to operate in the basic infantry role. A large number of NCOs and officers had to go off on courses to learn skills peculiar to that theatre of operations, and the support platoons were reorganised for their different function. By early September everything was geared towards training for Northern Ireland, and any reference to armoured warfare was sidelined as a low priority.

2

Invasion

'I came back first for my battalion and then to fight for my country.'

The Iraqi invasion of Kuwait took place on 2 August 1990, and at that time very few members of the Battalion even gave a thought to the fact that they might be sent out to the Gulf to take part in an operation to liberate Kuwait. Block leave, where half the Battalion at a time was to be released to take summer holidays, was programmed to start on 16 August and there was no suggestion that this should be reviewed in the light of events in the Middle East. One person who was more aware of the situation than most was Major John Rochelle, who was to command C Company. He was still working as a staff officer in the Ministry of Defence on the day of the invasion, and was privy to high-level briefings:

'I'd been working in a job in the MOD crisis management centre so I'd seen the initial briefings at the MOD. In fact I sat in on the intelligence briefing the night before the Iraqis invaded Kuwait, so I was very aware of what was going on. The briefing was given by the defence intelligence staffs to the Deputy Chief of Defence Staff (Commitments). They were well aware that Iraqi forces were massed on the border; the talks had broken down at that stage and they felt that Saddam Hussein had a number of options open to him. No-one was prepared to say exactly what he would do, that would be impossible; but of course we all woke up the next morning to find that the Iraqis were sitting on the Saudi border, or weren't far short of it.

'That was the start of my hand-over week at the MOD, as I was due to return to the Staffords. There were some attempts to delay my move but nothing came of that, and in fact at the end of it I was very glad that I came back to the Battalion. My colleague in the office, who was a Royal Marine, said, come on, put your money where your mouth is, do you think that the Army will deploy or even that 7 Brigade will deploy? This was because the initial reaction within the MOD seemed to be concentrating on naval and air force deployment in support of the embargo, which had been the steer which had come from the Government. And I said, very grandly, of course not. First of all 1 Staffords are going to Northern Ireland, so we can't possibly take 7 Brigade because they can't send 7 Brigade without the

Staffords. And secondly, one of the cavalry regiments is new to theatre and I very much doubt whether they'll be up to scratch. Of course I was proved wrong on both counts, much to the delight of my colleague, who I phoned up when we got back from the Gulf.

'We came back to work after summer block leave on about 6 September. There were already rumours as to some sort of Army involvement in the Gulf, and we all now thought that 7 Brigade were the most likely people to go because we had the two Challenger regiments and we had the Warriors with the Staffords. Rumours abounded, but we were told to carry on with the Northern Ireland training. So we reorganised, wrote our training programmes and were then told, right, there is an announcement the day after the visit of 3 Staffords [The Territorial battalion of the Regiment, which was training in Germany at the time]. People were not too concerned. I don't think they ever really got overly concerned, because a lot of soldiers saw it as a challenge, and that's one thing that I would emphasise throughout.'

Once the political decision to send ground troops had been taken, a number of deployment options were prepared for consideration by the Government. The details contained in these plans are classified, but any force of less than brigade strength would have been little more than a token effort, a gesture of solidarity, and would have ensured that the British commitment and influence in the conflict was of a minor nature. Subsequent events demonstrated that one of the options was to send an armoured brigade and, to everyone in the know, 7 Armoured Brigade was the likeliest choice. But as always with decisions of this import, the Chief of the General Staff, speaking on behalf of the Army, can do no more than advise and the final resolution must rest with the Government in their exercise of prerogative power. So even those in the Army who were aware of the details of the options could not be sure of the final outcome.

The Adjutant at the time, Captain Tim Sandiford, was one of the first to hear something more than pure rumour:

'Whilst we were battling with the problems of restructuring the Battalion for Northern Ireland, we were warned that Operation GRANBY might be in the wind, as were a lot of other people who were affected by the three options which were being considered. What we were told through the official channels was that the option was being considered, but it was a case of don't stop what you are doing at the moment; carry on, but at the same time could you look at this, that and the other, all of which pointed towards GRANBY. But everyone kept emphasising that it was only one of three options being considered, and if they did send an armoured brigade there was a good chance that it would be us, 7 Brigade.

'So we were then looking at where our shortfalls would be if we were to go back to the establishment for an armoured infantry battalion rather than that for Northern Ireland. And then eventually it was announced. Even the day before it was announced the Headquarters Infantry staff were coming up and saying, right, what are your shortfalls? They were saying, we'll keep doing this review but we're convinced you're not going to go; and we had a healthy, cynical view of what the politicians would decide. We were convinced that they would send a medium recce regiment, that being 96 "tanks" as far as the media and the public are concerned, and a company of Greenjackets. We were convinced that this would happen.'

There were not many in the Battalion who were prepared to believe they would eventually be chosen. Private Mark Ellis summed up the feelings of many of the soldiers:

'When we were on leave we were actually laughing and joking about it, saying, oh, that's where we're going next, but we didn't actually think that we would go.'

Private Stuart Smith agreed:

'On leave my Mum was asking, where are you going next, and I always thought automatically that they would never send us because we had Ireland at Christmas and so it wouldn't be the Staffords. But by the time the CO announced it to the Battalion the rumours were that strong that we knew what was coming next.'

Those who were serving away from the Battalion, either on courses or on postings with other units, had even less hard information to go on. Sergeant-Major Sammy Salt had just completed a Search Adviser's course in England in preparation for the forthcoming Northern Ireland tour:

'For the last 10 days of the course the Gulf situation was on the news more and more. We were talking to the Paras who were on the course, and they felt they were being earmarked to go. They were getting priority over kit. We were talking to one of their sergeant-majors and they were getting priority on everything; weapons, clothing, kit, anything. The more we heard, the more it looked like the Paras were going. We used to have side-bets as to which of them was going to be there first.

'On Friday lunchtime after our final exams we all departed and I was on my way back down the M1, and it came up on the radio that 7 Armoured Brigade were being deployed to the Gulf. The car swerved from one side to the other, and I pulled over and decided I'd better have a cup of strong tea, which I did. It was a shock, completely out of the blue. There had been no suggestion that we would be sent. I then phoned the wife from the motorway cafe. Obviously she was flapping slightly, she'd heard about it on the news at the same time that I did. But when I got home she was more concerned about me getting back here to Fallingbostel, because my ferry wasn't until the Monday and it was on the Friday that we found out.'

For Major Jim Tanner, who had been sent on a three month posting to Uganda, it was very different:

'I had handed over B Company to [Major] Chris Joynson on the Monday before this all started. On the day that the decision to deploy 7 Armoured Brigade was announced I was at Barons Court tube station dragging my baggage, with another officer, onto the tube. I saw the headline on the newspaper stand, "Desert Rats to the Gulf". I was so pissed off about that. While I was in Fallingbostel and subsequently at Warminster it was all speculation. I'd convinced myself that the Staffords would never go because they were going to Northern Ireland. I'd absolutely convinced myself of that. So I could shut myself off to it. I was so frustrated having just handed over my company but there's not much you can do about it.

'I sat and thought I'd write a letter to the CO wishing him luck. One of those letters that said, if ever you need me and that sort of thing, I'm stuck in Uganda. But it was only really wishing him luck because I just couldn't see that there was a position for me.

'We got to Uganda on the Tuesday via Brussels and Nairobi. We drove up to Jinja, which old Staffords who served there will know well, and then on the Wednesday I was summoned to Kampala and the DA said to me that I was going back to Germany. Well, I found it difficult to conceal my delight. Having said that, I stayed in Uganda another six days to set up the course I was out there to teach. So on the following Monday I gave the opening address to the course, and I told everybody including the Commandant that this would be the last thing I said and I was taking that afternoon off to have a look around.

'On the Tuesday I packed my kit and on the Wednesday I left. In one sense I was very sorry to go, I really was. Not sorry to be going back to the Battalion because if I missed this adventure that the 1st Battalion was involved in I would have felt, like most professional officers, that I couldn't show my face again. But sorry to leave Uganda, because it's such a fabulous country and the people are wonderful.'

Captain Chris Hughes had just relinquished the job of adjutant after two years in that appointment, and was on leave in France when the announcement came:

'I was aware of the general situation from the news. I didn't know of the options that were being considered but I did feel that if anybody was going to go, 7 Brigade was the likely choice. For about the last four days of my leave it was certainly a topic of conversation.

'I actually heard about it on Radio 4 in our holiday cottage in France. Then I phoned Tim [Sandiford, the new adjutant] who said, you're adjutant again, and suggested I got back straight away. So I did.'

The Battalion Padre, the Reverend John Tee, was also abroad when the news broke:

'At the time, I was sitting with my Swiss girlfriend in her flat in Berne. I was watching the news and obviously there had been a big American build-up; we always used to watch the news, not thinking for one moment that the Staffords would go out there. I remember jokingly saying to my girlfriend, that could be me, not thinking that it would be of course. Only to find on my return to my bungalow a warning order to greet me saying, you've got three days to get ready to deploy to the Gulf.'

A number of senior NCOs and one officer were serving with 3 Staffords, the Territorial battalion of the Regiment, as instructors. On the day of the announcement the 3rd Battalion was exercising in Germany and had been up to visit the 1st Battalion only the previous day. Sergeant-Major Baz Barrett was one of them:

'Listening to the news in the UK before we went out to Germany, I felt that something was going to happen, and I was in a position where my TA company commander worked for an ammunition testing establishment. He had said that there was a lot of Rarden ammunition being tested at this time [indicating that Warrior might be deployed]. They were obviously going to send the latest equipment and so I thought the Staffords might go. The sergeant-major who had taken over from me in the 1st Battalion had gone off somewhere on a posting, so I felt I might be dragged back if the Battalion had to go.

'When 3 Staffords visited the 1st Battalion, the rumours were flying round and I actually asked the Adjutant if he thought that I would be called back, and he said that he didn't think so; they would put somebody else in rather than call us back. But I still felt that it would happen.

'The next day we went back to our camp. It was R&R day and I went off to have a round of golf. About 1800 hours that evening I got back to the camp and, as we got to the guardroom, I was told the Adjutant wanted to see me. Then I was certain it was going to happen. I was told by you [the author] because the Adjutant had been called back as well and was packing his kit.'

The vast majority of those who were called back were delighted to have the opportunity to rejoin the Battalion. There were some serving with other units who were not called back simply because there was no need for them. Sergeant 'Dixie' Oliver was not content to let the matter rest:

'I was serving in Northern Ireland with the Ulster Defence Regiment. Through the grapevine I heard that the Staffords might be earmarked for the Gulf. So I obviously approached my OC and asked him about his feelings on me getting back to the Regiment. Because a lot of the training team were from other regiments within the division who know the Staffords well, there was a lot of envy that the Staffords had been chosen and their regiments hadn't. Also, I was in a safe desk job, and they couldn't understand why I wanted to rejoin the Battalion.

'I tried through the proper channels to get posted back, but to no avail. I even rang up the Battalion, and the Battalion said they were having problems finding me a job as a sergeant. I said I wasn't interested in being a sergeant, I was just interested in serving, and I had a lot to offer at any rank. And to be truthful, I would have come back and carried the mortar baseplate [a thankless task], I wasn't bothered. The Adjutant did tell me that if the UDR would release me it would be a lot easier. But I was on to a non-starter there. A lot of the UDR soldiers were very supportive, because they were doing for their country what I wanted to do for my Regiment. But they wouldn't release me.

'So in the end I found out that the Battalion was deploying, I knew the time limit through sources of my own, and I was on a tight schedule if I was to get back. I wasn't getting any assistance through the proper channels, so therefore I took it on my own bat to come back.

'I knew I had to go absent without leave to get back. We were on exercise at the time. My wife knew that if the Staffords went to the Gulf then I would go with them. It was hard for her to accept why I did it but she knew what my plan was though, which was, as a last resort I would return and then arrangements would be made for her to move back to the UK. It was all in hand.

'When we were on exercise I saw it announced on Newsnight that the Staffords were being deployed to the Gulf. I tried the proper channels again but I was just flogging a dead horse. It was becoming the local joke that I was in a safe job and yet wanted to rejoin the Regiment.

So anyway, I spoke to my family and took the decision. I just booked a flight, drove to the airport in my own car, locked it up and left it there with instructions for it to be picked up. I caught a flight at six o'clock in the morning and landed back in Hanover at half past one the following day. It cost me £300 to get back. When I arrived I reported straight to the RSM and he took me down to see the CO, who was very supportive, couldn't have done enough for me, which was welcome because I was expecting a right bollocking when I got back. I obviously needed a friend and Major Knapper was on hand and, knowing me well, he spoke for me and put my case forward. The CO was in a difficult situation, I had put him on the spot, and it's not until now that I appreciate the pressure he was under. However, he did discipline me in the sense that I was bucking the system and I had to go back to the UDR. It was hard to accept; I was gutted when I had to go back.

'I went back under a cloud of uncertainty. I was told that it would be 'overlooked' and I would probably get away with a heavy fine and a three month warning, and it would be put down to emotional circumstances or whatever. So I made it clear that I was willing to revert my rank, because that way I wouldn't be in a position to do the job I was sent there to do and therefore I would have had to be RTU'd [Returned to parent unit, ie. 1 Staffords].

'When I got back to the UDR I was put on close arrest, removed from my job and treated like a soldier under sentence. I didn't feel it was necessary, and it just put my family under additional pressure. I was then put on CO's orders [disciplinary procedure], reduced to the rank of corporal and RTU'd. Which was exactly what I wanted.

'I do realise that I put a lot of people in difficult situations, but the feeling was so strong because, although people say you fight for your country, in my eyes you fight for your Battalion first and then that all ties in, and ultimately you fight for each other. I wouldn't say I came back for my country, I came back first for my Battalion and then to fight for my country.'

The Regimental Sergeant Major, WOI Steve Huyton recalled the incident with a wry grin:

'Sergeant Oliver had telephoned me and I could read between the lines; he was going to end up here regardless. His RSM rang me up and said that he was determined to go and there was not a lot he could do to change his mind. The next minute he turned up here, walked straight into my office and said, sir, I'm here and I'm here to stay. I want to go to the Gulf. I did feel some sympathy towards him, but at the same time I had to look on him as a senior NCO and the thing that actually worried me most was that I just hoped that everybody else wasn't going to start doing this.

'At the end of the day it didn't turn out too badly for him, and I did respect what he did. He came back and got on with the job in a very professional manner. In his eyes I don't think he will regret what he did regardless of how his lost seniority will affect him in future years.'

Clearly, by the time that the formal announcement was made to the Battalion on Friday 14 September, many had guessed that they would be going. On the Thursday morning, the RSM had called a battalion parade in order to brief everyone on the visit of the 3rd Battalion later that day:

'I'd sent a message out to all the sergeant majors that I wanted everyone on parade. Now I'm sure that the guys who were on parade were convinced we were going to tell them something about the Gulf. In battalion headquarters we had an inkling that things were happening, but we didn't want to say anything until we actually knew what was going on. I remember going out there to brief them on cleaning up the camp and on the visit generally. I did my brief on 3 Staffords and then split them up to clean the different areas, and I could see all the boys looking round thinking, is he going to tell us or what? And I just marched off and left it at that. But that always sticks in my mind, because even some of the sergeant majors thought I was going to tell them something.'

During the visit of 3 Staffords on that Thursday, the TA soldiers could sense the atmosphere of suppressed excitement throughout the Battalion. All the messes hosted dinners or parties for the visitors, and the sole topic of conversation was the possibility of deployment. On Friday morning, the company commanders and senior officers of the units of 7 Armoured Brigade were gathered together in the Forces cinema in Fallingbostel to be told by the Commander of the 1st Armoured Division, Major General Wheeler, that the Brigade had been chosen to go to the Gulf. The Battalion Operations Officer, Captain Mark Steed described the scene:

'General Wheeler is quite charismatic and larger than life. He stood out at the front and talked to the 7 Brigade units and principal staff officers, as well as representatives from the units which were involved in the other options which had been under consideration. There were also a few outsiders, that is, not from 1st Armoured Division, in the audience. Wheeler spoke to us for maybe five minutes giving an introduction, saying what a great opportunity this would be if it actually cracked off. We had a team who gave a background talk about Iraq, Saudi Arabia and the Middle East. They talked about the geography of the countries and the state of play so far. Then Wheeler said, right, I just want to talk to people in my Division, everybody else, bugger off. And they did.

'As soon as the door closed at the back of the cinema he said, just before I arrived here I found out that it will be 7 Armoured Brigade who will be deploying to the Gulf. And actually it caused a real tingle at the back of the neck, and a real mumble went round the cinema as he said it. By the time it took him to wrap up there, which was a further two minutes, and for us to get back to the camp, the word was out with the boys that we were going.'

The Commanding Officer got the Battalion on parade that afternoon to tell the soldiers. He did not intend it to be a dramatic announcement, but it was not received with total equanimity by everyone, as Private Paul Wain recollected:

'When he first said it you could have heard a pin drop. It went all quiet and then everyone muttered, shit!'

But by the time the married soldiers had returned home to tell their wives, Tom King, the Secretary of State for Defence, had already released to Parliament and the media the fact that 7 Armoured Brigade would be going, and the story was being carried on radio and television in Germany. Emma Frankham was upset by this:

'At the beginning it came as quite a shock, because it was announced on the television before the husbands could come home and tell their wives. So I was sitting at home quite casually on Friday afternoon watching television, and it flashed up as a newsflash. I had agreed to meet my husband at the NAAFI later on anyway, so I went to meet him, and then we came home and had a long talk, and there were a lot of tears because we didn't know what was happening.'

Many of the wives felt that it was unreal and found it difficult to come to terms with straight away. Julie Huyton, wife of the RSM who was later awarded the BEM for her services to the families during the conflict, was typical of many:

'We had just moved into our married quarter, and that day Steve was told that the Regiment was going to the Gulf. It didn't really sink in at first. It was just like a dream. And then it did sink in, when we had to make plans about what was going to happen if he didn't come back, and he told me things about the insurance. In fact his brother came to visit us just before he went, and he stayed up with him when I went to bed. The following morning was the day Bobby, Steve's brother, was going back, and Steve said to me, I've had a good chat with Bob and if anything ever happens to me and I don't come back, Bob is going to come over with my dad and your mum, and it really did hit me then. It just seemed so different to planning your life and thinking, you know, he's got this Ireland tour and then he'll be back. This was something out of the ordinary and it really did come home then.'

Because the news of the deployment was of such fundamental importance to the families as well as the soldiers, the Commanding Officer arranged for the wives and families in Germany to be given the opportunity to attend briefings on the situation as far as the present state of knowledge and security restrictions would allow. A central presentation was held in the Fallingbostel cinema shortly after the announcement to the soldiers. The object of the briefing, during which questions were encouraged, was to ensure that an accurate picture of the current situation and likely future activities could be conveyed. This had some effect in damping down the rumours and speculation which inevitably accompany an event such as this. Additional briefings for the wives of their soldiers were conducted by each company during their remaining time in Fallingbostel.

Of course, some of the families were not in Fallingbostel at the time of the announcement. Similarly, girlfriends and fiancees were in England: the Army will not provide accommodation for soldiers to cohabit unless they are married. Sue Layton was engaged to her present husband that September:

'I was at work at the Nat West Bank and I had a phone call. It was Andrew and he said, Sue, we're going to the Gulf, I love you, 'bye! I just thought, is he going now? Is he going in two weeks? I didn't know what to think, I was a bit upset and I said to the manager, can I go home and phone, and talk to him and find out what's happening?

'You hear about it happening, but you never think it's going to happen to you. It was like, oh no, someone else will go, not you, you're going to Northern Ireland. I'll prepare myself for that, you're going there. And that was it really, it was just one big kick in the teeth.'

Liesl Temple, who is a teacher, was in a similar situation:

'The first idea I had of it was when I phoned Andy up and the person I spoke to said, oh, are you phoning up to find out whether he's going or not? I just never thought they'd actually go, because they were supposed to be going to Northern Ireland. So Andy came on the phone and said they'd know by this Friday.

'On Friday I was in my bedroom, and I'd turned on the news and it said they were going to go in. Then there was a knock on the door and someone said that Andy had phoned. So I went over to the staff room and the whole staff room emptied, with people saying, it's all right, it's all right. I suppose I realised he was going to go then, and I was quite upset. I was worried that he was going to get killed, that he was going to be away for so long, and worried about just not knowing what was going to happen. But everyone around me was very good, very supportive.'

Although a number of Staffords who were serving away from the Battalion were recalled to fill vacancies, it was impossible to take everyone who wanted to return. Captain Tim Sandiford, who had to deal with this delicate problem, explained:

'I had a very unhappy situation with Neil Mackintosh, one of our subalterns who was at the Depot. I phoned all of the training units, because the war establishment gave us an increment of a further eight officers, and asked for our officers to be returned. We were given everyone we wanted except Neil. The Depot said he still had a platoon under training and wouldn't finish until late November with them.

'However, the story that Neil Mackintosh got at the other end, which caused him to phone me, extremely upset, was that we hadn't asked for him. I was very angry that the Depot hadn't had the moral courage to tell him that it was them who had put the stops on it. He was then suffering a very severe crisis of confidence when he'd seen people around him, whom he considered to be at best his equals, being asked for, and him not. Understandably that shook him up and he went through a very rough patch. It was some time before I managed to get through and speak to him on the phone and explain the situation, but I think they really did him very badly there. All credit to him that he has stayed with us since.

'We also had a lot of ex-soldiers phoning up and asking if they could rejoin for

Operation GRANBY, and as it was, there were ten or eleven re-enlistments who gave up their civilian jobs in UK and came back to the Battalion. Some have since left again but some are still with us.

'I also had some ex-officers trying. Kevin Frowen, who was by then a TA officer with 3 Staffords, was up here the day before it was announced and hovered around like a puppy outside the door, popping his head round and saying, Tim, is there any way that I can come back? He was trying very hard to get back; so much so that he managed to corner the CO during the dinner that night, but to no avail. Also, I had the author of this book asking if there was any way that I could get him back without him being seen to have volunteered, otherwise his wife would leave him! Nearly every officer and soldier who was away on a posting tried by one means or another to get back.'

For any professional soldier, the opportunity to go to war and put into practice everything that he has spent his career training for is one not to be missed. However, the modern British soldier is not an unfeeling, unthinking robot, and the reality of the situation was apparent to everyone. For many of the soldiers, like Private Colin McDonald, the initial reaction was one of euphoria:

'Everyone was talking about it and everyone was being gung-ho. People were saying, yeah, I can do this and I'll do that, we've got all this good kit. Once we got out there everyone changed. They were saying, shit, we're here, what are we going to do? Everyone admitted they were scared to their mates.'

Corporal Melvyn Downes was also elated:

'At the start it was caused by ignorance. You could ask most of the squaddies to point out where Iraq was on a map, and most of them could get the rough area, but nobody thought much of the Iraqi Army. Everyone thought they were just a bunch of 'camel-jockeys' and was saying, oh, we're going to wipe the floor with these. But then, before we went, we saw more on the news and came to realise they had the fourth largest army in the world, and we could see all the equipment they had, and there was talk of chemical weapons. Then we started getting a bit more wary.'

Private John Hill agreed with him:

'I think that's when it really hit me. When we were doing the training, and they were saying the Iraqis have got the capability to do this, and they can use that sort of gas on you. And I thought, bloody hell! Am I going to make this or what?'

The reaction of the young officers was very similar. Lieutenant Andy Nye commanded 9 Platoon:

'It didn't really come as a surprise when the CO announced it. It came as a shock perhaps, because it had been speculation until then, and when it was actually confirmed it hit us. Most of us here were very, very pleased. Maybe proud is the right word, but anyway we were dead chuffed that we were the ones who were going.

'Lots of banter was exchanged and we were all sending friends in the Paras telegrams saying, we're going, you're not, and crowing about it a bit. Certainly, when we went back to UK on the weekends before we left, that sort of comment was exchanged on a personal level with individuals that we knew. Most of them were pretty hacked off that they weren't going, because they have always been the ones who have gone in this sort of situation; quick reaction and all that. It was nice for us to be able to have the opportunity to go and do it, and prove it. Purely to ourselves as much as to anyone else.

'It doesn't matter how long you train and where you go. Whether you go to Northern Ireland or Kenya or Belize, you just don't know. You can give the best set of orders, be the best fire controller, do the superbest platoon attack in training, but you just don't know whether or not you could do that under fire, and if there were real people to destroy. So everybody felt really chuffed that they had the chance to go and see, although we couldn't predict what the outcome was going to be.

'I was apprehensive. I hadn't got only myself to think about at this stage. My fiancee was already pretty aware, and apprehensive about me going to Northern Ireland. So I was apprehensive. The dates were pretty similar and she was all teed up for six months away, so the timing was OK. Also, in a way I was a little happier because at least we would be able to see the enemy in the Gulf. Whereas in Northern Ireland you don't know where it's going to come from; it could be a mortar attack, it could be a bomb. It's not a uniformed threat.'

Sergeant Major Nigel Whitehouse was very aware of this excited atmosphere on his return to the Battalion:

'I got back to Fallingbostel and came into the office, and everything was hype and aggression and everything else, and I brought it all back down to earth. I said, right, let's get rid of this gung-ho type of attitude. We're British. We're going to get on with the job. I want none of this gung-ho stuff. I wanted to bring everyone back to reality again. The comment from the Company Commander was, it's a good job you're back now, you've brought us back down to earth. The 'sensible sergeant major'.

The Colour Sergeant was saying to me, we don't have to worry about accounting for kit. We've just got to pack it all and go; it will all be written off when we go to war. I said, no it won't. We will account for every single little item. You will make your normal lists as if we were going on exercise. It turns out at the end of the day that it's a good job we did that, because everything has had to be accounted for.'

On a personal level, he had not anticipated the way he would feel when the announcement was made:

'I was actually at Dover docks on my way back to Germany from a course. I had the radio on and it was three o'clock on that Friday afternoon. The newsreader said the contingent going out to the Gulf is 7 Armoured Brigade, and then mentioned 1 Staffords. I have never, ever felt so much alone as I did then. I was there in the car on my own and I thought, shit! I felt really alone because I was away from the Battalion; away from the family if you like. We got back on the Saturday and of course I came straight in to work. Everything was buzzing, and it was great; I was back in.'

This strong sense of belonging was felt by others, like Private Mark Ellis:

'I was really just proud that the Regiment had been picked to go because I didn't think they would be. I thought they'd send the Guards or someone like that. So my first feelings were just pride that they'd picked the Regiment to go.'

It is, perhaps, a reflection of the high level of training insisted uponby the Staffords that many soldiers likened this initial few days after the announcement to the preparation for a peacetime exercise. Private Stuart Burton said:

'I was getting ready to go to Ireland, so it didn't really bother me. It seemed like an exercise, and I thought they would call it off.'

Corporal Darren Wilson also found the reality of the situation hard to grasp initially:

'Until we got out to Saudi Arabia, it was just like a normal, major exercise. I don't think anybody was really flapping about anything. The only difference was that when kit was wanted, it was here in five minutes. Not the usual peacetime wait of months and months for this piece of kit. If we needed a piece of kit, it was there.'

But he did have an acute awareness of his own mortality:

'Personally, I didn't want to go. I had had a brother in the Falklands and my mum went through hell then. And my mum would obviously have to worry again while I was out there. I wasn't worried for myself, but for the mayhem I'd leave behind if perhaps I died.'

Most of those who went to the Gulf freely admitted to a degree of apprehension or fear once the euphoria had worn off. Private Gary Stevens was:

'A bit apprehensive at first, whether it was going to crack off or whether it wasn't. And on the news when we were out there, one minute he was going to surrender and the next minute he just turned it all about again. You were on a high one day and then on a low the next.'

Private Simon Jones was more frank:

'I was frightened. But in a way I was glad at the same time, because ever since I've been a kid I've always wanted to do something like that. I got the impression that a lot of people didn't want to go because they didn't think it was anything to do with them. That's how they felt at first, but once the training started they just didn't seem to give a damn.'

Whatever each soldier felt, there was no opportunity to dwell upon these sentiments. The Commanding Officer decreed that the weekend immediately following the announcement was to be a working week-end, and the preparations for war began.

3

Preparations for War

'It didn't really hit me until that morning when Bill was walking out of the door.'

Once it was certain that the Battalion would go to the Gulf, considerable preparatory work, involving every department, had to be done to convert from the Northern Ireland role to meet this totally unexpected situation. Since its arrival in Fallingbostel in 1986, no-one had ever imagined that the Battalion would have to operate anywhere other than in north-west Europe. There were no plans prepared to move such a quantity of vehicles, personnel and equipment such a vast distance, and no thought had been given to the particular problems that operations in a desert environment would create. There was a need to provide intensive training for all the soldiers; both to refresh them in skills they already had, and to educate them in new skills appropriate to the impending conflict. Massive amounts of new equipment were ordered to ensure that everything which went out to the Gulf was in the best possible condition.

As far as the Commanding Officer was concerned, the immediate priority was to sort out exactly whom he would be taking with him:

'There was an awful lot of confusion about manpower, which caused a certain amount of stress. A very senior retired officer wrote a very silly letter to the Telegraph which mentioned the Battalion 'in dispatches' but in which he got all his facts and figures wrong. The plain fact was that we were a little under strength, but not badly so. We had to go to Operation GRANBY at 50 over our planned war establishment. So that was 875 compared to a peacetime establishment of about 801. Therefore there was a need for 75 extra, and we were 30 or so under strength, so that raised the requirement to about 100.

'Then we found we weren't allowed to take the under-18s. Once we got out there that rule changed, however we then had a problem getting our boys out to us. What they did was centralise all reinforcements, which included our under-18s; and so when you needed to replace someone, you didn't necessarily get a Stafford, though we fought bloody hard to do it. The first tranche of reinforcements came out with us and they were all from other units. Our boys were the last to go through the reinforcement training system that was set up, so they weren't available immediately. It was terribly frustrating; I had a real run-in with Brigade here in Fallingbostel. I wanted my boys out with me. I knew that there was nothing worse than being sat back here, the boys come back, and they haven't been part of the scene so to speak.

'We weren't allowed to take those people who were medically unfit for front-line duty. I then found out that the REME, for instance, count Fallingbostel as a home posting, which means that soldiers can serve here who are not medically fit for front-line duty, and 15% of my REME boys were unfit for a start. Then we had to leave a rear party to look after things back here, and that was another 51 soldiers. So we had a shortfall of 150 or so by the end of all this.

'Manpower management was a dreadful problem and I certainly got into trouble in some respects, because everybody wanted me to take my reinforcements as formed units, which I didn't want, and also I didn't have a requirement for them. I was only a few down in each area. For example, I needed only four sections of riflemen whereas the Grenadier Guards wanted to send me a formed company. I didn't want that, and I got away with it. Some other battalions that deployed later with 4 Brigade didn't get away with it. They had bigger manpower problems than we had, and I kicked up such a fuss.

'I must say that the units who supplied the soldiers were terribly helpful and very supportive. The problems that did occur were within the hierarchy. I heard mutterings that the Guards' Major-General in London was saying, Guardsmen must only be commanded by Guardsmen. Anyway, I didn't take a blind bit of notice of that, and it didn't seem to make any difference in the end.'

The Adjutant at this stage was still Captain Tim Sandiford. He had to deal with this particular problem:

'For days, the problem of our shortfall of 40 riflemen was bouncing about the system. I asked for four formed sections, which I thought would ease the problem for both sides. The Grenadiers were desperately keen to send a platoon and a section, and it was being argued backwards and forwards between COs and Division and Headquarters Infantry and so on. Fortunately one day I was phoned by one of the divisional staff officers who said, exactly what do you want? The CO wasn't there, and I said, well, four formed sections. So we got it. In the end, the argument was resolved by one phone call. We did compromise, quite rightly, in that we also took two of their officers into the companies those Guardsmen went to, to look after them.'

The Commanding Officer had decided that, in order to get the most experienced command team, he would move Captain Tim Sandiford back to the Milan Platoon, command of which he had only relinquished four weeks earlier; and Captain Chris Hughes would return as adjutant, the job he had done for the preceding two years. As soon as he returned from his holiday in France, Chris Hughes came into the office to take over:

'I got back on the Sunday evening and went into work the next morning. I felt quite sorry for Tim. He had been in the job for 4 weeks, and he had obviously got his teeth into the manning problems. He was well on the way to sorting them out, so it was quite difficult to snatch it back off him. But it made sense; particularly as he was needed to command the Milan Platoon more than I was needed as Adjutant.

'The handover took less than 12 hours. I went in in the morning and by two o'clock in the afternoon I had taken over again. There was nothing else to deal with, only GRANBY. Manning was certainly the main concern. It got very difficult at a much higher level than we were at, ie. we were given this war establishment with the GRANBY establishment on top of it, and literally every two hours, someone from Division and Headquarters Infantry at Sennelager would phone up and say, I want to check your figures with you. Then we would go through, man for man, every one of the 850. We would agree it, then the word came back that Margaret Thatcher had signed up to send a Brigade, and somebody had looked it up in the staff officers' handbook and found out that an armoured brigade in BAOR is something like 7,000 strong and suddenly we were sending 11,000. And apparently she had said, where the hell have the extra 4,000 come from?

'So they put a ceiling on it and said, right, you're trying to creep more people in for whatever reason; enough is enough. So they then came back and said, look, we may have to take five or six off you. It got to be a real pain; we never knew quite where we were.'

The manpower shortfall could not be made up by recalling Staffords who were serving on a tour of duty away from the 1st Battalion; it would have caused chaos, and in any case many of them did not have current experience as armoured infantry. The decision was taken to reinforce the Battalion with soldiers from other armoured infantry battalions serving in Germany. Understandably, these soldiers had mixed feelings about serving with a 'foreign' regiment. Some, like Lance Corporal 'Razors' Woods from the Grenadier Guards, knew very little about the Staffords:

'All I knew was that they were a Brummie line regiment.'

Private David Spence from the Prince of Wales' Own Regiment had:

'Never heard of them before.'

Sergeant Bob Martin from the Grenadier Guards had, however, come across the Staffords:

'One of the section commanders in the platoon that I went to was on Senior Brecon [a tactics course for senior NCOs] with me. Everything I had seen of them on courses was good. I got on all right with them.'

Most of the attached soldiers arrived on the Monday following the announcement. The Battalion was now working flat out preparing the vehicles for the Gulf, and reception arrangements left something to be desired in the eyes of some of those coming in. Sergeant Andrew Harding, a Grenadier, took a realistic view:

'It must have been hard for them because they were only expecting to do a week in Germany before deploying, and all of a sudden it turned into a month and a half. So it must have been chaotic for them. They put us up in an attic above the company block which was very basic. It was the only space available and it was a fast ball for them when we turned up.

'When we arrived, Captain Russell-Parsons, who was one of the Grenadier officers with us, went away and got hold of a B Company officer, and between the two of them they liaised with the CQMS, as you call him [in the Guards, he is known as the Pay Sergeant]. He got us this accommodation, but no-one seemed to know what to do with us. I was put in an attic in the Sergeants Mess.'

Lance Corporal Russell Finn of the Royal Greenjackets arrived with the other Greenjacket soldiers by Chinook helicopter from their base in Osnabruck:

'I thought it was a cold reception that we got. We were Greenjackets, they were Staffords, and we were on their patch. They were a bit stand-offish. It took a hell of a long time just to start talking. With us, some people might say different, but we think we are some of the friendliest guys going. We go up to people and talk. But with other regiments, especially the Staffords, what I found was that it took a long time for them to get to talk to you. There was a big stand-off, and then all of a sudden we got on fine.'

Captain Tom Wagstaff of the Prince of Wales's Own Regiment had no complaints about the reception he and his soldiers got:

'The reception was very good indeed. We were met by Mr Huyton, the RSM. My impression was of a great deal of hectic, controlled activity. One comment made was that the Stafford soldiers had been getting ready for a Northern Ireland tour and morale was only average. Yet the ones I saw were strutting around very proudly, and a Stafford officer said that there had been a complete change, from one minute being just another battalion going to Northern Ireland, to being *the* armoured infantry battalion picked to go to the Gulf.'

He felt that his soldiers did not find it too difficult to assimilate into the Staffords and become a part of the Battalion:

'I think, basically, the Staffords are a normal, bog-standard line regiment like ourselves. So it was easy for us, because although they're from the Midlands and they all speak with a Brummie accent, and we're from Yorkshire, we could relate to that. Whereas other units, such as the Guards (and I'd like to stress that I say this without knocking them in any way) are a different breed. The officers are a different breed obviously, but also the soldiers are, just by reason of the nature and type of work they tend to do. Also the Greenjackets are somewhat different. Out of the major units attached to the Staffords I would say that we got on better with them on the whole.'

It was the Guards who commented the most on the differences between their regiment and the Staffords. Guardsman 'Tankie' Knight, slightly tongue in cheek, said:

'Looking at a Guards officer compared with a Staffords officer, a Guards officer is more highly dressed. A lot posher in a way. The Staffords officer for example, might not shave for two days in the field. The Staffords officers just didn't look like officers. You could instantly tell a Staffords officer from a Guards officer, even in civvies. He looked like one of us and he spoke like one as well. It was more relaxed. With a Guards officer, it's always sir this, and sir that. It wouldn't have changed in our battalion if we had gone as a battalion to the Gulf. Number 2 Company went as a complete company to the Royal Scots, as did the Queen's Company. We visited 2 Company and it hadn't relaxed at all. You couldn't get away with anything. They were even doing drill in the desert to keep the discipline there!'

Sergeant Andrew Harding could, however, understand the difference in attitude, even if it did not entirely meet with his approval:

'The Staffords are a lot more relaxed in their system of discipline; for example, the way that a corporal would talk to a platoon commander. In our battalion he would be getting away with murder. If you look at it from an objective point of view, the aim was still achieved. The thing was done but, opposed to us who scream and shout, the Staffords would talk about it first, go away and have a quick brew, and then say, go and do that lads, or whatever. But in the end it achieved the same aim, although it was foreign to us.'

Guardsman Steven Penney found it refreshing:

'It was completely different, a different world. They talk between the ranks much more. In our regiment there's a lot of difference in the ranks. Guardsmen usually stick to Guardsmen, but in the Staffords a private soldier can talk directly, even to a company sergeant major. They seemed a lot more communicative and friendly between the ranks.'

Lance Sergeant Andrew Dillon made the most of it:

'Everyone called me by my first name; no-one called me Sarn't. The platoon commander called all of us Guardsmen by our nicknames, and I think the blokes related to it a lot more than if it had been more formal. It wasn't at all upsetting, and it didn't damage the rank structure or discipline. None of the blokes would call the platoon commander by his first name, it was always sir. Sometimes as section commanders we could have a bit of a laugh and joke with him, but there would still be that gap; he'd still be that much above us. The system works for the Staffords but you couldn't import it into the Grenadiers.'

Every regiment has its own culture and traditions, and all those who were attached to the Staffords felt very strongly that they wanted and needed to retain an element of regimental identity. Everyone was allowed to continue wearing their own regimental insignia and, although as time went on these soldiers did mix well into the Battalion, they were never fully absorbed into the Staffords. They never saw themselves as Staffords, and everyone agreed this was important.

One unfortunate incident during the initial training period in Fallingbostel was the result of differences in regimental recruiting practices. The Staffords have always had a proportion of coloured soldiers, a reflection of the demography of the counties from which they recruit. The Guards, on the other hand, have in the past tended not to recruit from other ethnic backgrounds, although, following recent media criticism, this unstated policy has been reviewed. Lance Sergeant Andrew Dillon explained:

'One of our company sergeant majors was down at Fallingbostel helping with the delivery of the vehicles which we were supplying. You must understand that we only have a couple of black blokes in the regiment. He said to one of the coloured Staffords that he was to call one of our drivers massa, master. It was meant as a joke but it got blown out of all proportion. It gave us quite a bit of grief within the company before we left, and that bloke never spoke to any of us again. I must say that we weren't like that. We got talked to about it and were told that it was racist. People's colour didn't matter to any of us, but with that happening it caused a little bit of friction that we didn't really need.'

Although the Battalion had been told they would definitely be going to the Gulf, no firm date for the start of their deployment plan was forthcoming. The commander of 7 Armoured Brigade, Brigadier Patrick Cordingley, flew out to Saudi Arabia with a small team to liaise with the Americans who were already there. It was only when he returned to Germany that a clearer idea of the timetable for training and deployment was to emerge. Because of this uncertainty and lack of information, all the preparation was done on a worst case basis. The worst case was that the Battalion would move out within a couple of weeks of the announcement, and on arrival the vehicles would drive straight out into the desert ready to go to war.

In peacetime every unit is bound to have shortages of equipment, resulting in vehicles being off the road or weapons being inoperable. As in any system, military or civilian, there is a time lag between the ordering of a piece of equipment and its delivery. Inevitably some spare parts will be in short supply, and the result is that the Battalion is never 100% fit for role. The Army supply system is geared to cater for operational periods such as Operation GRANBY by prioritising demands for spares, so units which are directly involved are dealt with as a matter of urgency. Within the Staffords, the burden of ensuring that the Battalion was fully equipped for the task in hand rested with the Quartermasters Department. The Quartermaster, Major Glyn Ireland and the Technical Quartermaster, Captain Douggie Forrest, were involved from the outset:

'Nothing at all had ever compared with the scale of Op GRANBY and the lack of time for preparation prior to being told we were going. It all started off with a conference on the Saturday morning at 1st Armoured Division Headquarters. It actually lasted about twelve hours. Basically what they had done was call together all the Divisional supply representatives to support 7 Brigade. People were told by the Deputy Chief of Staff, who chaired the meeting, you will provide this; there was no argument. We were given carte blanche. He said, what would you like to go with, what is your shopping list?

'We had a list of what we would like to have, and once we had done that we went through it and marked the things we would get, what we would probably get, and the things we would most likely not get. All during the meeting, the phone lines back to Fallingbostel were red hot. Colour Sergeant Williams was to-ing and fro-ing up and down the autobahn with the different documents that we required.

'We had spoken to people in the Battalion who had experience of the desert, and then we added our personal experiences of Bahrain and Sharjah. So we came up with things like Millbank water filters, shamaghs, goggles, sunglasses and chaguls to add to the basic list of kit we required to bring us up to wartime establishment, and to make up our peacetime shortfalls.

'We then raised the problem of having a mixed fleet of vehicles [Warriors and 432s] which was causing us great heartache and created the problem of having to carry two completely different sets of spares with us. So they agreed to increase our wheeled fleet in order to carry these spares. We also looked at replacing some of the 432s with Warriors, and started examining the problems of desert conditions, the dust and the heat, on these vehicles.

'After the conference, everything we needed was demanded in the usual way except that it was given a priority of 1; the highest priority you can get. The priority system eventually became a bit of a farce. Everyone in 7 Brigade was demanding on priority 1, and so they then sub-prioritised it. In the end the system just got clogged. There was also a daily conference at Brigade to iron out ongoing problems.

'The major equipments we were demanding were Warrior spares, chain guns, recovery vehicles and wheeled vehicles. When the announcement was made our wheeled vehicles were in a very bad way, because various supply problems had meant that no spares had been forthcoming for some time. So the demands were really flying in to bring us up to scratch. It was non stop. We had a 24 hour system working in the QMs department until the day we sailed. In addition to that, the majority of the troops in the department were working an 18 to 19 hour day.

'Everybody in BAOR couldn't have been more helpful. Not only did they give us what we wanted, they brought it up to us as well. We didn't have to worry about going to fetch it, they actually delivered it. And they delivered it to the point of excellence. Everything was in good condition. The Queens Own Highlanders, for example, were actually ringing us up and saying, do you want more kit? They had to go out to the Gulf in the end, so they eventually had to make up a massive shortfall of everything they had given us.'

The decision was taken to re-equip the Milan Platoon and the mortar fire controllers with Warriors, as it was decided that their 432s would not be able to keep up with a fast moving battle group. This decision was made some two weeks after the announcement, so the 432s which the soldiers had been working so hard to prepare were parked up and attention shifted to the Warriors replacing them.

The two major problems this caused were the need to retrain drivers for these vehicles, and the development of a system for stowing the

Milan missiles and firing posts in the back of the Warrior. Most of the drivers were supplied by the Grenadier Guards. As far as the carriage of missiles was concerned, a team from the Infantry Trials and Development Unit came out to Fallingbostel and rigged up a harness in the back of the Warriors to hold the ammunition. In fact, by the time the Platoon had experimented with this system in Saudi Arabia during their first period of in-theatre training, they had carried out some fairly major modifications to this prototype, tailoring the system to their needs.

As Battalion Second in Command, Major Jim Tanner was responsible for co-ordinating the training of all the soldiers prior to their move out to the Gulf, although this took second priority to vehicle preparation until the vehicles were despatched by ship from Bremerhaven:

'A lot of courses were arranged for the Battalion and other units by Brigade Headquarters. There were courses on desert survival, desert navigation and all those sorts of things peculiar to the theatre. We had outside instructors for all these specialist courses. Everybody wanted to talk to us. You felt that, for some of them, an afternoon on Clacton beach was enough to qualify them to talk to the soldiers of 7 Armoured Brigade about life in sandy conditions! They seemed to be coming from everywhere; out of the woodwork.

'We had some useful stuff. A team turned up from Sandhurst; some of the lecturers from the Military Studies Department, and it looked as if it would be vaguely interesting. But it was very good. It was a presentation all about the Iran/Iraq war, Arab/Israeli conflicts, and you got to understand, perhaps, a bit more about the Arabs. Having a sense of history, I found it useful to read a couple of books about that part of the world. The campaign in Mesopotamia in the First World War was useful. Not that it would teach us many lessons at all; maybe the need to have a firm logistic base, for example. But nobody needed to read the book to find that out. But you could learn about the Arabs, and what the climate could be like.

'One officer sent all his warm kit back to Germany, including his Army sleeping bag. I said to him, you wait, you just wait until the winter comes. And when it did come it was freezing. We had frost and the rain was just atrocious. So we did need all that stuff, and reading about it helped me to keep all my kit.

'There was quite a lot to do during the training period in Fallingbostel. The soldiers were trying to fire all their weapons, although there were bits and pieces like .50 calibre machine guns which we were due to get, but never saw in Germany. Eventually, when we did get them in Saudi, we got the US Marines to train us on them.

'It was fairly clear that although the soldiers could do everything, because an infantryman is a jack of all trades, unless you can have an intense training period prior to a conflict, as we did, there is no great depth of skill. They can all do it: they can all put their NBC kit on; they can handle all their weapons. But they never have the time to devote themselves to absolute skill. So the concentration in that very early stage was on individual training and just honing up those individual skills. No attempt was made to do any unit or formation level training at all. We had already done that at BATUS.'

Sergeant Major Nigel Whitehouse took part in all the training, as well as having to cope with the extra administrative workload that came his way as A Company Sergeant Major:

'Different regiments around BAOR were told to set up and run ranges for us. We simply had to turn up. The RAF provided Chinook helicopters to ferry us down to Sennelager training area, in order to save time which would otherwise be wasted moving down there in trucks or on coaches. We would come in around six o'clock and move down the road to the area we had turned into the 'airstrip'. We'd be picked up there, fly down to Sennelager, do whatever it was we'd got to do down there, which could be throwing grenades or going through live platoon attack ranges, and then be picked up again and fly back at the end of the day.

'Of course, during the day briefings had been going on, so we would need to get the details of that. If anything needed to be actioned, we'd have to do it that night ready for the next day. My family coped pretty well with these long hours. I mean, at the end of the day, Diane's done nearly as long as I have in the Army. She understood that I was working and I had got to get ready for the Gulf. It was as simple as that.

'Fitness training was very important. I took the Company running every single day. At eleven o'clock, every man jack in the Company stopped work and fell in, and I took them on a run. The Company Commander just slotted in and let me get on with it. It's always been my thing, ever since I've been with the Company. I've always done that anyway. We used to do between three and six miles in full kit. We even did the eight mile Infantry Combat Fitness Test in NBC kit. That was extremely hard, that was. It was a very hot day.'

Following the revelations in the media about the size and capability of the Iraqi chemical arsenal, NBC training, which is a traditionally unpopular subject with soldiers, was undertaken with unprecedented diligence and enthusiasm. Captain Jack Ferguson, Second in Command of A Company, summed up what many of the soldiers felt:

'Being old and bold, the one thing I always used to hate was the NBC aspect of training. But that became a priority, and I made sure I went on all the training with the soldiers learning all about it. And I was extremely happy to be doing it. In the past I would not touch NBC; I'd have nothing to do with it. But certainly, come the announcement, I took a great interest in it!'

As Private David Travis found, the training in Fallingbostel was intense and directed towards the enemy they expected to encounter:

'There was a lot of fitness and we also worked hard on our armoured vehicle recognition skills. By the time we went in there, I can honestly say that everyone in the Platoon could recognise every wagon that the Iraqis had. We used the Milan Platoon NCOs to teach us.'

The Mortar and Milan Platoons carried out a great deal of live firing on the Bergen Hohne and Munsterlager ranges, as part of their preparations. The Mortar Platoon fired over 3,000 rounds of ammunition during this period; normally, five years' worth of training ammunition. As well as the standard high explosive round, training included intensive practice with the illuminating round: a parachute suspended flare designed to light up the battlefield at night. A large number of white phosphorous smoke rounds were also fired.

By now, Captain Tim Sandiford had handed over as Adjutant and was once again commanding the Milan Platoon:

'We fired 288 missiles in two and a half days. I can't reveal what they cost apiece, but that was equivalent to some millions of pounds down the range over that period! We fired against all sorts of targets. The ranges were run for us, which meant that the commanders could be trained. You can't normally do that because your NCOs are having to act as safety staff on the range. We literally just turned up on the day and did what we wanted.

'There were some operators who fired 10 or 12 missiles in that brief period, when usually they are allocated one or two a year because of the cost. The soldiers were able to treat them in the way that a rifleman might look at his small arms ammunition on the range. That was a very great shift of emphasis because they were quite prepared to try different methods of engaging targets. There was none of the normal feeling that you must not try anything too radical otherwise you might have wasted your one missile of the year. We were able to try very short range shoots which are not normally practised, and they could also practise flying the missile along a circuitous route to the target. We had the luxury of being able to 'waste' one or two missiles by these experimental, for us anyway, firings.'

Even when the training day had finished, there was work to be done out of hours. Most commanders believed there was a need to talk to their soldiers outside the structure of the formal training programme, to discuss everything from personal fears and expectations to pay or financial problems. Lieutenant Stephen Neale talked to the soldiers in his platoon about the delicate question of writing 'final' letters before they set off for the Gulf:

'We had platoon discussions every now and then. They just seemed to develop naturally from the training process. It was a way of finding out what they felt, what they wanted to do. I wanted to understand how the whole of the platoon thought, and not just the section commanders and others I normally worked closely with. We talked about tactics as well as more emotive subjects.

'The subject of letters to relatives was something we talked about quite a bit. Should we or shouldn't we write these letters? One or two did ask my advice, but most people just wanted to be left to themselves to write them. It was decided by most people after the discussion that it would be a good idea to do it, and I think most were written before we left Fallingbostel. When the air war actually started, the half a dozen or so who hadn't made that arrangement did so then.

'I wrote one to my dad. When I first joined the Army he wasn't very happy with my decision; he basically wanted me to stay at university. So I just said to him, don't be upset by the fact that I'm dead. I'm happy doing what I'm doing; it's what I chose to do. No matter what you had done, there was no way you could have stopped me choosing the course of action that I did, and not to feel bad about it. It was along those lines.

'It was difficult to put into words. I had in my mind exactly what I wanted to say, but when I actually came to putting it on paper it sounded very stupid. It took me two or three attempts before I ended up with something. Even then I thought it was only passable. I was trying to be matter of fact about it, but I don't think you can help but be emotive when it comes down to actually putting it on paper. Ultimately, if the worst happens, these are your final words to your family.'

One soldier wrote the following letter to his fiancee:

'Dearest,

Things haven't worked out quite as well as they should have, have they.

Above all you must be strong. You must walk tall, with the pride and dignity that I did when we went out anywhere together. You were, and still are, the light of my life and you can take pleasure in the knowledge that you alone were the catalyst which forced me on in the face of adversity.

I dearly hope that you never have to receive this letter. Although it signifies my departure from this earthly life, you must never forget that you are a part of me, as I am of you and nothing can stop that. You can't quantify love, and you can never destroy it. It's always there around us.

You must, as I said, be strong and you must mourn me and carry on living your life. I dearly want you to be happy and the one way that you can make me happy, while I'm flying around with my cloud, is by remembering me with happiness, not with remorse and sadness. You are my life.

Take care my darling petal,

I love you,'

Personal preparations were, as far as possible, assisted by the Army. Will forms were distributed, and every soldier was advised to make a will before departure if they had not already done so. Although a will made orally on the battlefield by a soldier is a rare exception to the legal rule that a will must be made and witnessed in writing, it was prudent to have it formally made out to avoid any potential problems in the event of the death of the soldier.

The Battalion Pay Office issued advice on the allocation of pay to wives whilst their husbands were away, and were able to give examples of pensions and gratuities which would be payable on the death of an individual. Inevitably though, it was financial matters which caused the most aggravation, as Captain Chris Hughes explained:

'The insurance guys not playing ball with the soldiers caused me a lot of concern. They would happily take money hand over fist from them in the first instance, but then it reached a stage where they wouldn't issue new policies or add life cover to existing ones. I understand why they did it but it's an unpleasant side of the financial industry. I still find it reprehensible.

'The banks were concerned about people's overdrafts and people's loans. The soldiers obviously wanted to go down to the bank to make sure their wives weren't going to have a problem while they were away. So if they'd got a one or two thousand mark overdraft they just went down and said, right, I just want to make sure this overdraft is good for while I'm away. But it wasn't quite as simple as that. They said, no it isn't; we want it settled. What happens if you die? We can't sue your wife for it, we will lose money.

'I had that conversation with the bank manager myself. At the end of the day, to be fair to him, he offered me a glass of spirits, which is the first time he's ever done that, and was very decent about it. But this was after I'd talked to him for about 20 minutes and explained life to him.'

During this period of preparation, the medical capability of the Battalion was expanded to cope with the numbers of casualties that might result from a war with Iraq, particularly if chemical weapons were to be used. Every soldier received additional instruction in advanced first aid, including the administration of morphine to casualties and the establishment of saline drips on the battlefield for those who had lost blood. This was to prove a life-saving technique during the war, although in most cases drips and morphine were used on Iraqi casualties. It is interesting to note that the technique of rectal insertion of drips, which was recommended during the Falklands War as being simple to apply on the battlefield, was not adopted. The soldiers were trained to insert the drip intravenously, and in many cases practised on each other under medical supervision.

The Battalion Band are trained in peacetime to act as combat medical assistants, and as soon as the announcement was made they downed their instruments and willingly set to, brushing up on their medical skills. At the same time, the Regimental Aid Post, which in peacetime is run by one doctor and a small number of medics, was augmented by an additional two doctors and a large number of soldiers and NCOs. Captain Richard Gale, the Medical Officer of the Royal Greenjackets, was posted into the Staffords for Operation GRANBY:

'We had two things to concentrate on initially. One was generally running around, getting the boys fit and doing specialist training. The other was the medical side, in particular vaccinating everyone. I had to run the garrison vaccination programme, which vaccinated roughly 3,500 blokes in three days. People had anything up to six jabs. If you hadn't got your medical documents to show which innoculations you'd had were current, you got everything. We then ran training courses for the bandsmen to get them up to speed. And we were also running the first aid training for all the soldiers.'

As the weeks in Fallingbostel dragged on, there was intense speculation about their eventual deployment date. When the announcement had been made, no date had been set, but everyone was under the impression that the Battalion would move out to Saudi Arabia very quickly; perhaps within a week. It was particularly difficult for the soldiers who were attached from other regiments. They had said their goodbyes to families and friends before setting off for Fallingbostel, and now found that they were allowed back to their units for a weekend after three weeks of training. At the end of this weekend farewells were again made, only for them to find themselves once again allowed to return home a fortnight later for another weekend. There was still no definitive deployment date.

The situation in which the soldiers found themselves caused some to reconsider relationships which, until that point, had received little adverse pressure. The Padre, John Tee, saw one particular aspect of this:

'We saw an absolute barrage of people wanting to marry fiancees before they went, partly for romantic reasons and partly, probably, because if anything did happen to them, their girlfriends would be entitled to all sorts of goodies in the event of their death. Normally we have this ruling of three months before people can get married. Obviously the paperwork could never be completed in time, so I was actually advised by my senior chaplain not to bother with anybody who wanted to get married.'

Vicky Lane, however, saw things rather differently:

'We had planned to get married on 3 November, but then everything cracked off in the Gulf. So I came over to Germany in September. We wanted to get married but Padre Tee said there was no way it could be done. That really upset me. Then a new padre arrived, Brian Richards. We went up to see him and he said he'd do his best. We had to send off to England to get my birth certificate, and when it arrived, it was really at the last minute. They sent a driver all the way down to JHQ at Rheindahlen with the paperwork, and then the padre said okay, we can do it now. How about Wednesday at three o'clock?

'That was it. Somebody lent me a wedding dress, and we went off to Walsrode and bought a wedding ring on the Monday. We hunted high and low for stockings and eventually got some. So we got married on the Wednesday and everything went off brilliantly. The only sad thing was that our families couldn't be there, but we're going to have a service of blessing for them now.'

At last, it was decided that an advance party from the Battalion would fly out to Saudi Arabia on 11 October. The Warriors and other vehicles had left by ship some weeks earlier, and the role of the advance party was to prepare reception arrangements for the Battalion and its equipment. Lieutenant Colonel Charles Rogers, the Commanding Officer, led this small group:

'We knew that we were going to be under command of the American Marines. We were flying into the port of Al Jubail; I'd never heard of it before in my life. The theory was that we would go up-country as a brigade to defensive positions, and take over from US Marine units. The threat of invasion was still the greatest problem at that stage. But there was an awful lot of discussion going on between the American Marines and the American Army as to where their boundaries were. The Marines wanted to have a bit more ground so they could fit us into the front line, and the Army were digging their heels in.

'A US Marine came to Fallingbostel before we moved out and briefed the whole brigade, which was super. They were very helpful, and when we got out there the Marines were very welcoming and looked after us extremely well.'

This was the moment when the first group of soldiers from the Battalion had to say their final farewells, knowing that, this time, there would be no possibility of an extra few days or weeks in Germany. The flights were booked and waiting for them. Captain Nick Foster, the Regimental Signals Officer, was on the advance party:

'Fiona, my wife, took me up to the gym, which was where the coaches were due to pick us up. We had already said our goodbyes at home and we were determined not to have any sort of public farewell. Quite a few people had families who waited until they drove off and it was very tearful for them. Without wanting to overdramatise it, the picture that I had in my mind for a long time out there was my son, Daniel's face, looking at me out of the back window of the car as they drove out of the car park. I don't think he realised what was happening, but that certainly stayed with me all the time I was out there.

'We then got onto the coaches and were bussed down to RAF Gutersloh to fly out. As soon as we got away from Fallingbostel, and everyone had taken a few breaths and got over the goodbyes, it was like going on exercise. Spirits were high, people were talking shop; nothing else was talked about. I wouldn't say that wives and loved ones had been forgotten, but they had been put into second place now, and the task in hand was the thing that we were all considering. So it was a very lively bus going down to the airport. Indeed, it was a very lively journey all the way across there. Everyone was talking to each other; jokes, speculation and generally talking shop. I think everyone had done their reflection about the separation, and in one, purely military sense, they were quite relieved to get away from the families so that they could start doing the thing that we had all been psyching ourselves up to do.'

The main body of the Battalion began to fly out on 20 October. The flights were a mixture of hired civilian aircraft and RAF VC10s and Tristars. Most of the married men experienced similar emotions to those Nick Foster described. They also appreciated how difficult it was going to be for their families. The soldiers had a job to do, and would be fully occupied, with little time on their hands for brooding. They would also find themselves constantly in the company of their friends, with whom they would be able to share emotions and worries. The families, on the other hand, although living in close proximity to each other, were to have an indeterminate period of nights at home on their own, bereft of a husband or a father. They had to find ways of coping with this. Geraldine Cottam's husband flew out with the advance party:

'It didn't really hit me until that morning, when Bill was walking out of the door. That morning I couldn't believe it. That day I never went out and I just spent the day crying. I think everybody felt the same. I honestly didn't think he would walk back through that door again. It was really, really frightening.

'They think because we're here in a garrison town, that we were all in the same boat and there would be plenty of company. During the day it was great, but because I had young kids, I couldn't really get out at night. Also, being winter as well, by five o'clock it was dark and the kids were in. And once they came in and the door was closed, that was it until the next morning. I really, really hated the nights. I don't mind sitting at home at night normally, but five and a half months of sitting on your own got a bit much. You could phone your friends, or they could phone you, but it wasn't the same as actually having somebody to sit there and talk to you.

'The children had to cope with it as well. The eldest was asking, why do they have to go? And they were asking if their daddy was going to die. Questions I couldn't really answer, although I answered them as best as I could. The first month was very, very difficult. They kept asking, when is my daddy coming home? Then they just got used to it and they still kept asking, but not as much. And I kept saying, Daddy's at work, Daddy's away, but he'll be coming back soon. And the three of them accepted it and I had no problems with them. It was just the loneliness.'

4

Desert Training

'If we had to go in somewhere for real, we knew the Staffords would just rip them apart.'

All the trooping flights landed at Al Jubail airport in Saudi Arabia, which exists to serve the nearby commercial port of the same name. For most of the soldiers, including Captain Nick Foster, this was their first experience of the Middle East:

'We had noticed the difference in temperature when we had refuelled in Cyprus, but it was nothing like the airport at Al Jubail. The humidity and the heat were appalling. This was night time. We'd been there less than half an hour, and we were wet through: everyone was sweating buckets. It was the humidity which really affected you; that horrible clammy feeling when you've got a heavy, damp atmosphere.

'The reception was well organised, there was transport there to meet us, and we were bussed down the coast to the port of Al Jubail in a rickety old bus. We had been given lunch packs and drinks, and they were rapidly consumed. Everyone was clamouring for water. Boxes of bottled water had been placed at strategic points in the aisle of the bus, and people were encouraged to drink as much water as they wanted.

'In Al Jubail port we went through the reception process, which basically consisted of documentation of next of kin details and mundane things like that which we had done a hundred times already. We were given some cash and then had a briefing on the layout of the place, a security brief, and an update on what was happening with the vehicles. Then they showed us across to the accommodation where a small pre-advance party was waiting to meet us.

'They were already established in a large shed on the harbour edge which had been earmarked for the Staffords. It was just a huge expanse of floor space. Everyone was sleeping on the floor: there were no camp beds, they arrived a little bit later. It was vastly overcrowded. How we didn't get any major illnesses ripping through the Battalion, I don't know.'

Private Paul Lister was similarly unimpressed with the accommodation, which was christened 'The Pig Pens':

'It was an infested area. It was very hot and fly-ridden. I remember blokes going to sleep with their socks off, and their feet being black with flies having a meal on them while they slept. Food was an experience. They were feeding quite a few of us. We had this breakfast; it wasn't a solid, honest breakfast, it was a liquid meal. The Americans had cooked it up for us. It looked as if somebody had had a go in it! It just wasn't worth getting out of bed for.'

Hygiene was a major concern for the Battalion Medical Officer, Captain Richard Gale:

'With the whole Battalion being in a hangar with another 2,000 guys, just packed in, there was a major environmental health problem. There were only four toilets for over 2,000 guys, and limited washing facilities. We were just waiting for diarrhoea to start at one end of the building and see how quickly it would reach the Colonel. It didn't actually happen, whether through good management, good environmental health procedures or luck, who knows. Probably luck!'

Nick Foster was a member of the advance party which had some 10 days to wait before the first main body flights began to arrive:

'The only vehicles we had at this stage were Land Rovers. While we waited for the main body of the Battalion to fly out we were able to get away occasionally, for a couple of hours at a time, to the beach which had been put aside for the Americans to use. They laid on small buses to get us there, and we were responsible for our own security which we covered by taking armed guards with us.

'There was some hanging about and the boys found things to entertain themselves. We tuned into Radio Baghdad, 'The Voice of Peace', which was always good for a laugh. It was their propaganda station, but it had a completely unintended effect. I remember someone coming on one day and saying, American and British soldiers, you must all go home now. You will all go home in bodybags if you stay, and your wives and girlfriends will not be waiting for you at the airport! We are now going to put you over to real American general who will tell you exactly what morale is badly like in front line American troops; General. And then a strongly accented voice came on, I am true American general. I can honestly say that morale very badly is!

'It had us in stitches, it was hilarious. They played some very good music as well to get the boys listening to it. The Brigadier came round one day and we were all huddled around this radio. He said, hello, what are you listening to. And I thought, oh shit. I said, actually sir, it's a propaganda station from Baghdad. He said, really? He had a listen to it and then said, this is jolly good stuff isn't it? I think by the end people were listening more to that than they were to the BBC World Service.'

The armoured vehicles and large pieces of equipment had been loaded on board hired civilian freighters in Germany. It was not possible to place everything the Staffords needed to take out on one ship, so the arrivals were staggered over a period of some days. As far as possible, the main body flights from Germany were timed to arrive in Saudi Arabia coincidentally with the vehicles, so the troops spent the minimum time possible in the overcrowded port area before moving out into the desert. Even so, with a move of this size and complexity, there was bound to be some waiting around.

One of the early arrivals was Major Tim Gatfield, Support Company

Commander. His task was to prepare a training package for the Battalion in conjunction with the 7 Brigade staff and the US Marines:

'We were in the Pig Pens, which I hated, and so I jumped at the chance to go out and help clear and set up the ranges. The principal brigade officer setting up the ranges was a Royal Artillery major, assisted by an officer and warrant officer from the tanks; and they were orientating the ranges towards their specialities. So I banded together with the Small Arms School Corps QMSI, who was out there, and we basically decided how we were going to set up the ranges for the Staffords.

'We had one dedicated infantry range which we called Career Hill. It was called that because so much personal safety needed to be exercised that careers were very definitely on the line. Then there was a series of set piece ranges: anti-tank range, gallery small arms range, 30 millimetre range, light mortar range; and they were available to all arms. There was also a combined arms range which included an infantry sector. There was an armoured vehicle fire and manoeuvre area which also included an infantry trench system objective.

'The sappers actually built them once we had designed them. Given that the sand was extremely soft and they were very busy anyway, I think they did an excellent job. Later on we enhanced them with work parties from the companies. I then wrote the range orders for the infantry ranges. We were told that General de la Billière had accepted the fact that we might take casualties on the ranges, and was prepared to cope with that should it happen. So the orders that we wrote were the absolute minimum necessary, and really came down to common sense.

We relied a hell of a lot on the individual being his own safety supervisor. We purposely used the minimum number of safety staff to reduce the numbers wandering around amongst the bullets. We just impressed on the blokes that it was up to them whether they pulled that trigger or threw that grenade. And when we got down to it, there were some very close calls, to say the least.

'I would like to see that level of realism and reduced safety in peacetime training. It would require a sufficient degree of build-up training; but we would have to accept that there might be a number of casualties. During the training in the Gulf, it was pure luck that there were not two or three fatalities, and there were some quite serious injuries. I honestly believe that there is no substitute for realistic field firing. Simulation and blank ammunition have a part to play in the training process, but ultimately there is no substitute for live ammunition. The improvement in the standard of weapon handling, in the awareness and alertness of the troops, and confidence in their weapon systems, improved three or four hundred per cent. There is no doubt in my mind that, by the end of it, they were ready for war.'

Brigadier Patrick Cordingley took a keen interest in the planning and construction of the ranges, and was acutely aware of the question of safety levels:

'Having realised that there was a potential safety problem on these ranges, the next thing I did was to go and talk to General Peter, who was my direct boss, and say to him, we're in a situation now where we could kill soldiers during training. To which, because he's such an experienced man with so much practical knowledge of the sort of situation we were in, he said, of course that's understood. You may well kill people. You then look back into the history of the Second World War, and they had figures for the number of people they could kill during training before people started to raise their eyebrows. So it took an enormous amount of pressure off me, knowing that General Peter would support me if somebody was killed. Then one immediately started looking at the training package in a slightly different way.'

From Al Jubail, the companies moved out 40 kilometres west of the port into the desert area around Al Fadili. This is an unpopulated plain, rising gently to the Jabal Al Fadili in the north. Although there are no permanent settlements of note, exercising troops had to be constantly alert for the Bedouin tribes which roamed throughout the area. The surface is fine, soft sand blown into dunes, and the whole area was described by one soldier as 'real Lawrence of Arabia country'. Bounding the area to the east is the Al Qaysumah/Al Qatif oil pipeline and associated tapline road. To the south and west, the desert stretches away to the horizon with no recognisable boundary. The range areas were marked out on the ground using painted oil drums where no obvious landmark existed, and then overprinted onto maps by 14 Independent Topographical Squadron of the Royal Engineers. The Battalion was allocated an area of some 50 square kilometres with the rest of the Brigade deploying around them.

The first few days were spent working on the vehicles and testing them out in this unfamiliar terrain. The companies moved out from Al Jubail on Saudi low loaders as soon as their vehicles were disembarked from the ships, and so arrived at Al Fadili over a period of five days. C Company was the last company to deploy on 1 November. At the same time the soldiers were acclimatising, and the command team was putting together a coordinated training programme for the Battalion.

The training commenced with a short battalion exercise on 3 November, which was designed to shake out the cobwebs and give the vehicles a run. C Company's war diary noted that,

'It was essentially a very simple exercise, which proved that we did know what we were doing – a good confidence booster.'

Following this, the Battalion moved to a concentration area north of the ranges, from where they were to operate during the next eight days while they undertook the live firing training 'package'. It was intended that the ranges would be open all day so their use could be maximised but, in the event, the Saudi authorities restricted firing to two 90 minute periods each day; from 0815–0945 and 1500–1630. The negotiations to be allowed even these limited timings extended until 6 November, so it was not until the following day that the Staffords were able to commence their training in earnest.

The most demanding ranges were those which placed the live firing within a tactical scenario, known as field firing. The soldiers had some experience of this, particularly from BATUS, but as Corporal Melvyn Downes explained, this was not quite the same:

'The ranges were the most realistic that I have ever been on. I've done courses like Junior Brecon [a tactics course for Junior NCOs] and that's supposed to be quite realistic, as is Canada, but they were nothing compared to these ranges. And that brought everything a lot closer to home. There were hardly any safety staff, you just had free run of the range.'

Private Warren Blacker could hardly believe the amount of latitude given to them:

'Some of the trench clearing exercises were amazing. You would have a section running down past you and you'd be shooting in front of them and over their heads. Then someone would shout, move now! You'd run down past them and they would be shooting just in front of you; all the rounds were landing just yards in front of the whole section as they ran through. If someone had been just a bit out, they could have taken someone's head off. But that was excellent.'

Private 'Mac' McDonald was a Warrior gunner:

'We did one attack where we stopped right in front of a trench. While the soldiers who had debussed from the vehicle were firing, we had to fire over their heads. Some people were popping their heads up out of the trench and looking, and as the rounds went down, they could see the explosions as they hit the sand in front of them. It's the first time I've seen blokes really crawl through trenches as we fired over their heads.'

Down in the trenches, Private John Hill could not initially maintain quite the same composure as his colleagues in the turret of the Warrior:

'I don't know about the rest of the blokes, but I shit myself during the first live firing trench attack that we did. I thought someone was bound to get hit. They had told us that the safety levels had been lowered on these ranges. But after the first one it was a case of, well, I have got confidence in my section commander firing behind me or something like that. You'd done the first one and no-one had been injured and I thought, well it's going to work because we've just done it and I haven't been shot.'

C Squadron of the Queens Royal Irish Hussars joined the Staffords on the largest field firing range to take part in a company/squadron group attack. The Squadron Second in Command, Captain Charles Alexander, found the experience heartening:

'That attack gave us so much confidence in the Staffords. Watching them with live ammunition, what they were doing was unbelievable. The amount of hand grenades and ammunition fired was staggering. The assault itself was nothing short of spectacular. One of the troop sergeants said that as they actually went in with bullets flying all over the place, he stuck his head out of his hatch to try and get a clearer idea of where he was. He said that that was the last time he would do that, the whole thing was quite terrifying. We couldn't believe that no-one had been hurt. Also, quite a lot of the tank crews driving along had Milan missiles come whizzing past their ears, some only about ten yards away. It didn't worry me in the slightest because I knew it wasn't aimed at me, and someone was guiding the thing.

'If we had to go in somewhere for real, we knew the Staffords would just rip them apart. A little later on, we did a dry exercise with the US Marines, and the Staffords were like lunatics. The Staffords were attacking us. They drove up in their Warriors, flat out, scattering Marines in all directions, and then piled out and gave them a good kicking.'

Although the Staffords suffered no fatalities on the ranges, there were some casualties. Most were of a relatively minor nature; quite a few people were burnt by white phosphorous grenade fragments. The grenade's primary function is to provide an instantaneous local smoke screen. As soon as the white phosphorous comes into contact with the air it burns, releasing a cloud of dense, acrid white smoke. The grenade is also a very effective anti-personnel weapon when thrown into a confined space such as a bunker or a trench. Anyone close to the point of the burst is horribly burned. John Hill was close to his section commander when he threw one in training:

'Corporal Downes threw one, but the wind had changed so a few small pieces came back down among us. The Platoon Commander got a piece, I got some, and a couple of others did as well. We weren't badly burned, it was like a fag end, but it was enough to make you flap. When it happened I was nearly sick because of the smoke. Then people started screaming because nobody realised how much they had got on them. The piece that hit me was only the size of a pencil head, but I got my kit off that fast it was unbelievable; the lot came off in one go.'

To their embarrassment, the Commanding Officer, Second in Command and RSM all received wounds from high explosive L2 grenades during this range period. WOI Steve Huyton was the most seriously injured:

'I was a safety supervisor on the range. As I ran along the back of one of the trench systems that C Company were clearing, they posted a grenade into another trench. What I believe happened was that it rolled along the top of the trench instead of into it. The next minute, bang! it was only a little piece, but I was flat on my back. It hit me about six inches above the knee and another piece went round the back of my leg and lodged in there. It looked a lot worse than it was at the time. It was like getting a good kick in the leg during a football match, and I knew exactly what had happened. The next minute, the radio op from the company commander's vehicle came over and stuck a field dressing on it. Then I saw Major Tanner taking photographs!

'I was evacuated back through the casualty chain, and I was dreading it because I didn't want to lose touch with the Battalion. I ended up in Al Jubail at the tented hospital where two colonels came in to look at me. One said I would have to have an operation and the other said it would just need a course of antibiotics. In the end I had the antibiotics, thank God. They were very good and very professional in there, but they did seem to want to keep me in for ever. The most embarrassing moment was when I was dying to go for a pee but I couldn't get up off this bed. A nurse brought me a bedpan up and said, here, you can use that. Christ, I was in a right state trying to have a bloody pee in that. And this nurse was running in and out all the time. It's strange, really, because for the last few weeks I'd been quite happy to have a crap in the open desert with soldiers all around.'

Captain Mark Weir was the Staffords Medical Officer, working in conjunction with Captain Richard Gale who was attached from the Greenjackets. One of his jobs was to instruct in and, if necessary, deal with, cases of battle shock:

'We didn't have anybody directly lecturing the troops. We did have 60 Field Psychiatric Team come up and speak to the officers and senior NCOs about it. Their job was to do no more than instruct on the symptoms and immediate treatment. I think that the impression we got was, look out, the psychiatrists have been let out of the asylum! I think the commanders did understand the potential dangers though. It's not really a medical problem anyway: it's a problem of soldiers being knackered, scared and hungry.'

Major Simon Knapper felt no need for this sort of preparation in A Company:

'There were two main fears in the Company. The first one was that it would all be over before we got there, and the other was that nothing would happen at all. I think people were more frightened of missing it; I mean, these guys had joined to be soldiers, and here was the opportunity to do it. There was the possibility of substantial casualties, and I'm sure the married men knew that and were slightly more concerned than others, but actually I would say that everybody was really keen to get in there and find out how they would react in those circumstances. There were no fancy seminars. We refused to see the psychiatrists; I thought it would be of little benefit to the Company.'

The Commanding Officer felt the seminar the psychiatric team held with all the commanders was a valuable exercise. It served to confirm that the attributes of a county regiment: good leadership, camaraderie, and a straightforward approach to problems, were a sound basis from which to confront the problems of battle stress.

Navigation was a great problem in the featureless desert. The Saudis have historically retained an extremely tight control over the issue and ownership of maps of the country as a means of deterring subversion. Because of this, topographical teams from all the forces involved in the conflict had to produce up-to-date mapping of the relevant areas. The lack of recognisable landmarks on the ground and the flatness of the desert surface meant these were often described as 'not much more helpful than a piece of sandpaper with grid lines on it'.

Sun compasses were issued, which were not affected by the magnetic field of an armoured vehicle in the same way as a normal magnetic compass, but these were fiddly to use and not popular. The best technique was found to be to take a bearing as best as one could and then follow it for a set distance, measured either using the vehicle's odometer or, if moving on foot, by counting the number of paces taken. Major Tim Gatfield had worked in the desert before and was well aware of the problems they would encounter:

'Navigation is really the principal problem when you're working in the desert. You can generally tell where you are within a few kilometres, but the ability to know where you are accurately, gives you an incredible advantage as a soldier. I actually bought my own satellite navigation system before we went out, which cost £1,200. It was worth every penny.'

By the time the Battalion crossed the border into Iraq, satnav equipment had been issued on a fairly large scale and undoubtedly contributed to the speed and flexibility of movement of the Allies. Most commanders were convinced it was a battle-winning piece of equipment. At this early stage of training, however, the more traditional methods were learnt and practised.

The process of acclimatisation was not confined solely to getting used to the temperature. Before leaving Fallingbostel, rumours of deadly scorpions and venomous snakes which sought refuge in discarded boots or sleeping bags were rife. Corporal Darren Fern quickly realised there was little to fear from the desert wildlife:

'The camel spider had a bad reputation when we first arrived. It's a bit like a scorpion in appearance, the only difference being that it has a double set of jaws. It's meant to inject flesh with some form of anaesthetic, and then it eats the flesh away because you can't feel it. It's meant to live off the fat of camels because they're so thick-skinned it doesn't do them any harm. There were rumours that people woke up with their ears chewed off and that sort of thing. So that didn't help; blokes were sleeping on top of their vehicles all the time. At night, you'd hear them rolling off and going thump onto the ground. It was quite funny in retrospect.

'At night, you'd see the blokes wandering around the vehicles with torches looking for scorpions and lizards and things like that. Private Reeves had a pet scorpion called Horrible. It was a fair size. We used to have fights with them, anything to keep us amused. We'd get a mess tin and put in a scorpion and perhaps a camel spider. We'd prod them a bit, really vex them up, and then knock them towards each other. Sooner or later, one would be injecting the other with some venom. Then they did fight. The camel spider usually won because the scorpions could inject them to their heart's content without any effect. When the camel spider got the scorpion in its jaws that was it. Horrible lasted quite a while though. It had its pincers taken off in a fight and all sorts, but it was still going. After a while, though, it got boring and we binned them. I don't think anyone wanted a tin full of scorpions falling down on them as they were driving into Kuwait.'

Robert and Vicky Lane – hastily married

Major John Rochelle speaks to his company before G Day

Vehicle preparation at Fallingbostel

The Royal Greenjacket contingent who fought with the Staffords

The 'Pig Pens' at Al Jubail

R and R at Al Fadili

SADDAM
RULE'S !!

General Boomer, US Marines, visits the Milan Platoon

There were few showers in the desert

C Company Orders Group

Training at Devil Dog Dragoon

The overwhelming feeling towards the prisoners was pity

Inside an Iraqi bunker

Staging area

Destruction on the Basra highway

Without exception, everyone was pleased to be away from the unexciting, mass-produced, American food which was the staple diet in Al Jubail. In the desert, each vehicle was issued with standard British Army composite rations, known universally as compo. These come in six different menus, and are designed to supply a large number of calories whilst being simple to prepare and reasonably palatable. Most soldiers supplemented their compo in one way or another. Corporal 'Barney' Barnett was the Battalion Headquarters clerk, and, by default, chief cook for the Second in Command's Warrior:

'My particular culinary skill ended up being curries. Major Tanner insisted on 'hot' meals. He's not a meat and two veg man, and he wouldn't let us cook those. So we were always having chili con carnes, bum burners, and curries. Once you'd gone through all the menus, it became dead hard to give the lads something different. There's a limit to what you can do with compo and curry powder. Everything ended up with some sand in it. By the time we came back, you were almost missing that familiar crunch in your meals. We did make some good dishes though. Most of the lads had some extra stuff sent out from their wives and families, and that supplemented our rations.'

The British Army has always had a reputation for being a great consumer of tea, and the Staffords were no exception. This proved to be a constant headache for Company Sergeant Major Bron Malec:

'The Warrior is worth a quarter of a million, half a million pounds? Whatever it is, it's the most expensive kettle in the world. The only reason they ever turned a Warrior on at night was to run-up a BV [Boiling Vessel]. It's just a container with an element in it which you can plug into the vehicle and the contents heat up. If you don't turn the engine on, it sucks all the juice out of the batteries after a while. On stag [sentry duty] at night, people were either not turning the engine on so in the morning the Warrior wouldn't move, or they were running the vehicles. We were trying to instil battlefield discipline into the company at the time, so one of the things I would do would be to run round the vehicles and stop people running them. The worst culprits were the platoon commanders. They'd always got a brew on. They can't breathe without a brew! At the end of the day it was all pretty futile. People could see that it made no difference. The vehicles were running all night and all day once we started the ground war.'

It was considered vital to maintain a high level of personal and communal hygiene. The temperature created the ideal environment for germs to reproduce, so all cooking and eating instruments were thoroughly washed and inspected after each meal. With the Warriors parked in static locations for some days at a time while the soldiers trained, strict rules were enforced regarding the disposal of dirty washing water, at least 75 metres from any vehicle, and the siting of toilets. 'Pee posts' were established well away from the vehicles. These ranged from a simple tube stuck into the sand, to more elaborate urinals constructed from a series of empty plastic water bottles with their bases cut off and wedged together. These could be manipulated and shaped according to the designer's fancy, and there are apocryphal stories of one construction which managed a full loop along its transparent length.

Privacy was an impossible luxury in the desert as Lieutenant Colonel Rogers found:

'In Battle Group Headquarters we dug our own khasi. It was always funny. I'd just be sitting there on my throne, and Private so-and-so would come and have a chat. It completely put me off my stride! So in the end, I did allow myself the luxury of my own bucket. I decided that really it was just too much, talking to the whole of Battle Group Headquarters when I was trying to think great thoughts on my throne.'

Although much new equipment had arrived in Fallingbostel before deployment, a steady stream of stores was arriving while the Battalion conducted its initial training. Particularly sought-after were the new desert combat suits. The British Army did not hold a reserve of this type of clothing, and firms in the UK had been commissioned to produce thousands of sets. Until they arrived, the soldiers were wearing green, camouflaged jungle suits. Although these were lightweight, they were clearly the wrong colour for desert operations and a number of people suffered from uncomfortable sweat rashes due to the synthetic material chafing moist skin. The new combat suits were made from cotton and were far more comfortable.

The Staffords are no strangers to inappropriate tropical uniform. In 1707, the 38th of Foot, predecessors of the present day Staffords, found themselves on the West Indian island of Antigua without any appropriate tropical uniform. During the 57 years that they remained there, they adopted a local sackcloth as the basis for their uniforms, and this is commemorated today by the wearing of a buff holland patch behind the regimental badge. At Al Fadili, the wait was not so prolonged, and by early November every man had at least one suit.

Other equipment which arrived during this period included basic essentials, such as racks which bolted onto the Warriors to allow them to carry the extra water jerrycans needed, and operational ammunition stocks which were carried by every man and in every vehicle. This ammunition was not used for training; it was issued purely to ensure that, if deployed at short notice, the Battalion was capable of fighting for a limited period without resupply.

New weapons like the luchair rifle grenade were fired on the Al Fadili ranges. This high explosive round was slipped over the muzzle of the SA 80, the standard infantryman's rifle, and could then be accurately fired at targets at ranges of 500 metres or more. It proved to be an extremely popular addition to their arsenal, as Private Paul Martin explained:

'It was a really accurate weapon. It was the first time we'd ever seen it when it arrived in the desert. We had one introductory lesson on it, and then fired a few practice rounds which made chalk puffs instead of explosions. Then we did about three attacks all in one day firing it live. It was a really easy weapon to learn, basic.

'We also had a thing called Mini Viper. It was used to clear a path through anti-personnel minefields for soldiers on foot. You put it on the end of the rifle and it worked like the Giant Viper. It just laid out a high explosive hose on the ground, and when that detonated it cleared all the mines beneath it.'

Basic items like goggles, sunglasses, desert camouflage nets and desert boots also began to arrive. The first boot issued was ankle length suede, and was not popular because it let in sand over the top. Later a revised version was issued, which had a higher top over which trouser bottoms could be fastened to provide a more effective seal. Combat body armour was issued. This waistcoat, constructed from Kevlar, was capable of stopping low velocity rounds and shrapnel splinters. It was relatively lightweight, if a little bulky, but most people were prepared to tolerate it because of the extra protection it conferred.

NBC training was still one of the most frequent activities as media speculation increased about the possible use of chemical or biological weapons by the Iraqis. The latest version of NBC suit, the Mark IV, was issued to everyone. These were, however, still camouflaged in green as they had been designed for use in north west Europe. By the time the ground war started, NBC suits in desert camouflage had been issued.

New air filtration canisters for respirators were in abundant supply, and roll upon roll of CARM (Chemical Agent Resistant Material) was handed out. These huge sheets were stretched over the armoured vehicles, underneath the camouflage nets, and provided a high degree of protection from contamination by droplet or aerosol-based chemical agents. They had the additional benefit of being waterproof, for which the troops were particularly grateful when the heavy rainfall started after Christmas.

Although a great deal of preparatory work had been done on all the vehicles before they left Fallingbostel, there were bound to be some teething problems associated with the high temperatures and soft sand in which they now had to operate. Lance Corporal Neil Peacock was a REME vehicle mechanic with B Company's Fitter Section;

'We had a lot of problems initially with sand ingress; sand getting into the air filters, power packs blowing up because of the excessive wear on pistons and cranks. Warrior was tested in the desert before it was issued in Germany, but ours were fitted up for European operations. The dust was getting in through the gaps in the air filters, so we had to put extra padding in to hold the filters down. The boffins from GKN who manufacture the vehicle said it was sand ingress causing the packs to blow up. We think it was the extra work we were demanding of the vehicles in the soft sand. There was also a problem to start with, with the engines overheating, but this was overcome by a simple modification to the thermostatically-controlled fans.

'Because the companies were dispersed up to 500–600 metres apart when they were in static locations, we had to walk over to do any repairs carrying a toolbox, weapon, webbing, respirator and body armour. That was knackering. Then when you got there and realised you had to go back to your vehicle to get a spare it really got hot. It was very hard to motivate yourself.

'The crew, drivers and platoon sergeants were excellent. In the six months we were there, they learned more about that vehicle than they would have done in ten years in Fallingbostel. You could grab any one of those crews and they would know all about the routine maintenance and minor repairs to Warrior, because they had to.'

Towards the end of the live firing package, the Battalion paused on 11 November to mark Remembrance Day. The C Company diarist, Lieutenant Peter Horne, noted:

'The Battalion attended a Remembrance Day service at 0530 hours. A rather rushed affair, as we had to prepare for Exercise Ferozeshah [a company/squadron group live firing exercise]. However, as one gazed around the hollow square, one couldn't help but wonder how many of the same faces would be at next year's Remembrance day – assuming that we went to war.'

The Staffords then joined up with the rest of the Brigade to take part in the first brigade level exercise in the desert. Nicknamed Exercise Jubail Rat, it started on 14 November. Until now, the two tank regiments had been conducting their own training in different parts of the Al Fadili area, although they had 'lent' troops and squadrons of tanks to the Staffords from time to time to provide fire support on some of the field firing ranges. One of the aims of Exercise Jubail Rat was to get the separate units working together as battle groups as they practised the various operations they expected to have to conduct against the Iraqis.

The exercise started with the crossing of an obstacle belt which had been constructed to simulate the Iraq/Kuwait border defences. This did not go smoothly by all accounts, but the purpose of the exercise was to identify problem areas, and these were exhaustively analysed afterwards to improve procedures and techniques. The Brigade then advanced across the desert, coming across 'enemy' positions en route which required clearance by tanks and infantry. It was a short, sharp affair, and ended at 0930 hours the following morning.

There was a constant stream of journalists and visitors to the Battalion while they were training. The Adjutant, Captain Chris Hughes, was responsible for coordinating these visits:

'The CO was very keen on PR. He was thinking of the wives and families particularly. And they were asking, why do we keep seeing the Queens Royal Irish Hussars on television every night? Where are the Staffords? The wives got very upset about it, and that was really what drove the CO to become very keen on PR. So we wanted them in, yet when they were there some of them were quite difficult. It was a matter of trying to share them out amongst the companies.

'Sometimes it was quite difficult because they knew what they wanted to see. They didn't want to see what you wanted them to see. For example, once they wanted to see the mail delivery. There were two film crews and a couple of journalists who went to A Company and then one letter arrived! It didn't make the Nine O'Clock News.

'The top journalists like Kate Adie are very chameleon-like. That's how they get their information. They assume your attitudes when they're talking to you or the soldiers, so that in about one minute flat you think, hey, I'm talking to a friend here. And of course you're not at all. You're talking to someone who has the potential to be fairly dangerous. Yet people were very keen to have somebody to talk to. It's very flattering if somebody takes a great interest in you. You just had to bear in mind what they were after; they were after selling press.'

Captain Jack Ferguson was also wary of the press, but he did concede that they were not all tarred with the same brush:

'The Express did an excellent piece on the Battalion. It was honest, and accurate, and they didn't misquote us or quote out of context. They were living in a hotel in Al Jubail, and they were prepared to get messages back for the guys' families. The journalist would get the telephone number, phone back to UK and say, I've just spoken to your son, he's fine, he's in the desert and you've got nothing to worry about. He didn't have to do that.'

Kate Adie was undoubtedly the most popular journalist amongst the soldiers, and she was very good at allowing herself to be photographed with platoons or sections. It was a Stafford soldier who made the oft-quoted remark that they knew war was not imminent because Kate Adie had not yet arrived. She had thought hard about her role before flying out to the Gulf to report the conflict:

'It's quite an interesting kind of relationship which the press have with the army. When a man gets a gun the relationship changes; it's as simple as that. When it comes to your own army, there are a lot of moral questions about: loyalty, support, patriotism and not rocking the boat. Then on the other side: objective journalism, telling the truth, and giving people the full picture. All of those things are an amazing problem.

'Things were much improved on the Falklands. The only problem I had, as regards censorship, was with the Foreign Office, not the army. That was a question of Saudi sensitivities. This time, what we did do, and what I think is a good pattern for the future, is that we argued that whatever censorship there had to be, it was done by people in the field; not by people behind desks at home who are influenced by politicians.

'Sometimes there were minders around when I was reporting, but I ate minders for breakfast! I said, if you don't trust me to actually talk to them, to be with them, then you can't trust me. Anyway, I don't like somebody hanging over my ears when I'm talking to somebody, so I got rid of the minders. The problems were only with the civilian minders. The people in uniform were much more realistic; much more confident in their men. They knew what they were like.

'The soldiers were very bright; and talking to the lads, it was clear that a lot of them were very, very browned off about the fact that they were treated by the tabloids as a bunch of tabloid-reading oiks. They objected to this. I'm not suggesting that the entire army sits down and reads the FT every day; they don't all absorb Telegraph leaders. But these days, they are much better educated, much brighter, much smarter. All of them were following the news on the world service. They didn't like being portrayed as a thick, rather simple, Tommy Atkins type. Quite a lot of soldiers said, we're not "their lads". They rather objected to being appropriated.'

When she did come, her visits created more interest than those of many high ranking officers or politicians and she received constant attention, but not always to her benefit, as Lance Corporal Neil Love recounted; perhaps somewhat tongue-in-cheek:

'I was going back to Al Jubail with some paperwork, and we saw her behind a Land Rover. She was about to make a report and she was looking all nice, spick and span. Then she ruffled up all her hair, rearranged her clothes and said to the camera, I have just come out of the field . . . ! We just looked at her, and she knew we were looking, then we buggered off.'

Major Simon Knapper had fairly strong views about the media:

'I don't like the press, I'm never comfortable with them. I think they're parasites. It's all fine words, but at the end of the day they're doing it for the money. They give you all the spiel about public information, freedom of the press, all that crap. They're in it for the money. They're highly paid and they are a bloody nuisance. They are amateurs in the sense that, although they may be professional journalists, they are amateurs because they don't know what the hell they are seeing or writing about, and they can do so much damage by a stupid phrase or word.

'The dilemma is, should you be honest with them and accept the fact that they might decide they don't like you and tear you to bits? Or should you not be honest with them and only give the half the story? They'll take what you say; a couple of facts, a bit of fantasy, a bit of guesswork, and there's the story.

'I do think though, that the Regiment handled the press very well. Very little bullshit, take us as you find us. After four and a half months or so I felt that our relations with the press were entirely honest. Therefore, the press preferred to interview grim-faced Jocks, grimly sharpening bayonets, and they weren't actually interested in Staffords just getting on with being good, solid soldiers, not bullshitting, just getting on with life. And this wasn't sensational enough.'

Chris Hughes also looked after the many visitors to the Battalion:

'We had some good visitors. It was nice to see people like the Chief of the General Staff, General Boomer from the American Marines, the Commons Select Committee on Defence, and a group of American politicians including the congressman for Disneyland!

'They landed in two US helicopters and they poured out, and it was like seeing 'Fear and Loathing in Las Vegas'. These Hawaiian shirts and some rather large women, and there was a guy in a baseball cap with a video camera. They all looked like tourists. We laid on a demo for them. Then this guy with the baseball cap and video camera went up to Captain Richard Wootton and said, hi, I'm the congressman for Disneyland. And Richard said, yup, and I'm Mickey Mouse! The guy just stared at him. He was not quite sure how to take it.'

There were no telephones in the Al Fadili training area, and therefore all communication with friends and relatives at home was by letter. The Forces aerogramme, the ubiquitous 'bluey', was the preferred method, although normal letters and parcels could also be sent through the system. Mail is traditionally something very important to soldiers on operational postings and Operation GRANBY proved no different. Morale was more easily influenced by this than by any other factor. Lance Corporal Neil Love was the Battalion Post NCO:

'I was based in the field with A2 Echelon. Incoming mail was delivered at a rate of easily 40 sacks a day, and it was first sorted in camp by Corporal Stanley into company sacks. I would deliver it to the company colour-sergeants, and they would take it forward to the troops. At the same time, I would take any incoming mail, sort it all out, and then distribute it to the Royal Engineers Postal and Courier Regiment. We handled classified documents, recorded mail and signals, as well as all the personal mail. I was quite busy.

In the first month or so there were some complaints that the mail wasn't getting through, and I think they were justified. It mainly applied to mail from Germany. The RAF kept saying that the plane had broken down, but I reckon they were stopping off for a pint in Cyprus! The main problem was actually that when 4 Brigade started moving out, the mail took a lower priority to 4 Brigade's kit, so all the mail was accumulating at Gutersloh airport. There were a lot of complaints from guys that they weren't getting mail, but in fact we found out in many cases that it was caused by their wives not writing to them.'

Sergeant Major Sammy Salt, Company Sergeant Major of B Company, took a keen interest in the mail:

'We used to make the guys write two blueys a day; one in the morning and one in the afternoon, just to get them into a routine. It lasted a couple of weeks and then it ceased to be compulsory. The blokes then were writing on their own. Most guys on exercise don't write or phone home, and I wanted to get them out of this syndrome. It did seem to work because the guys were screaming for more blueys.'

For the families in Fallingbostel, the mail was just as important as it was for the soldiers. Fiona Foster felt the need to emphasise this to her husband, Nick:

'The letters did become very important; you really did look forward to getting them. Nick would write and say, your letters are really important and I'd say, well in fact, it's just as important to me. I know he was working hard, I know he didn't have the time to write that I did, but I had to make him realise that getting letters from him was just as important for me as it was for him. To be fair to him, he did actually get a lot better – I was getting probably a couple a week.

'I tried to write about three times a week. Some people wrote every day but I couldn't do that. I didn't really feel that I had enough to say. I'm a dreadful letter writer anyway, so it took quite an effort to get into the idea of writing even three letters a week. All my friends went completely by the board, nobody else got any letters at all.'

Private Stuart Smith enjoyed receiving the unsolicited letters which flooded in from all over the United Kingdom:

'We had some very saucy letters, and some other lads in the company had some right dirty pictures sent to them. The letters were passed round the guys, and we stuck the photos inside the back doors of the Warriors. During the war we had two prisoners in the back of the wagon. When they saw the pictures they loved it. They had big smiles on their faces, and they kept pointing at them and talking to each other.'

Some soldiers believed their outgoing mail might have been subjected to censorship, but the Adjutant refuted this:

'At the start we thought the mail might be censored, but there was an awful lot of stuff going out and I think that was probably the biggest problem. In fact it was the telephone calls which concerned us more. There were a lot of people in Al Jubail and even Riyadh with access to phones. I did hear a suggestion that a week before we went in they would rip the phones out, but it didn't happen in the end.'

In Fallingbostel, the mail was proving to be a lifeline for the families because telephone calls were so difficult to make. Some wives took comfort in withdrawing into the solitude of their immediate family, but for the more gregarious there was the opportunity to participate in functions arranged by the Battalion wives' club. This unofficial and voluntary organisation has existed for many years, but the departure of the men effectively forced it into a higher profile. The club is run by a committee chaired by the Commanding Officer's wife, who has a power of veto, but the executive functions and day to day running are performed by other committee members led by the RSM's wife. Julie Huyton arranged a very structured team with representatives from a cross-section of wives whose husbands were of various ranks. Carla Hughes described how the club worked:

'There is an implied obligation if you are a company commander's wife that you will do your bit; be it entertaining your officers, entertaining the senior ranks and their wives, or coffee mornings. There is also an implied obligation to go to wives' club things. Some people do it happily, some people do it under sufferance, and some people don't do it all. There is nothing that can be done to make someone do it. Some people say it can affect your husband's career, but I don't think it can do really. I have just always found that it makes it a lot easier if you know the soldiers' wives.

'At first, when the men had left, it was all very ad hoc. Some of the companies were doing a lot more with their wives than the others were. Although I was the Adjutant's wife, there was nobody to look after Support Company [the company commander was a bachelor] so I volunteered to pick them up. Then, because Sue Dennis, who was organising Headquarter Company, and I lived next door to each other and were very good friends, it seemed a good idea to do things together. So then our functions became combined Headquarter and Support Company ones.

'We had a number of meetings with the wives who were interested, to find out what they wanted to do. The most popular request was to have a function with a male stripper! We didn't do that. Then they suggested a karaoke night. We advertised that around the Battalion, but we only had about six people sign up for it so it was cancelled. Similarly with a ten pin bowling night, we tried and failed on that one. I think people preferred just to go out, and have a drink and something to eat, and be able to talk to each other. The nights that we had like the Chinese evening, where there was food, a bar and a disco were much more succesful.'

On 16 November, 7 Armoured Brigade was declared operationally effective. Within the Battalion, this milestone appears to have been received with equanimity; it is likely the declaration was made as much for its public relations value as anything else. The emphasis now shifted from work-up training, which was deemed to be complete, to continuation training.

The plan was that the Battalion would work a 15 day training cycle. The companies would train for nine days, concentrating on individual skills and low-level training. This period included work with tanks from the Irish Hussars and the Scots Dragoon Guards. There would then be a three day battalion level exercise coordinated with the other brigade units. This was to practise and test the tactics and skills which had already been tried out at company level within the context of battle group operations. Finally, each company would have a three day rest period in Camp 4.

Camp 4 was a large hutted camp in Al Jubail. It had been built as a transit camp to house immigrant workers in Saudi Arabia, and during the conflict it was given over exclusively to the British forces. The Americans had similar facilities. Lieutenant Nick Todd described it:

'The accommodation was all hutted, and the guys were in four man rooms. There were three large dining rooms, one of which was given over exclusively to the staff of 33 Field Hospital who were based there. That caused some frustration because all the pretty nurses were in there and we weren't allowed in. They even posted Regimental Policemen on the door to make sure we didn't get in. Even so, quite a few of the guys said they were medics and got in that way.

'The facilities were pretty good. The greatest luxuries were the hot showers, and real toilets which you could sit down on. There were two burger bars, sports facilities like volleyball, and a gym which had some weight training kit in it. All the rooms were air-conditioned. Telephones were available, although they were rarely all working at the same time. The queues were usually enormous. There were also "choggie shops" where you could buy everything from a razor blade to a can of pop. They ran trips down to the beach, to the American camp which had a pool, and to another pool in Al Jubail. You could also go out shopping if you wanted.

'From Camp 4 they ran the "Scrub a Squaddie" programme. Blokes could go out to expatriate families in the vicinity, who would take them in for the day and feed and water them. Some were pretty good, and would wash their clothes and ply them with the sort of luxuries that they hadn't seen since they had left Germany. It was just a nice break; a chance to forget about what was going on.'

Permanently based in Camp 4 were the B Echelons of the 7 Brigade units. Commanded by the quartermasters, these were the organisations which provided administrative and logistic back up to the fighting soldiers. From here, pay was issued and associated problems were sorted out. The Battalion Chief Clerk worked with a small team to keep track of the individuals who were posted out of the Battalion as casualties or for other reasons, and those who arrived to take their place. The issue of new equipment and replacements for consumables was coordinated. It was also from Camp 4, before Christmas, that an anonymous Stafford soldier telephoned the Baghdad Sheraton Hotel and made a reservation for a suite in one month's time.

The continuation training out on the Al Fadili area continued to emphasise the need for a high level of proficiency in NBC training, and a team from the Defence NBC centre at Winterbourne Gunner in the UK travelled around the companies, instructing and practising them in the latest techniques modified for desert operations. As Private 'Mac' McDonald noted, there was no lack of enthusiasm amongst the soldiers:

'Everyone put 100% effort into the training and approached it in a totally professional manner. Most of the time, people didn't think they were getting enough training and were asking for more. That's the first time I've ever heard a private soldier asking for more training. Overall we did enough training. After a while we were just repeating things, which could get monotonous. But as soon as we had a break and weren't working quite so hard, that's when people started asking to do more.'

On 2 December the routine of the training cycle, which was now running fairly smoothly, was rudely interrupted. Captain Tim Sandiford recorded the incident in his diary:

'As we were being briefed for an exercise, we had a no-duff Dress State 1 [orders to dress in NBC protective clothing but not at that stage put on the respirator]. This was followed by an announcement that the satellites had picked up the launch of three Scuds from Iraq, outgoing towards Israel. As we changed we were all rather stunned and pensive, feeling nervous and uneasy. Moments later we got 'Gas, Gas,

Gas' from Brigade. There was one second of stunned disbelief, then a dash for the respirator. It doesn't take nine seconds!

'When you think it's for real, it suddenly doesn't feel as if your mask fits, and the velcro fastening on the new suit digs into your throat and makes you gag. It appears that a Naiad went off in Brigade as the dress state was upped. The Scuds impacted in Iraq and were only a test firing; was he trying to provoke the Israelis? From the first report until the report of impact, we were sure that the war was about to start, and to be the nightmare scenario of Israel turning it nuclear at the outset.

'After the Gas Clear, we were all very jovial and full of witty comments. The whole feeling was a pretty calm apprehension, but when you are putting your NBC boots and gloves on whilst masked up, you are on your own and there is time for reflection when you can only think, oh shit!'

As part of their own training packages, the companies ran self-contained exercises. These practised the desert skills they had been taught, such as survival and navigation techniques, as well as the more usual infantry tasks, including patrolling and escape and evasion. Most commanders were keen to take the opportunity to separate the soldiers from their vehicles and get them working on foot. It is very easy to become dependent upon the Warrior as an armoured infanteer. It can carry your food and water and has the facilities with which to cook it. It transports all your equipment, and is a shelter from both the elements and enemy fire. There was a need to remove this protective mantle every once in a while during training.

The first battle group exercise of this phase took place from 2–4 December. It started with a night march on foot, prior to a dismounted night attack on a simulated enemy position. The whole thing was done dressed in NBC suits and wearing combat body armour. Once the attack was completed, the Warriors rejoined their troops and a defensive position was established. From that position, the following night, a mounted night attack with tanks in support was made onto a further dug-in position. The exercise ended after the Battle Group had reorganised on the objective.

It would be misleading to say that all these attacks went perfectly. The night attack is probably one of the most difficult operations carried out in war, and the commanders rapidly realised that it could only succeed if the plan was kept very simple. In addition, the chances of success are greater if the procedure is reduced as far as possible to a series of drills. This is not to say that the commander on the ground has his flexibility curtailed; rather, every possible manoeuvre must be practised over and over again under all sorts of conditions, so each individual is confident of the part he has to play in the battle.

The particular problems identified after this exercise were the need for each soldier to carry a plentiful supply of water to combat dehydration, which will occur rapidly when dressed in NBC suits and body armour; and the difficulty of accurately fixing the enemy positions on the ground. The vehicle night-sights could be degraded by fine dust, mist or rain, and it was all too easy to overrun the position or miss it to one side or the other.

These, and many other points which were raised, were thoroughly analysed after each exercise in debriefing sessions which took place at every level of command. While the Commanding Officer was debriefing his command team, section commanders would be talking through the exercise with their soldiers. There was much cross-fertilisation of ideas, as the section commanders would have the opportunity to pass on their thoughts to the platoon and company commanders, and similarly, the Commanding Officer's points would be passed back down the same chain to the soldiers.

Close links were established with the American forces during the period leading up to Christmas. It was originally intended that 7 Armoured Brigade would come under command of the 1st (US) Marine Division once the Brigade was ready to deploy. The Division was based on the coastal strip of Saudi Arabia, north of Al Jubail and well to the east of the Wadi Al Batin. They were eventually to assault into Kuwait from the south-west when the ground war started.

The Milan platoon carried out cross-training with the TOW Company of the 2/18 Infantry, while C Company, with the Milan and Recce Platoons, acted as enemy for Task Force Ripper, the US Marine Force, during a major dry exercise in mid December. But by 20 December the possibility of the Brigade moving west and coming under command of the US Army as opposed to the Marines, was being discussed at high level as a probable course of action.

Whatever option was to be chosen, it was clear that the British forces in the Gulf were going to work hand in hand with their American allies. As the Staffords got to know their counterparts on the ground, the Commander British Forces Middle East (CBFME), General Sir Peter de la Billière, was becoming well acquainted with the Allied Commander, General Norman Schwarzkopf:

'He is a large man physically. He is a very dedicated, highly trained and experienced soldier, having gained battle experience in Vietnam and other campaigns. He is a first rate general with very firm ideas as to how to conduct a battle, very much formulated on a basis of a diet of history as well as his training. He has a sharp mind, and a lovely sense of humour. He is a man who, on the whole, has the intellect and the ability to control things fairly tightly himself.

'And then, with all that, what he has, and what was very special and necessary out there, is the ability to be a politician, and the greatness to see that in the campaign, the failure of the coalition was going to be the failure of the whole military operation, and that therefore he had to keep the coalition together, if necessary at the expense of some of the military preferences he would like to have gone for. He was always prepared to do that. He was always prepared, if necessary, to make political concessions to the military idealism in order to ensure the cohesion of the coalition and therefore the cohesion of the military machine.

'The Staffords had these mugs which were presented by the people of Staffordshire for Christmas. The CO gave me one which I carefully cherished all the way through the Gulf, it was my mug in the Gulf. Now I alternate between the Staffordshire mug and the Free Kuwait mug. I then thought I'd present one to Norman Schwarzkopf, so I asked the CO for a second one which he very kindly gave me. Regrettably, the truth of the matter is, the moment never arrived to present it to Norman Schwarzkopf and I've still got it!'

Influencing the planning at this time was the announcement that 4 Armoured Brigade was to deploy from Germany to reinforce the British ground presence in the Gulf. The two brigades would now come under command of the 1st Armoured Division, commanded by Major General Rupert Smith. The announcement had been made on Thursday 22 November by the Secretary of State for Defence, Tom King, and the 4 Brigade units were due to start arriving around Christmas.

In one sense, the majority of the Staffords were disappointed to hear they were to be reinforced. Until now, they had been the focus of attention as the only British infantry battalion in the desert, but this was to shift as the 4 Brigade units began to arrive in theatre. A very strong sense of pride in the Brigade had developed, a form of elitism, and although the Staffords remained a part of 7 Armoured Brigade, they had to develop a new loyalty towards the 1st Armoured Division of which they were now a part.

But this was purely an emotional reaction. The deployment of another brigade could only benefit the British troops, bringing with it, as it did, valuable additional firepower in the form of Royal Artillery MLRS launchers and heavy guns. While the Staffords continued with their own training, they planned briefings and familiarisation visits for the men of the Royal Regiment of Fusiliers and the Royal Scots, the two armoured infantry battalions in 4 Brigade.

With this massive reinforcement underway, and the American build-up continuing inexorably, as well as the deadline imposed by the UN Resolution 678, it was clear there could be no thought of initiating a war with Iraq before mid January at the earliest. The Staffords therefore planned to give the soldiers as good a Christmas celebration as was possible. On 21 December, the Battalion celebrated Ferezoshah Day. It is a regimental custom that the Battle of Ferozeshah, which took place in 1845 during the First Sikh War, is celebrated with a battalion parade and trooping of the colours. The colours are no longer carried into action (during Op GRANBY they were secured in Fallingbostel), so a regimental flag and Union Jack were paraded in the desert in their place. The 1/7 Battalion of the US Marines was invited to the parade, which was followed by sports fixtures against the Americans and a barbecue lunch.

Christmas and its attendant celebrations were always destined to be a low-key affair. Contrary to media speculation at the time, religious services were held for those who wished to attend. Alcohol, an important feature of the festivities in peacetime, was banned. Ever inventive, a number of soldiers had found a way around this, as one anonymous interviewee explained:

'There was a little booze in Camp 4 at Christmas. I had some whisky sent out to me in a shampoo bottle. I took the top off it, and shared it out amongst about six of us. I took the first swig and immediately spat it out blowing bubbles. They hadn't washed the bottle properly beforehand!'

Those companies which did not go into Camp 4 for Christmas Day maintained the tradition of the officers and senior NCOs serving 'gunfire' to the other ranks before breakfast. Gunfire is usually hot sweet tea liberally laced with rum or whisky. Sergeant Major Bron Malec was determined the soldiers of his company should not miss out on this annual treat even though there was no alcohol officially issued to fortify the brew:

'I prepared the tea personally using all the resources at my disposal, and then the company commander and I went round and served it to the soldiers. I think they all enjoyed it. We also had a bugler dressed as Santa Claus who played reveille for us. So that was something a bit different for the soldiers.'

Many soldiers described Christmas as probably the lowest point of the tour for morale. These attempts to invest the festival with an air of normality were one way of bolstering flagging spirits. Sergeant Gino Pulizzi was a platoon sergeant with B Company:

'People were beginning to get a bit pissed off at that stage. It was hardest for the married ones with kids. I had a lad in my platoon and he just didn't want to know, so I thought the best thing to do was just leave him. I wouldn't say morale was particularly low, but you could see that people were getting a bit fed up. All the platoon sergeants and officers kept a pile of the parcels that we were getting sent through, so that the lads would have something to open on Christmas Day. We threw them on the back of the ambulance and drove round the position with party hats on, dishing the presents out. On the whole though, morale was kept up.

'We really just wanted to get on with it. Just get out there and have a go at the Iraqis. We didn't rate any reports about the Republican Guard. We didn't rate them at all. We knew that we were better, man for man, than they would ever be. We weren't worried at all. Every man in my platoon just wanted to get on in there. We'd had intelligence briefs about them, we knew they had decent kit and we took them seriously, but we were very confident. We just wanted to get in there and fight them.'

One of the brighter moments for B Company was the visit paid to them paid by the British Joint Force Commander, Lieutenant General Sir Peter de la Billière. The company watchkeeper, Lieutenant Nick Todd, had reason to remember the visit:

'He spent Christmas night with us and had a bit of a chat with the boys. He's a very easy man to talk to. He had dinner with us in the command post and I was duty chef that night. I'd just pulled a can of carrots out of the BV, opened them up and the can was getting a little bit hot. So I went to put it on the edge of the table, but I missed it and they went all over his leg. Amazingly, he said he enjoyed the meal! Afterwards, he went off to talk to the boys and then he just set up his camp bed and went to sleep. The next morning he came on a run with the company.'

The General enjoyed his visit:

'It was a great treat to go out and stay with a battalion for any length of time other than a short visit. I always like to talk to the servicemen, as many as possible gathered together, tell them what is going on, how events are progressing, what we were trying to achieve and what their job was, that type of thing. Then the most valuable part of any of these talks was questions afterwards. Now with many units you didn't get questions for one reason or another, some units gave you quite a lot, but the best set of questions I ever had in the Gulf came from the Staffords. The interesting thing was that they collected them together in the dark, in the desert, on a sand dune. So they couldn't actually see me, and I suspect that this broke down the barriers of rank and they felt much freer to come back at me. They knew they couldn't be identified by face anyway. I had a very long question session which I found immensely valuable, because then you find out what the serviceman's thinking and what he wants to know. That was a tremendous moment, talking to them under the stars in the desert. After that we went on and watched a film, which I think was the only film I ever watched in the whole of my time in the Gulf!'

C Company arranged some entertainment for their soldiers over the Christmas period. Lieutenant Andy Nye was 'volunteered' to coordinate it:

'We had a revue at Christmas. I've always been interested in that sort of thing and I brought it up in conversation, and the OC turned round and said, right, you're in charge of the revue, I want it on Boxing Day. Initially, it was a nightmare trying to get people interested. But then I got my platoon to put on two sketches in the field. No props or anything, really basic, and I invited the reps from the other platoons, then they got really keen. Then the LAD found us some lights, and I asked OC B

Company if I could borrow his bandsmen medics so we had a six piece band. The Pioneer Section constructed staging and a curtain, because we were doing it in one of the dining halls in Camp 4. I met a couple of nurses and my opening line was, can I borrow your suspenders, and they then lent us a couple of dresses and make-up.

'We practised and practised, and by the end of it the blokes were saying, look boss, it's not funny, because we'd done it so often. But the very first sketch, based on 'Blind Date', went well. When the blokes behind the scenes heard the rest of the company go berserk, because they'd just not seen anything for so long, everybody then had the right spirit. It was brilliant. 7 Platoon did the 'Desert Rat Rap', each taking the mickey out of a personality in the company, and that went down a treat.'

A mobile cinema was made available to the Battalion, and most soldiers who wanted to were able to visit the nearby quarry which served as a natural amphitheatre and watch the films projected onto a makeshift screen. A couple of fortunate soldiers were given the opportunity to travel down to Bahrain on Christmas Eve to participate in the BBC live satellite link-up with Fallingbostel. Sergeant Major Bill Crowder was one of those selected and his wife, Lin, welcomed the chance to take part:

'That night I was just excited, very excited. The link worked straight away; I think they'd been working on it all day. We were there a bit early of course, the girls who were speaking to their husbands, because they weren't sure if the husbands had actually made it. Anyway, fortunately they all did.

'As soon as the first hymn started we could all hear our men singing, and that was the most exciting part of it. There was a big screen so you could see the men; it was just overwhelming, you could never explain how you felt. And then you were ushered up onto the altar and spoke to your husband, but all through the service you could see your husband, so that was nice. You didn't get very long, anyway; I think it was 45 seconds each. But the people from the BBC actually said to us, make sure you've got written down what you want to say because the minute you see him it'll be so emotional, it will go completely out of your head and you'll just stand looking at each other. So of course we'd done all this, but when I stood up there it all went to pot, I didn't say any of it. I just said, hello, merry Christmas, happy anniversary, and things like that. So it was a bit silly really.

'I think I was too excited to be choked at the time, but afterwards it was very upsetting. It's not the first time we've been on our own for Christmas, it was just different. We all knew it was going to come to a war, really, so it was just the waiting and the worry, the anxiety. Bill was the same as me. He phoned me afterwards; it was about three o'clock in the morning and he was really upset. I think it was just emotionally traumatic for all of us.'

A couple of weeks before Christmas, every unit in 7 Brigade had been allowed to send a representative back to Fallingbostel to update the wives on the situation in the Gulf. The Staffords sent Captain Chris Hughes:

'I wasn't keen to come back. It was quite a difficult thing to do in many ways.

You'd said your goodbyes, and we'd been there two months and settled into the absence if you like. So it wasn't quite as wonderful as it sounded. Of course I was delighted to see Carla and to have the chance to talk to her.

'I presented to the Stafford wives on two nights, and went down and did the same with the Grenadiers in Munster and the Greenjackets and the Prince of Wales's Own in Osnabruck. I think they found it useful, because a lot of the wives weren't getting told anything. You couldn't say in your letters where you were, but you could say what you were doing. Some of them hadn't heard a dicky bird.'

Many of the families had taken advantage of the MOD offer of free flights to return to UK from Fallingbostel to spend Christmas with relatives and friends. Those who were left held a wives' Christmas party, which Ellie Banks attended:

'The wives' Christmas do is an annual event where the blokes serve the wives. I didn't think they'd have one but they did, and it was all videoed and sent over to the men. It was brilliant, a real highlight. It wasn't the same obviously, because the blokes weren't there, but they did their best and we thoroughly enjoyed it. It must have been a great comfort to the blokes seeing that the wives were alright, drunk again!'

The children of the soldiers were encouraged by their teachers in Fallingbostel to write to the single soldiers in the Gulf. Neil Loftus was a teacher at Shackleton school:

'A girl in my class designed a Christmas card that we sent off. A lot of the soldiers wrote back saying how much they appreciated it, and a lot of the kids got individual blueies from these soldiers; that was nice for them. They could feel as if they'd done their own little bit really. One of them is still in touch with the soldier she wrote to. After the war finished, her mother asked her to keep writing to him.'

Mike Bennet was the headmaster:

'The Families Office sent me a list of all the single chaps in the Gulf, and we sent them all a card. I know that they went down well; I got a letter from one of the single lads saying how the letter from the kiddie cheered him up, but these are things teachers do anyway. I do think though, that the Army could have taken the opportunity to send out a letter to all the schools thanking us for our contribution. I'm saying that for the profession, not for my school, not for me; we only did our job, but we did it well.'

Before Christmas the Brigade had been warned it would have to move north, away from the Al Fadili training area, over the New Year period, in preparation for the likely resubordination to VII (US) Corps who were deployed north-west of Al Fadili. Once the festivities were over, attention focussed on preparing the vehicles for the move, and planning further training on the strangely named 'Devil Dog Dragoon' range complex which had been constructed by the American Marines at Abu Hadriya, some 70 kilometres up the coast. As the Staffords passed through Camp 4 over Christmas, and came across the newly arrived soldiers from 4 Brigade, they felt very much that they were already seasoned campaigners in the desert, wise to the conditions, competent desert soldiers with confidence in their equipment and colleagues.

5

Redeployment and the Air War

'It had gone on long enough, and he needed to be brought to heel.'

As the Staffords prepared to move north along the coastal road from Al Fadili, people in England, both military and civilian, returned to work after the Christmas break. At Whittington Barracks, near Lichfield in Staffordshire, Lieutenant Colonel Crichton Wakelin supervised the running of the casualty notification organisation:

'In the early stages post deployment, the casualty notification was being coordinated by the Staffords' Regimental Headquarters [RHQ] down the road. When I arrived in this job in October, we started to get an ops room set up, and we got Captain Ian Harris, who was a 'spare' officer at the time, to run it on a day to day basis. Once it was up and running, it became quite clear that RHQ would not be able to cope with the substantial number of casualties that might be incurred, were the worst to happen.

'There is a laid down procedure for this sort of thing, but it was so rusty because people hadn't used it that we ended up relying on trial and error, meetings, discussions and phone calls to build a system that was actually going to work. There was a distinct stage where we went from doing it pretty much on our own, to it being picked up at district level and then UKLF and Army-wide. Then the procedures began to be looked at in a more detailed way.

'Once we felt that war was pretty likely, we began to train people. We identified visiting officers from those serving officers in the area, TA officers and retired officers. We produced briefing packs and held seminars for them. At these, we got "guest speakers" who had experience of dealing with the situation of telling people that their relatives had died. We had a captain from the Parachute Regiment who had dealt with the Falklands casualties, a lady from the local Hospice who was very good indeed, we had the padre, and we had a social worker. I think it was quite an eye-opener for a lot of people.

'We also worked very closely with the local Gulf support group who had all the contacts in the county. They knew of other families in the area who could go and help anyone who was bereaved, give them advice or just hold their hands. They had amazing contacts all over the place; people offering accommodation, transport, telephones, everything. The workers there were all volunteers, mostly soldiers' wives or families, and they did an absolutely marvellous job.

'In the New Year we had a national rehearsal during which we had to deal with 99 simulated casualties, and that was very useful. Once the war started we began to get the really minor stuff, like flu and swollen testicles, and we had to go and tell the parents. We found that a bit difficult, because people saw somebody coming along and they thought it was to tell them some terribly bad news. When they heard it was swollen bollocks they were quite happy!'

A similar system had been established in Fallingbostel, where the next of kin of most of the married soldiers remained during the conflict. Carla Hughes was, like many other wives, involved in the contingency planning:

'People were worried about how they would find out if their husband was killed. There was a lot of debate about whether we would be told as soon as it happened. The Army used to say that wives or dependants would only ever be told between certain hours; I think it was between eight in the morning and ten at night. That seemed to me to be sensible because I didn't feel that somebody coming round at three in the morning and telling me that Chris had died would be of any benefit. There wouldn't be anything I could do other than just be hysterical at three o'clock in the morning.

'But then a lot of the wives said, no, they didn't agree with that. They wanted to know immediately. Immediately is relative of course, because it probably would have been two or three days later anyway, but a lot of wives felt they didn't want somebody in Fallingbostel knowing their husband was dead if they didn't know. It was finally decided that we would be told when it happened, that is as soon as they knew. It was then firmly stressed that you could go along to the Families Information Centre and say if you didn't want to be told in the small hours. I did do that.

'You could also name your friend if you wanted to be told by someone, or alternatively if you didn't want to be told by someone else. I think it ended up being more of a negative list, that is people naming those whom they didn't want to cross their threshold. There was a big feeling amongst the soldiers' wives that they didn't want some pushy officer's wife coming round to tell them. I didn't think we had enough casualty visiting officer's assistants, which is what we were called, who were soldiers' wives. Originally, only officers' wives were asked to do it, and I didn't agree with that. So I did make a point of saying, let's open it up to all ranks, which was done. I spoke to the colonel in charge of organising it all, and fortunately he was of my opinion that compassion isn't a rank-structured thing, and that some people are much better at it than other people. Just because you may be a major's wife doesn't mean that you are the right person for that particular job.'

The local newspapers all had teams in Saudi Arabia covering the activities of the Battalion, and consequently there was a high degree of awareness within Staffordshire of the part being played by the county regiment. Major Mac McLean, the Regimental Secretary, was the link man between the county and the Regiment:

'There was tremendous support from the county: a heck of a lot of phone calls of goodwill, letters of goodwill, and that sort of thing. People saying, what can we do? It's very hard when you're working 25 hours out of every 24 to have any bright ideas about what they could do. The bright ideas factory went into abeyance.'

This geographical and historical tie, unique to the British regimental system and particularly strong in Staffordshire, was appreciated by the soldiers. Lieutenant Colonel Charles Rogers was taken aback by the sheer volume of mail:

'Around Christmas time, lots of parcels started to come through. The vehicles were choc-a-bloc with parcels and Christmas presents. The county was wonderful, lots of presents and lots of letters from people one's never heard of. I remember a lovely Christmas card from a seven-year-old saying, God speed, we wish you well and go and kill Saddam Hussein. A staggering amount of letters. They were fabulous. I can't emphasise enough how great the county was in support of us. If there's one great example of why regiments must be geographically tied to somewhere, I should imagine this is the proof of the pudding.'

On 2 January, the Battalion moved from the Al Fadili training area. The C Company diary noted:

'The first day that it has rained since we arrived in Saudi. Admittedly, it was a fairly pathetic attempt, however it did send people scuttling for their vehicles and battening down. The weather has changed dramatically. There is now a constant northerly wind and the only thing that varies is its strength. As the ranges are on the eastern coastline of Saudi, we now find ourselves having to wrap up quite tightly against the chill winds, especially at night and first thing in the morning.'

That day was also to mark the first fatal casualty the Staffords witnessed during Op GRANBY. The soldier who died was not a Stafford: he was an NCO from 16 Tank Transporter Squadron, and was assisting with the loading of A Company's Warriors onto the massive tank transporters. Lieutenant Simon Banton was at the scene:

'He was near the winch area on one of the transporters, and one of the Warriors was being put on. The Warrior was being directed by another RCT guy on the ground, and I believe he got crushed between the Warrior and the winch system. His chest was completely caved in.

'This cry came down, get a medic! I ran down with my two medics to where he was and started giving him mouth to mouth. We continued for about 45 minutes before a doctor turned up. Once he turned up, within about two minutes he told us to stop. We knew he was dead, but you had to keep going until the doctor arrived.

'It's the first time I'd ever seen anybody dead. I found it exceedingly upsetting. It just seemed such a waste, it really did. I was a bit withdrawn for a couple of days afterwards, I kept myself to myself. We were prepared for death, in that we knew it was probably going to happen if we went to war; people would die, but I just didn't expect it in those sort of circumstances, and I didn't expect it to be as it was. One minute somebody's walking about and the next, he's got his chest caved in and he's on his back. Every time you pumped air into him, his vomit came back up into you. Then the doctor arrives and he's just a corpse on the ground. It was shocking.

'I think it did bring home the reality of the situation we were in. I mean, you'd drive around the desert and see all this British kit everywhere, people everywhere, and you'd realise you were part of something which was unique. But up to that point, although when we deployed we were expecting to go straight in and we were all very hyped up, it was all still very much 'Boys Own'. For me, from that night, it really came home. I'd actually seen someone die, and there were only two weeks left to George Bush's deadline. There was a haste about everything, and huge convoys on the road, and I suddenly realised that war was approaching.'

When the Battalion arrived in Abu Hadriya, they once again harboured up in the desert. The facilities of Camp 4 were still available, and the training cycle was planned to allow the companies to continue to rotate through it, but no-one was sure how much more time would be available to take advantage of this. The Devil Dog Dragoon field firing was due to start on 5 January, and the preceding two days were given over to vehicle maintenance and administration. For the medical team, coordinated by Captain Mark Weir, there was a busy time ahead:

'The biological warfare innoculation programme was a big one. We took a large team around all the companies; it was just a big circus. They lined up and we banged them in. It was the medics and the bandsmen who were actually doing the injecting. We managed to do the whole Battalion in about four hours on that day, and that was two injections per man. We then repeated the whole procedure a few weeks later on 29 January. I can remember threatening to give them a third innoculation as they got onto the planes to come home. That went down like a cup of cold vomit! The side effects were minimal. Some of the blokes felt a bit unwell, but we don't think that was caused by the vaccine itself. Looking at the numbers we did, it was quite a small proportion.'

Every soldier carried morphine in the form of an autoject. This is a device like a small pen which is simply placed against a fleshy part of the anatomy such as a buttock or leg, and then a button on the top is depressed. This causes a spring loaded needle to shoot out, piercing any clothing, then delivering a dose of morphine intramuscularly. It gives rapid pain relief for the more serious wounds. Unfortunately, Mark Weir found they were not 'soldier proof':

'There was one incident where a soldier accidentally injected himself. He was showing the troops how to use it and, after saying that what he was doing was for demonstration purposes only, and that they should not try it, he then did. He was taken off to the RAP feeling a bit woozy. When he was asked, who is your company commander? he replied, I don't know, but he's a wanker! He was stoned out of his mind; it's a good hefty dose.'

The range complex at Devil Dog Dragoon was constructed by the US Marines and Royal Engineers from the 1st (UK) Armoured Division, having been originally planned by a team from 7 Armoured Brigade, later assisted by advisers from the Division. It was a larger training area than Al Fadili, and there were less restrictions placed on live firing. There was a mix of infantry and tank ranges, as well as a portacabin 'village' for practising FIBUA (fighting in built-up areas). Being right on the coast, the danger area extended out to sea, and one of the duties which fell on the Staffords from time to time was to provide sentries on the beaches to keep a lookout for coastal craft straying into the danger area.

If anything, these ranges were even more realistic than those at Al Fadili had been. Captain Tom Wagstaff acted as a safety supervisor:

'It was the most unbelievable range package I have ever seen in my life. In the British Army we're used to pretty realistic live firing exercises; we had an American Marine with us who just spent the entire time on his belly, he couldn't believe it. People were throwing live grenades at night, which they just don't do.

'The range was big enough to be able to have one battle group live firing and a second battle group dry firing, the idea being that you went through a dry run the day before you did a live run. So actually, it was the Brigade Commander running it, and he tried to run it as a brigade exercise. It was unforgettable, we had fighter ground attack, artillery, and engineers all firing live during these attacks. They were saying that if you train past the safety limits you are prepared for virtually anything apart from, of course, the actual psychological reality of war – the fact that somebody is physically shooting back at you. There was everything else; cross-fire, overhead fire, flying all around you.

'On one particular range there was an incident with the LAW 94. We'd just got onto the edge of the FIBUA village and the guy, Private Stokes, took up a position to fire at a target about 125 metres away. He was concentrating on the target so he didn't see an oil drum about 25 metres in front of him. He fired his spotter rounds and hit the target okay. Then he switched to main armament and fired it. Because the rocket is a lot bigger than the tracer round, it hit the oil drum and of course blew up, and he got fragments across his stomach, arms and legs.'

Major Mark Auchinleck was the Second in Command of the Scots Dragoon Guards:

'That was a wonderful range, very good indeed, and much more realistic than BATUS. Safety restraints were lifted and safety distances were shortened markedly. I've never seen a night training battle with live ammunition flying everywhere, all in a controlled fashion, like it. BATUS is very tame compared to that, and it was pretty much expected that we would kill a couple of people. Fortunately there were no serious casualties at all. There were one or two journalists from a media reporting team who filed up and said, no, this wasn't for them, could they please go home, which caused a certain amount of amusement.'

The highlight of the period was a full blown battle group attack which took place at night; something which had never been done in peacetime training before. This was widely reported on television in the UK and Germany, and the BBC subsequently made a short video of edited clips of that attack, set to the music of Phil Collins' 'Something in the Air Tonight', which was not broadcast. Some copies of the video were distributed to the Battalion at the end of the war. Major Jim Tanner was in charge of the range that night:

'It was pitch black, there was very little in the way of artillery or mortar illumination, and the only light we had was the cylum chemical light stick which was carried by each of the safety staff and attached to the antenna of each safety Warrior. All the other vehicles were blacked out. Hearing grenades going off, and people shouting, and bits of shrapnel whizzing about; you can't protect yourself against that, you've just got to get on with it. And all the soldiers realised that. You could see the look on their faces. They weren't frightened, they just got on with it.

'We finished that attack and went to do the second attack with C Company, who slightly missed the position, came in at it from a funny angle, and really went for it. Then I realised that as two platoons were going down two separate trenches of this triangular trench system, the trenches then came in on one another, so they were shooting at one another. And then shooting at us, standing on our Warriors trying to control it. Then they all realised what they were doing and started to crack on again. That night, which was the most dangerous night, there was not one injury at all. Nothing. The soldier controlled himself in the end. He knew what his job was; and, whatever it was, he knew that he could not afford to ignore what was going on to the left and right of him and in front of him. He had to be sure of where he was firing if he didn't want to hurt his mate. And likewise, you don't get yourself in a position where you're going to get blown away by your own side.'

The BBC journalist, Kate Adie, was invited to cover the exercises at Devil Dog Dragoon ranges:

'The reason we were sent on these live firing exercises was not only PR; it was a bit of, as they say, 'police horse training'; innoculation. In fact, I knocked out a couple of people from my outfit who couldn't take it. I don't think many journalists have been around the kind of war where there were so many tanks and artillery; that was new.

'I was staggered by what we saw with the Staffords. For a layman, watching people scream and yell, and mean it; going up and down these trenches with live ammunition; it's extremely disturbing. It's alien to anything you have ever seen. It doesn't equate to a fight. It doesn't equate to anything. It's raw, battle spirit. They were not putting on a show for us; we were totally aware of that. They were absolutely ignoring us; to the extent where we were dragged through very determinedly if we were getting in the way. Oh boy, was I frightened. They were completely and utterly intent on it. We could have been invisible.

'I was absolutely fascinated by it. It is one of the things I specifically remember. To someone who has never seen anything like that, it's quite shocking. I had no doubts at all that this is how they would operate for real.'

The training at Devil Dog Dragoon continued until 9 January, and by the end of it most of the soldiers felt they had once again honed their individual and team skills to a fine edge after the blunting effects of the Christmas period. Sergeant Major Baz Barrett was Second in Command of the Milan Platoon:

'I felt that the soldiers would perform well in war after the Devil Dog ranges. The individual soldier getting on with his task and knowing his job I was quite happy with. The fitness and the skills were up to scratch and attitudes were okay. I did still feel that there were things that we needed to do as a platoon, things that we needed to practice and to coordinate with the companies and the Battalion. Also, we had only just received the pintle mount and we needed to get out there and fire some missiles off it. We were constantly badgering people about this. In the end we ran ranges for the 4 Brigade Milan platoons, and got the chance to fire it then.'

While the doomed talks between James Baker and Tariq Aziz were taking place in Geneva on 9 January, Major Jim Tanner was fighting a losing battle to remain with the Battalion. Major Geoff Moss, the officer who had always been due to become the battalion second in command, had now been released from his job in Northern Ireland – something which the Battalion had requested back in September – and he was, not surprisingly, keen to rejoin the Staffords as soon as possible. To allow Jim Tanner to stay in the Gulf, he was posted to 7 Brigade as the staff officer in charge of plans.

He was not the only person to be moved at this late stage. Major Richard Dennis, who commanded Headquarter Company, was sent back to England, kicking and screaming, to attend the Army Staff Course. He had been heavily involved with the logistic planning from the outset, and naturally was loath to go. The Adjutant, Captain Chris Hughes, narrowly escaped a similar fate.

Other personnel had to be replaced because of injury or sickness, and reinforcements came to the Battalion from a central pool of soldiers held and trained in Saudi Arabia. It was possible for the Battalion to specify the particular skills they required of one of these replacements, for example Warrior driver or mortarman, so that minimal familiarisation training was needed on arrival.

On 11 January the Battalion received firm orders that it was to move, with the rest of the 1st Armoured Division, to resubordinate under command of VII (US) Corps. Lieutenant General Sir Peter de la Billière explained the rationale behind this move:

'The whole objective of our military presence out there had changed gradually from defensive to offensive thinking. It wasn't a decision made overnight, we grew into it gradually, but you could see it coming. As this was a major contribution from the British, I wanted the Division to be in a place where this contribution was going to be significant in terms of the overall battle, and not on a peripheral operation which was what the Marines were tasked with, which was a diversionary operation. I felt that this was important to the British people.

'When I looked at the plans that the Americans were conceiving, it became clear that the best place for the Division was going to be as a part of VII (US) Corps who were going to be responsible for the main thrust. So I discussed this with the Americans and got General Schwarzkopf's eventual agreement to the Division becoming part of the main thrust in VII (US) Corps, which gave them not only the independence of command, but it gave them the opportunity to take on a task which employed their forces on a much broader front and a much deeper front. It also made sure that they weren't going to get tied up in all the oilfields and pipelines which existed in Kuwait, and which weren't suited to armour.

'A further bonus that accrued from this was that the Marines, who were marvellous chaps and whom 7 Brigade were actually very happy with (it was a great agony for them to be moved) didn't actually practice NATO procedures because they weren't NATO troops. VII Corps of course were NATO troops and practiced the procedures, so the whole of that slotted in much better than it did on the east coast.'

The redeployment involved a move of some 350 kilometres inland, north-west of their present positions. Advance parties would recce positions for each company, and the main body was due to move on 19 January. This was bound to test the logistic capability of the Battalion, which the Technical Quartermaster, Captain Douggie Forrest, felt was already at a somewhat unexpected disadvantage:

'In my opinion, the Masons were influencing the priority of issue of certain items out in the Gulf. I could tell who they were. Not because they squeezed my hand, because they know I don't like that sort of thing, but just through observations. A few of the more senior men on the logistic side were Masons. I was rude to them, and in the end, by being rude, people made the effort to give me more than perhaps I should have had, just to keep me quiet.

'I don't want to over emphasise it, it was only certain things. For example, we would come up with a demand for something and people would say, that's a good idea, we want one of those. The kit would come in and then we'd be the last to get it! I got a bit pissed off with that. On the whole, though, the logistic set-up worked extremely well out in the Gulf. Brigade HQ gave us all the support we could have asked for.'

Because all the Allied planners were forecasting a fast moving and violent ground battle when it came to it, a requirement was identified for the companies to have their immediate resupply of Combat Supplies travelling with them. In north-west Europe these stocks of fuel, ammunition and rations are carried in lorries which travel behind the battle group, ready to move forward on request to top up the fighting troops. The grouping is known as the A1 Echelon, and is commanded by the motor transport officer. In the Gulf, the A1 Echelon was formed and carried out its role very effectively; but, in order to make the companies self-sufficient for a greater period of time over the sandy terrain, they were all allocated two American-designed tracked vehicles, the 548, as stores transporters. Sergeant John Frearson was sent to pick one up:

'I went down on a Chinook helicopter to pick it up. There were 15 or thereabouts for the whole battalion. They are big, like a four ton Bedford on tracks. We took two guys down for each vehicle and we were told, there they are, away you go. And that was it. We knew nothing about their maintenance or what spares they might need. We got inside them and had a look at the bit of a dashboard that they had, worked out how to start her, how to put her in gear, and then we moved off and that was it. We had been issued a book about them some days before, but I had done like everybody else and left the book behind. We had been told that we were going to have 24 hours of instruction on the vehicle before we took them over. We just drove back 80 to 100 kilometres to the Battalion.'

As the UN deadline of 15 January passed, many soldiers began to feel that Iraq was left with no possibility of escaping a war against the Allies. For some, religion provided a comfort, and the Battalion Padre, John Tee, found himself faced with a variety of spiritual problems:

'I did question my own faith actually. It's funny, I never really remember questioning it much when I was out there, but talking to parishioners who had letters from me, they said there were times when I mentioned recriminations or questioned whether I should be a priest or not. There were times when I wondered, what the hell am I doing out here, because they weren't exactly all giving their lives to Jesus.

'Having said that, the attendances at church services increased as we got nearer the land battle. Also, the closer we got to the land battle, more and more soldiers came to me for counselling about death and life and God and the Devil. Suddenly, these informal confessions of various things they'd been getting up to before the war were all starting to come out. They wanted to, as it were, clean their consciences.

'People also wanted Old Testaments. They wanted to get into the prophetic writings to find out how the war was going to pan out, the Book of Revelations and this sort of thing, and the Anti-Christ and Armageddon. There was that kind of feeling about the war at this time; could this be it? The war to end all wars. I mean, this was the rhetoric: we were listening to, the mother of all battles and so on, which is actually the same sort of sentiment that you hear in some of the prophetic writings of the Bible.

'There are soldiers who became Christians or recommitted themselves while they were out there, and who now continue to go to church. Having said that, there's an awful lot who did go to services while we were out there who haven't been since we got back. We were in such demand out there that, if they were Catholics, they came to see me for mass or confession because they might not see a Catholic padre from one month to the next. We couldn't really go in for the luxuries of inter-church fighting. All the rules and regulations of the church, and all those church issues that get everybody so excited over here, became quite meaningless when faced with your own mortality.'

Corporal Melvyn Downes found his convictions changed as war approached:

'I've never been religious like, I'm not mad on religion now; but my wife's more religious and she sent me these little prayers, and I used to say them every day. Come the end of it, everybody in the section used to say this little prayer every day. It just proves its strength when you've got nobody else to turn to. A lot of us confessed our sins to the padre, at least twice. Once you come back home, it's all forgotten about. I never say these prayers or anything. I suppose it's just a sort of insurance policy.

'I was superstitious. I had my baby's sock stuck on my helmet and my baby's spoon which I ate all my meals with. When I lost the spoon I was going mad, all round the vehicle until I found it.'

Major Simon Knapper also carried a memento from his family:

'I'm not superstitious. I believe in the power of the talisman, but not as an external power, I believe in it as a comfort like a baby's dummy. It doesn't do anything, it doesn't make the baby less hungry or direct any sort of energy into it, but it comforts it. Before I went, my little girl made me a shield out of a bit of paper and I carried it with me. I kept it in the back of my little book and I kept that in the turret under the gun. So yes, it was at the front of the turret.

'But this whole religion thing is over-hyped in my opinion. When you go into battle, you will not take chances. You will carry your rabbit's foot, you'll throw salt over your left shoulder, you'll write all the right letters and say all the nice things, and if there's an option to go to church, you might go to church. You don't take chances with anything, just in case it's the wrong one. You don't offend anybody. And that, to my mind, is why people turn to religion. I did have church services in the company and I actually had two soldiers baptised. The services were all voluntary.'

In B Company, Major Chris Joynson took a different view:

'I am a practising Christian and I take my faith very seriously. We arranged regular church services with compo boxes as altars. One day, John Tee was doing communion and he set up all the stuff on the back bin of the Warrior; he dropped the lid to the horizontal and put a stick underneath it. I didn't realise why the stick was there and I whipped it out, and the whole lot went onto the sand. John was not too pleased. I encouraged religion by making it available to people, but I didn't force it. For myself, during the Gulf I got closer to God, there's no doubt about it. I had an inner strength from it, particularly when you didn't know what was around the next corner. It was a comfort to me.'

Major John Rochelle was the only company commander who held compulsory church services:

'The services were mandatory, but where there was communion afterwards, which was voluntary, increasing numbers came to it, many of whom were not confirmed in the church. I think religion can co-exist with superstition. Some people treat it as life assurance, but I think that if at that stage they say that they believe in God, then that's fine. You can't knock a guy for that. If he subsequently says when he comes back, well, that's got me through that bit, at least he will always be tempted to come back to do the same sort of thing if there's a next time.'

In Fallingbostel, attendance at services held in the garrison church was much greater than it had been before the war. Superstition too had its part to play, as one soldier's wife related:

'Back in England we were out shopping and we passed this gypsy's caravan. Now it's not like me, but I said to my friend, shall we go and have our fortunes told and cheer ourselves up? So in we went, thinking it's all rubbish. The woman actually didn't tell me much, but everything she said came true. She said to me, oh, your man's surrounded by danger, those were the first words out of her mouth. And I thought, oh God, I've done the wrong thing here. She said, he's very far away across the sea but he's going to be alright, your man's coming back. And she said, he's going to be hurt, but not with blood, and I didn't have a clue what she was on about, I was just shocked. I thought, I wish I hadn't come in here. When he came back, I found out he had been burned. I think that and some other things she said were pure coincidence, but I wouldn't go back and have it done again.'

At 0200 hours on the morning of 17 January, Lieutenant Steve Neale was asleep by his Warrior:

'We were all getting our heads down. Travis, who was my radio op, was stagging on. I heard the field telephone ring and said, Oi Trav, what was that? He just turned round and said, nothing of importance sir, I wasn't going to wake you. I said, what is it Trav, let us know? He said, well, the Americans have just launched 200 Cruise missiles at Baghdad. At this point the whole crew of the vehicle got up and started battering him for not telling us.'

Lieutenant Nick Todd was also woken up to be told that the air war had started:

'Everyone was put into NBC state Medium, which meant putting the suits on. We were told to start taking the NAPS, and then about two hours later the first gas alert came in. So then we had to mask up, and everyone took it very seriously indeed. That happened three times that first morning.'

For Sergeant 'Dixie' Oliver, who had been promoted in the field the previous month, it was the first really worrying moment since he had been in Saudi Arabia:

'It was the first time we had had to mask up, fully expecting something to be coming at us. I was apprehensive because things were happening a lot quicker than expected. I thought that the Scud attack, which in the end turned out to be a false alarm, was quite sharpish of him. I thought the Iraqis had really got their act together. When we were sitting there with masks and suits on and not really doing a lot, I thought, where do we go from here? I was apprehensive. I've not felt like that before; I'd say it was fear of the unknown. We wanted to do something but we couldn't do anything. All that time preparing, and they had us by the bollocks!'

C Company were in Camp 4 at the time, under the watchful eye of their Company Sergeant Major, Bron Malec:

'When the Scud alert happened, all the Dukas, the Filipino workers in the camp, decided that because they didn't have the NBC kit that we were walking around in, that they weren't playing this game, they were going. So they dropped everything and went. Consequently, all the dhobi was stuck in the dhobi shop, the whole company's clothes. We were all walking around in shorts and tee shirts while the uniforms were washed. Also, the choggie shop was left open when they ran. So people were just hitting the dhobi shop and grabbing what clothes they could. My soldiers were caught with boxes of coke from the choggie shop. They reckoned they'd got it because they were bulk buying or something; they told the provost sergeant that they had been bulk buying in case there was a shortage later!

'People ended up with a shirt that was either two sizes too big or too small. That was horrendous to sort out. Then we went to the cookhouse, and there were no chefs because they were all Filipinos. So we then had to get two army chefs in to cook for something like 2,000 men. And that again was horrendous. I was sent for by the RSM of Camp 4 to receive a bollocking on behalf of the company.'

The journalists with the forward reporting teams were based at the Divisional Administration Area. Kate Adie was one of them:

'At 2.10 in the morning, there was this amazing moment when Corporal Walls arrived and said, ladies and gentlemen, I have to tell you, we are at war. We all froze with fear. Then at about 3.15 there was the dreaded yell of gas, gas, gas!

'We thought the stuff was actually coming from the air on top of us then and there. I cannot describe what happened in that journalists' tent when we found we hadn't got a bloody light bulb! It was the worst 15 minutes of our lives. We couldn't find anything. We were in total, silent panic. We crashed into each other every few seconds, and fell over. We were utterly scared, and of course, when you're in that state you can't get anything on; you're all fingers and thumbs.

'There were rather desparate sounds coming from outside. People were saying, where are the journos? Finally, we got all our stuff on and we were told to get out and jump into trenches. I do remember, having gone through 20 minutes of total panic, as I got outside a voice said, right, jump in it Kate. I said, what? It said, jump in. And I went, oh no, I'm not going in there. But I got kicked in! I went nose first. I remember lying at the bottom of that trench going, I hate war. Filming was the last thing anybody could do. It was not a bad lesson, though, in fear.'

The frequent Gas warnings and Scud attacks were the clearest indication to the troops on the ground that the air war was going on. They did notice an increase in the activity of friendly aircraft over their locations, but it was only later, when they were nearer to the Iraqi border, that the sights and sounds of war began really to impinge on them.

Planning for the move to the 1st Armoured Division concentration area, which was codenamed Keyes, continued. Advance parties left by road on 17 January, and this led to the claim of the Quartermaster, Major Glyn Ireland, that he was the Stafford closest to the front line with Iraq when the Air War started. He had been forward carrying out a reconnaissance of the logistic deployment in Keyes at that time.

The concentration area was nothing more than a large area of desert situated to the north-east of the town of Hafar Al Batin. It was just on the eastern side of the Wadi Al Batin, a dried up water course which, as it extends further north, forms the western boundary of Kuwait. To the south of Keyes and running south-east/north-west through Hafar Al Batin is the tapline road. This arterial route runs from the settlement of Ar'Ar, deep in the northern desert, to the port of Dahran. Alongside it runs the trans Arabian pipeline. The road became the main supply route for most of the Allied stores and vehicles heading up towards the Iraqi border, and was given the codename Route Dodge. Because of the density and speed of the traffic which flowed along it 24 hours a day, the Staffords preferred to call it Route Dodgey.

The main body of the Battalion moved up to Keyes on 19 January. The Warriors were loaded onto transporters for the journey, and the soldiers were taken by bus to the airport at Al Jubail where Hercules transport aircraft ferried them up to the airbase at Al Qaysumah, near Hafar Al Batin. Here they were reunited with their vehicles for the final short drive into Keyes. A move of this distance and complexity, involving as it did the whole of the 1st Armoured Division, was a staff officer's nightmare. Things were bound to go wrong and it was C Company which encountered problems, as Company Sergeant Major Bron Malec recounted:

'It always seemed to be C Company which had the problems with transport. If we had to travel anywhere there was a cock-up on the transport side. On this occasion we set off in a Hercules from Al Jubail. We came to land at our destination but he couldn't put it down because of the fog. So we turned around, but instead of returning us to Al Jubail, he dropped us off at the King Khaled Military City. We didn't know where the hell we were. We'd started taking NAPS that day which made you feel really rough. Headaches, dizziness; really, really poorly, like a migraine. And I was feeling like this when we got dumped at this airfield on the tarmac. The RAF guy said, this is it, somebody will pick you up in a minute, and he was gone.

'So everyone sat around on the tarmac, and there were aircraft coming up and down past us. Of course, by this time the boys had got the brew kit on, the hexamine cookers and the number two cookers had come out, and there was a bit of a party starting. A hundred men right on the strip. And as they were brewing up, they were trying to stop the cookers going out every time an aircraft landed or took off. That's what it was like, there was nowhere we could go.

'So this was all going on, the OC had gone off to try and sort things out, and I was sitting on my webbing feeling in shit order. Then I started seeing the blokes with these little white boxes. And I thought to myself, I haven't seen these things before. So I had a peer in one of them, and they had crackers and butter and tins of pilchards, and that sort of thing. Then all of a sudden I started to see soldiers with great big cartons full of these little white boxes. I went off to find out where they were coming from, and as I got up, I had one pushed into my hand. I thought, food. We'd been there about three hours by then, so I put it in my pocket.

'I walked up to this shed, like a lean-to, and there were hundreds and hundreds of these packed lunches. And as I walked round the corner and came across these boxes, and started to tell people to put the stuff back because I realised it belonged to somebody, it wasn't meant for us, the next thing I saw was a big, fat Egyptian brigadier. He came running out, flicking these boxes all round the shed, and screaming and shouting. He was trying to find out who was in charge. He kept saying, look at this, look at this, you pay, you pay! And all I could think of doing was to keep saluting him, because this seemed to calm him down a little bit. I was saying, the major's gone, but I'll help, and I was in his office at this stage, stood against his desk. I could see him calming down a bit, so I stayed standing to attention; I thought I'd better not relax because it was obviously helping.

'I got the soldiers to put back what we could; it was all a bit embarrassing because we'd stolen their rations really. Then the OC came back and said that the lorries were coming. But we waited and waited, and they didn't turn up. Then the Egyptian brigadier, he must have got that pissed off with us being there, he said, look, I'll give you two damned buses! But eventually the eight tonners turned up and, once we'd refuelled them and gone through three Scud alerts, we set off to meet up with the Warriors.'

B Company had managed to get to Keyes pretty much according to the plan, even though they had come across their Warriors travelling along the route in the opposite direction, seven hours after they had set them off. Major Chris Joynson had a chance to look around his company area at first light:

'The terrain there was very different from Al Fadili or Devil Dog. It was almost flat, gravelly sand; much better for the Warriors. We were on an old Egyptian position which had been dug-in before, and we used what was already there if it was habitable and fitted in with our plan. Then we dug in the Warriors with engineer assistance. We were actually able to make ourselves quite comfortable down there.'

Once established in Keyes, the Battalion prepared a contingency plan to defend the area against any Iraqi incursion; they were now only 60 kilometres from the border. At last, the Trimpack satellite navigation sets were issued. For the Reconnaissance Platoon, commanded by Captain Richard Wootton, the ability to navigate accurately was of crucial importance:

'Trimpack was undoubtedly a battle winner for us. It meant that we could move accurately by day and night, in all weather conditions. The battle group could carry out complex manoeuvres and you could be sure that everyone would end up in exactly the right position. We ended up with two in the platoon, which limited us to an extent, but at least I could split the platoon into two halves if I needed to. All you had to do was press a button and it would give you a 10 figure grid reference of your exact location. You could also programme in the grid of a position you wanted to move to, and it would tell you which way to go; you know, left a bit, right a bit, and so on. It would tell you how far you had to run as you were going; it was an excellent bit of kit. At certain times, usually twice a day, it would go down when the satellites were out of alignment. But that would only last for half an hour or so.'

By now, the Staffords had been living cheek by jowl with one another for over three months. Officers and NCOs did not have the normal peacetime separation from the other ranks, when they can retire to their messes at the end of the working day. There was little privacy for anyone, as Captain Chris Hughes found out:

'It got desperately difficult to get a bit of peace and quiet. You could get it at night because the darkness gave you your privacy, if you like. I slept outside on a cot bed for the first half of the tour. Then it started pouring down and Sergeant Miller belatedly told me that there was an extra crew shelter in the cage; after watching me getting soaked through for a night! And I put it up, and I always used it from then on; not because of the weather, but because I suddenly discovered this privacy. You could zip yourself up, and sometimes during the day I would retire there for half an hour. You needed a bit of privacy, everybody did; not just me, the soldiers did as well, and it was very difficult to come by.'

Across the ranks, the soldiers got to know each other far better than they ever had done before. Sergeant Dave Donnelly was a mortar fire controller (MFC):

'I had myself, a lance-corporal who was my Bravo [deputy] MFC, a driver who was a lad from the Prince of Wales's Own, and my gunner was a Guardsman. We just mixed in, it was great. The gunner and the driver slept in the vehicle, me and the Bravo slept outside all the time. We had no problems with who was cooking or doing the chores. We'd just be sitting there and somebody who was bored would say, I'll do the tea or whatever. Obviously we had our frictions. Silly things would bug me and them. Corporal Smart used to say to me, if I was going OTT, Sarge, there's no need for this, and that would be it.

'He called me Sarge all the way through. They all did. With me, I called them by nicknames. My gunner was Arnie, my driver was Ray and I called Corporal Smart Billy. But they always called me Sarge except for Arnie. Because he was a Guardsman, he wouldn't call me Sarge, it was always Sarn't. Everything was Sarn't. He'd never say yes to me because they can't say yes. But if I was giving them a bollocking, or I wanted something doing now, I'd use their rank and name.

'I think the rank structure stayed pretty rigid all the way through. Captain Spragg was my boss and I would say, right boss, what do you want to do now? That was when he was using me as a taxi. But if there were people around, it would always be Sir.'

The Milan platoon used sports as a way of letting off steam. Corporal Darren Wilson explained:

'We had a few good games of American football out there. If somebody had a beef with somebody else then that's where it would come out. You'd put on your helmet and body armour so you were fairly well protected. Even so, I left one game with my body armour ripped to bits and my hand smashed up as someone worked off a grudge against me. But that was definitely the best way of doing it. You've got to let the tension out somehow.'

Lieutenant Andy Layton encouraged a more relaxed atmosphere in his platoon:

'I always wanted to be close to the guys and I have to admit, it was a lot closer than I ever thought it would be. There was none of the formal, yes sir, no sir, and to be honest, that slipped within the first month. Sergeant Rogers always wanted to keep it but I was insistent that I didn't want it. His job is totally different from mine and I agree with him that he needed to maintain the formality as platoon sergeant more than I did. Other than the exercises and any of the major moves we did, Sergeant Rogers effectively ran the platoon. I was there as a figurehead. It was only when we got out of the back and started using tactics at the end of the day, he always looked to me to take the lead. We agreed very much on most things anyway, so it was a very close relationship. We didn't have any real problems at all.'

Andy Layton's company commander was Major Simon Knapper:

'We are purely down to earth officers and men. We're not hunting, shooting, fishing types, we're just a good solid infantry regiment, and actually the gap between our soldiers and ourselves is very small. We come from the same towns and areas, in some cases the same street. The discipline of the battlefield with its drills and its structures is paramount and yet, living in the back of a vehicle with your soldiers for five months, that officer has got to become part of the crew. He's got to take his turn with the cooking, the vehicle maintenance, the washing up, whatever's going on. As long as the living together doesn't affect the battlefield drills then there's no problem. And it didn't.

'There was no policy on using names. I would use nicknames occasionally; in conversation, if I was talking about my driver, I'd refer to him as 'Spike'. But we maintained the framework of the structure without standing on ceremony. I didn't get saluted for five months, which was great. My arm has felt really funny since we came back! There was no bullshit; there was a job to be done and we got on with it.'

In C Company, Company Sergeant Major Bron Malec felt it was part of his job to maintain the rank differential:

'I was the traditional type of company sergeant major, gripping people whenever it was necessary. The problem was this living so close together all the time. Platoon sergeants, platoon commanders, even the company commander living in the field with the soldiers, non-stop for five months. It is hard work for them, particularly for the company commander, and he was out there all the time with the soldiers. He never snuck back to camp once, and that's good going considering he is the senior officer there. The blokes appreciated it.

'We had to be careful that there wasn't too much familiarity. I was pulling the platoon sergeants away every now and then and saying, look, this must stop. I never saw anything that really worried me; they wouldn't do it when I was around. But it was obvious that it was happening from time to time. You couldn't get away from it, because the boys were living in the same vehicle as the platoon commanders and sergeants. It really is important to keep a degree of separation between the ranks. At the end of the day, when the platoon commander says go, or the platoon sergeant says do, they have got to do it without thinking, oh come on, what about such and such. And that's what you had to be careful of developing, because of the closeness of our living conditions.'

Once the Battalion was established in Keyes, a major programme of up-armouring the Warriors, which had begun at Devil Dog Dragoon ranges, continued. Trials had been done in December with bolt-on panels of Chobham armour, and the success of these trials had resulted in the production of enough sets to equip every Warrior. The additional armour was designed to enhance greatly the ability of Warrior to survive a direct hit by an anti-tank weapon. Lance Corporal Neil Peacock was a REME fitter with B Company:

'It was a right pain fitting it. We had to redrill and rethread existing holes in the Warriors. Then we bolted on the new slabs of armour. They said it was going to take about 12 hours per vehicle to do, but we got it down to about four hours working like a production line all through the night. We put up floodlights and generators, and the vehicles just passed through from one end of the line to the other. We did the more technical jobs to start with, and then we showed the crews what to do and they then took over. We just supervised from then. It wasn't technically difficult, it was just like reading a big Airfix model plan.'

On 30 January the Americans laid on a rehearsal for the operation that would be required to breach and pass through the Iraqi border defences. This was attended by all the commanders in the Battalion down to corporal level. Each platoon sent one Warrior, which drove down the route allocated for tracked vehicles to the simulated border area. All other personnel were carried in lorries along the wheeled vehicle route. The idea was to push as many vehicles through the simulated breach to validate the movement plan, while at the same time letting everybody see how it was intended to lay out the crossing area for the real thing. Involving as it did representatives from every unit in the British 1st Armoured Division as well as the VII (US) Corps units, it was a massive operation. At the end of it the Staffords were able to visualise, probably for the first time, how the breakout into Iraq would be conducted.

While this rehearsal was taking place, reports were coming through of an incident near the town of Ras al Khafji on the Saudi coast. The battalion war diary simply noted:

'Incursions along Saudi/Kuwait with a major incursion in Ras Al Kafghi [sic] – initial reports suggest a brigade-sized force.'

On the following day the diarist was able to comment:

'Possibly two brigades from 5 Mechanised Infantry Division attacked Ras Al Khafji outflanking Saudi National Guard and American Recon. Battle to retake the deserted border town still ongoing.'

This is in stark contrast to the massive international television and newspaper coverage the battle for Khafji provoked.

By the beginning of February it was apparent that the emphasis of the air war had shifted. The raids deep into Iraq, striking at air-bases, logistic centres and lines of communication, continued, but an increasing number of attacks were being made onto the Iraqi ground forces dug in around Kuwait and southern Iraq. The Allies had complete air supremacy and flew by day and night. There was plenty for Private Simon Jones to see:

'We had so many planes going over every day: Tornadoes, F15s, everything. We could see them refuelling above us, bold as brass. Loads of B52s went over and then you'd see them flying back after their mission. That was good when you saw those going over because you knew someone was going to get a good kicking. There was one point when we were in Keyes when we had two American Apache helicopters come over us. They had no lights on or anything, and they were about 20 feet off the floor. It scared the shit out of us. We were in the trenches, sleeping, and these two black things just appeared overhead. We didn't hear them until they were right on top of us; we shit ourselves. Then they flew straight past us and turned their lights on as they headed home.'

Having seen the plans for the breakout, the Commander of the 1st Armoured Division, Major General Rupert Smith, decided to conduct his own exercise to rehearse the procedures involved. It was called Exercise Dibdibah Rat, and took place from 4–6 February in the immediate vicinity of Keyes. Essentially it was an exercise in coordinated movement, practising the control and flexibility that would be required to move the Division up to the breach site, and then through it and on to break-out positions on the edge of the bridgehead which the Americans would form to the north of the Saudi/Iraq border.

There was little for the soldiers in the back of the Warriors to do except sleep as the vehicles rumbled on through the day and the night. Occasionally the Battalion would stop for a few hours, and then the fighting troops would spill out into the desert to dig shell scrapes and man sentry positions. The vehicle commanders were kept fully occupied with navigation and the constant attentions of the radio, via which orders and changes to the plan were passed, but for the soldiers in the back it was two days and nights of boredom. In Lieutenant Andy Layton's vehicle the monotony was rudely interrupted, as he described:

'We'd done a major move through the night and it was just getting light when the boss said, shake out into assault formation. That meant we had to go left, but we hadn't gone 50 metres when there was this massive great big ditch. We were doing about 30 kilometres an hour when I saw this ditch. I said, brake, brake! Hank hit the brakes, but it was too late, and we just went straight down into it and stopped dead. It felt as if someone had got a hammer and hit me on the knee.

'The first priority was to get out and check on the guys. Corporal Bailey had a gash on his head, but the others were relatively OK. I got on the radio and told the platoon to get on with the assault, and then I sat down and noticed a rip in my NBC suit by my knee with a lump of flesh hanging out. I looked at it and thought, oh hell. The medics came and took me away, and then I just seemed to continue moving down the casualty evacuation chain.

'Initially they closed it with three stitches to hold it together. That was at 22 Field Hospital, where they kept me for about three days. They told me I would have to go back to England. I must admit I felt sorry for the poor old matron there, who had to close her ears to me because I was ranting and raving, effing and blinding because I didn't want to go back. Then they told me I was going back to the evacuation hospital at Riyadh. There they said definitely I would be going back to England.

I have to admit, for a while I was pleased. I thought, great, I'm going home, I'm going to see Sue, that's fantastic. But that was the only time I felt like that. After that I thought, oh hell, the boys. I don't know what it is. It's something I've never been able to explain to Sue. It was the family, the Regiment. I felt really lonely. I can remember crying one night and just thinking I wanted to be back with the boys.

'Then for some reason, someone mentioned that I might not be going home after all, and from then on it was difficult to stay still. Eventually they said, you can go back, but not to the Battalion. You're going as a battle casualty replacement to the holding pool. I said, no chance, but they said, you've got no choice. So I played along with it, but only to a degree.

'The next morning at six o'clock, I got onto a flight to Al Jubail where the holding pool was. I could just walk without crutches by now. We got to Jubail, and then instead of going to the holding place I found another plane heading north. So he took me to Al Qaysumah, which was quite close to where the Battalion was. There was a Sea King helicopter there which was going to the divisional RV, so I hitched a lift on that, and then found the Quartermaster who got me back to A Company. Ironically, I came across the guy who had been sent up to replace me; he was a Scots Guards officer. I told him he wasn't needed and that was that. When I got back to the Company the boss said to me, look, you've got to do yourself and your platoon justice. If I don't think you can do it, I won't let you have the platoon. But it recovered OK; we had enough time before we went in, thank God.'

Although the Battalion had media 'Forward Reporting Teams' working with it, a great deal of secrecy was imposed to prevent the Iraqi intelligence organisation from deducing the Allied plan. In conjunction with this, a coordinated deception plan was launched to fool the enemy. Many of the details of this remain classified, but Captain Mark Steed, the Battalion Operations Officer, was privy to some of the plan:

'We knew that the 1st (UK) Division was being played on Emcon [Emission Control – radio traffic which simulated that normally propagated by the Division] further east, as if we were still grouped with the Marines near the coast. I've been told since that this was very effective. Also BFBS, the Forces radio station, used to transmit to us in Al Fadili and Devil Dog, but once we had deployed further west we couldn't get BFBS any more and there were whinges and gripes about this. But apparently it was part of the overall deception plan to convince the Iraqis we were still over there.'

Once the Battalion received orders to move from Keyes, the clock began to count down towards G Day, the day that offensive ground operations against Iraq would commence. On 11 February orders were received to prepare for another movement exercise, this time codenamed Exercise Dibdibah Charge. Unlike the earlier exercise, though, the Battalion would not return to their positions in Keyes. They were to move west again, 60 kilometres across the Wadi Al Batin, to a featureless piece of desert designated Forward Assembly Area Ray. It was from here that the British and American units would eventually move directly north to the chosen breach site on the Iraqi border.

The Battalion was complete in Ray, with the rest of the 1st Armoured Division, by last light on 14 February. It was also on St Valentine's Day that Saddam Hussein chose to announce that Iraqi troops would comply with the resolutions of the United Nations, and would therefore start to withdraw from Kuwait. Within a few hours of making this announcement it was clear the conditions Saddam wanted to impose as the terms of his withdrawal would be unacceptable to the UN, and the initiative rapidly dried up.

For the soldiers in the desert this was not as great a let-down as might have been expected. The failed diplomatic initiatives of the previous months had engendered a cynical conviction that such gestures were not going to be the solution to the problem. Sergeant Major Nigel Whitehouse had developed a personal view:

'I felt that at one stage we were becoming puppets of the Americans. No matter what Iraq offered, the Americans weren't going to back down. They wanted to take on the fourth biggest army in the world and get them out of Kuwait. They had the Vietnam stigma to get rid of. As long as Saddam was there, they were not going to accept any concessions that he put up. I think that at this particular stage, when it nearly happened, what they were asking wasn't that far out. But they couldn't agree because America wanted to fight that war.'

Sergeant Dennis Rogers disagreed:

'I don't think it was because of Vietnam. I think the Americans were looking at Iraq as being the most unstable nation in the Middle East, with the power to tilt the balance either way. Iraq could either gain more support from the other Muslim nations around it, or, if it had been left any longer, to work out a plan with themselves and Iran combined, they could have drawn the Americans into something bigger and worse. I think the Americans realised this, and needed to make a decision. They didn't want any peace plans for the simple reason that they had to destroy what was in Iraq. Nobody in the world, apart from the Americans, had the bottle to do it. We couldn't do it because we weren't powerful enough. America is a superpower.'

Although they may have differed on the motives of the diplomats, most of the soldiers wanted to get on with their job. Major Chris Joynson summed up the feeling of the soldiers in B Company:

'By this time we were all very frustrated by it, but we all realised that it was very necessary. But now we felt it had gone on long enough, and he needed to be brought to heel. Certainly the boys felt as if they were the pawns in the game, and were going to end up sitting in the desert for six or eight months. Saddam Hussein would eventually withdraw, having gained concessions of X amount of oilfields or whatever.'

In Fallingbostel, the wives were more susceptible to what appeared to be good news. Lorraine Mortimer remembered that day very clearly:

'That was the worst day for me, when they said Saddam Hussein was giving up. We were in the office, it hadn't been announced on the news or anything, and one of the lads from the information centre came in and said, we think it's all over. So obviously we felt as though a weight had been lifted. I walked down the road and there was a woman leaning out of the window shouting, it's over. When I got home I ran and told my friend Kerry and then, half an hour later, we sat down to watch it on the dinner time news. It was all a hoax. It felt as though you'd been slapped in the face. You were back to square one. This weight had been lifted off you and then it was all pushed back down again.'

It was a different incident which caused Carla Hughes the most distress during this period of waiting:

'The very worst part was when the RAF men were taken prisoner and displayed on the television. Foolishly, I hadn't addressed that at all. I had thought about what I would do if Chris was maimed, or severely handicapped or badly scarred, and I had thought about what I would do if he died. I had never contemplated that he might be a prisoner of war. It hadn't entered my mind at all.

'Even now, I can see the television screen; I can see them as clearly as anything. It just seemed so barbaric, so horrendous. It seemed to me that they had been tortured. I knew what I felt the Iraqis would have to do to Chris to get him to say anything. To know that their wives were somewhere in Germany watching that as well; I just felt it was so barbaric and horrific and dreadful. I went into the wives' coffee shop later on that morning and it was on the television then, as it was constantly, and I had to walk out, I couldn't stand watching it again. Even now when those pictures reappear, I still feel exactly the same.'

At last, on 19 February, the Battalion received the news it had been waiting for. The soldiers were told that it was now G−3: three days before G day, the date when offensive ground operations against the Iraqis would commence. Because of the continuing last ditch diplomatic peace efforts, the countdown to G day was suspended at G−3, so each following day would be designated G−3 until the countdown recommenced. What it meant to the troops was that the details of the plan were now revealed to them.

The following day, Allied artillery began to concentrate fire along the border, ranging in on Iraqi positions in an attempt to provoke the Iraqi artillery pieces to open up in response. As soon as they did so, sophisticated radar equipment picked up the shells in mid-air and instantaneously plotted their trajectory. These data could then be used to give a very accurate grid reference of the position from which the guns were firing, and these locations were immediately subjected to withering counter-battery fire from Allied artillery units waiting in reserve.

The increase in artillery activity was apparent to the soldiers as they waited by their Warriors during those last few nights. The spectacle was enhanced by the sight of American B52 bombers systematically neutralising positions along the border defences with their enormous loads of high explosive bombs. Private Danny Nokes was one of those who found the spectacle fascinating:

'You'd be told on the land line, watch out at half past ten tonight, and there'll be a bit of a fireworks display. When you had a clear sky, there'd be hundreds of planes you could see going over. It was very reassuring. You could watch them go past, then hold your breath and you'd hear the bombs all going up. You could feel the ground move and all. You felt a bit for the Iraqis underneath them, but it was really a case of, if it's got to be them or me, it's going to be them.'

The closeness of combat caused many people to review their affairs in case anything should happen to them. Private Warren Blacker wrote to his parents:

'The day before we went in I wrote to my family saying, you might not hear from me again because we're going in tomorrow. I put at the end, if all's well, you'll hear from me again but this is the last letter before I go to war. They said it was a bit of a shock, like. My mum was in tears and all that because I was just pretty straightforward about it.'

Corporal Melvyn Downes did not agree with writing 'final letters':

'We talked about these sort of things quite a lot then. I didn't encourage anybody in my section to do it because to me it seems like a deathwish. It seems as if you're writing out your last rites. By rights you've got to look at it as if to say, right, I'm going to come through this, we're all going to get through it. Whereas if you're writing letters like that it seems as if you're thinking to yourself you're going to die, as far as I'm concerned.'

Many of those who did opt to write a letter for delivery in the event of their death must have experienced similar emotions to those Sergeant Dave Donnelly described:

'I'll tell you what, it was heartbreaking. It really gets to you. You're writing it, there's a lump in your throat and you're thinking, shit, this could really happen. It was all make sure the kids don't forget me, that sort of thing, as well as, don't think about what's happened now, think about the future. Look forward, don't look back. I told my wife just what I wanted my family to do in the future. You write all these daft sentimental things like, I wish we'd done this, or, I know I've sat in front of the telly on a Saturday afternoon watching Grandstand when I should have been out with the kids. Mind you, now I'm back from the Gulf, after the first three weeks, that started again anyway!'

On 21 February the countdown to G day recommenced. It seemed to everyone that there would be no turning back now. Dave Donnelly found himself parked in the middle of the Battalion, surrounded by other Warriors:

'When they said that we were going, everybody was saying, this is it. You could see people walking up the line of vehicles shaking hands with their mates, saying, see you at endex. Everybody was saying, keep your head down, even to your worst enemy who you'd probably hated all the way through.'

Like everyone else, the Adjutant, Captain Chris Hughes, had to wrestle with conflicting emotions:

'There was discussion on the radio about last minute peace talks, and you got really trapped in your own mind then. You can't imagine what it was like. You just lay there every night thinking about it. You didn't think about anything else. So you'd get stuck by this thought, I just want to go home. Then the next minute you'd think, I do not want to go home before I've gone to war, that's what we've come out for, and I want to see some action. Then, no I don't, I just want to go home, no I don't, I want to be a hero!

'I was talking to Simon Knapper one night, and we talked for quite a long time. I said to him, I have this feeling that when this is done I don't want to do anything else dangerous for a long time. I don't want to drive fast on the motorway, I don't want to cross the road if it's busy, I just want to get home and be safe. I'm quite happy to do all this, but the constant feeling that you may not come back or your friends wouldn't come back left me feeling like that. Simon said that was exactly how he felt after the Falklands.'

It was by no means totally sombre during these last few days. Corporal Ford from C Company lightened the atmosphere when he was interviewed by a correspondent from The Sunday Telegraph. As far as his possible death in action was concerned, he told him:

'I'm going to get myself cremated and my ashes put in a jar. Then my boys can play cricket for me every summer.'

Unless there were any further delays, 24 February was to be G day. The plan called for the Americans to break through the border defences and establish a bridgehead in Iraq on the first day. The British troops would be called forward once the bridgehead was established, and it was expected that they would break out of the bridgehead and start to advance through Iraq in the early hours of G+2. The orders for the operation had been worked out in some detail and were ready to be issued to the Commanding Officer's Orders Group, the collection of officers and senior NCOs through whom information and orders are passed down to the soldiers. Lieutenant Colonel Charles Rogers did not feel that it was a particularly dramatic moment:

'You must remember that, for this initial phase, it was nothing more than a complicated and lengthy move up through the American breach to our breakout position. Hughes banged on for two hours with the movement order; God it was boring. The only exciting bit was when he said, oh shit, I've got the figures wrong. It woke people up for about two minutes. It was the most boring set of orders I've ever attended.'

Captain Chris Hughes always knew it would not be a riveting set of orders:

'Move orders are an extremely important aspect of an operation like this one, but unfortunately they are also intensely boring. The Commanding Officer in particular did not need to become bogged down in details like these, so it was inevitable that he would find it tedious. The rest of the orders were brief because what was going to happen was either unknown, or relatively straightforward in that we were going to go and do what we'd always done.

'Then I made a cock-up in one of the sets of timings. I'd been doing them for about seven hours beforehand and had worked out all these timings, there were hundreds of them. I'd done something like subtracted an hour instead of adding it in one small batch of timings. Half-way through delivering them I realised my mistake. I swore with some conviction then, but actually it wasn't significant and it was a simple matter to correct them at the end. It was rather depressing, though; it would have been nice to get the whole lot right first time.'

Once the company commanders had received their orders, they passed them on to their soldiers. This was done by giving orders to the platoon commanders who then in turn gave their orders to their sections. In C Company, the Company Commander also took the opportunity to address the whole company, as the Company Second in Command, Lieutenant Peter Horne recalled:

'John got the company together after the O Group and said, right, we're going. These are the important timings. Then he read the speech from Shakespeare's Henry V, the night before Agincourt. The one about Englishmen abed, Saint Crispin's Day and so on. It was quite good, because he read it out and then he translated into contemporary English for the blokes. It wasn't melodramatic at all. I'd read it beforehand and thought it would be really good, and it was really apt.

'Then he spoke separately to the officers and the NCOs. To us he said that when he found out we were going on Op GRANBY he was quite apprehensive because we were quite a young team. I was the oldest at 25. But now, he knew that we would have no problem at all going to war, and he had every faith in us. I presume he said the same sort of thing to the others. It was very reassuring to hear.'

The final diplomatic effort to avert war, initiated by the Soviet Union, had now failed. There were no further suspensions of the countdown to G day, and at 0200 hours on 24 February VII (US) Corps began to assault the chosen breach site 60 kilometres north of Ray. The ground war had begun.

6

The Ground War

'It was an awesome sight, something I'll never forget.'

Acting on the presumption that there would be no further delays to the countdown, a number of sub-units from the Staffords had already moved off to prepare for their particular roles in the offensive. On the 23 February, G−1, A Company had regrouped to come under command of the Royal Scots Dragoon Guards. At the same time, B Squadron of the Scots Dragoon Guards and C Squadron of the Queens Royal Irish Hussars had moved across to join the Staffords.

The three fighting battle groups of 7 Armoured Brigade now consisted of the Staffords who had two rifle companies, B and C, and two tank squadrons; the Scots Dragoon Guards, who had three tank squadrons and one rifle company; and the Irish Hussars, who had three tank squadrons and no infantry. Supporting the battle groups were a number of other 'teeth' units, including the Royal Artillery Regiments, and field and armoured engineers.

On the same day, the Recce Platoon and the Battalion's Alternate Headquarters moved up to join the American 3 Armoured Brigade headquarters. Their task was to mark and coordinate the move of the Staffords Battle Group through the American breach site and bridgehead. Major Tim Gatfield was commanding Alternate HQ:

'We had our final briefing that night from the American brigade commander. Then myself and a couple of the guys went in and watched the film from RPV [remotely piloted vehicle – like a large radio-controlled model aircraft; fitted with cameras which transmit real time film of the objective over which it is flying back to the operator] flights which had been taken the day before over the positions that we were due to take. They were interesting in that they showed the standard of the positions.

'Up until that time, we really thought we were talking about deep trenches. We'd heard that they'd been making reinforced concrete girders and shipping them in, and that they actually had bunkered strong points. We expected to see Soviet-style trenches, interlocking and based on good hard strongpoints. And we

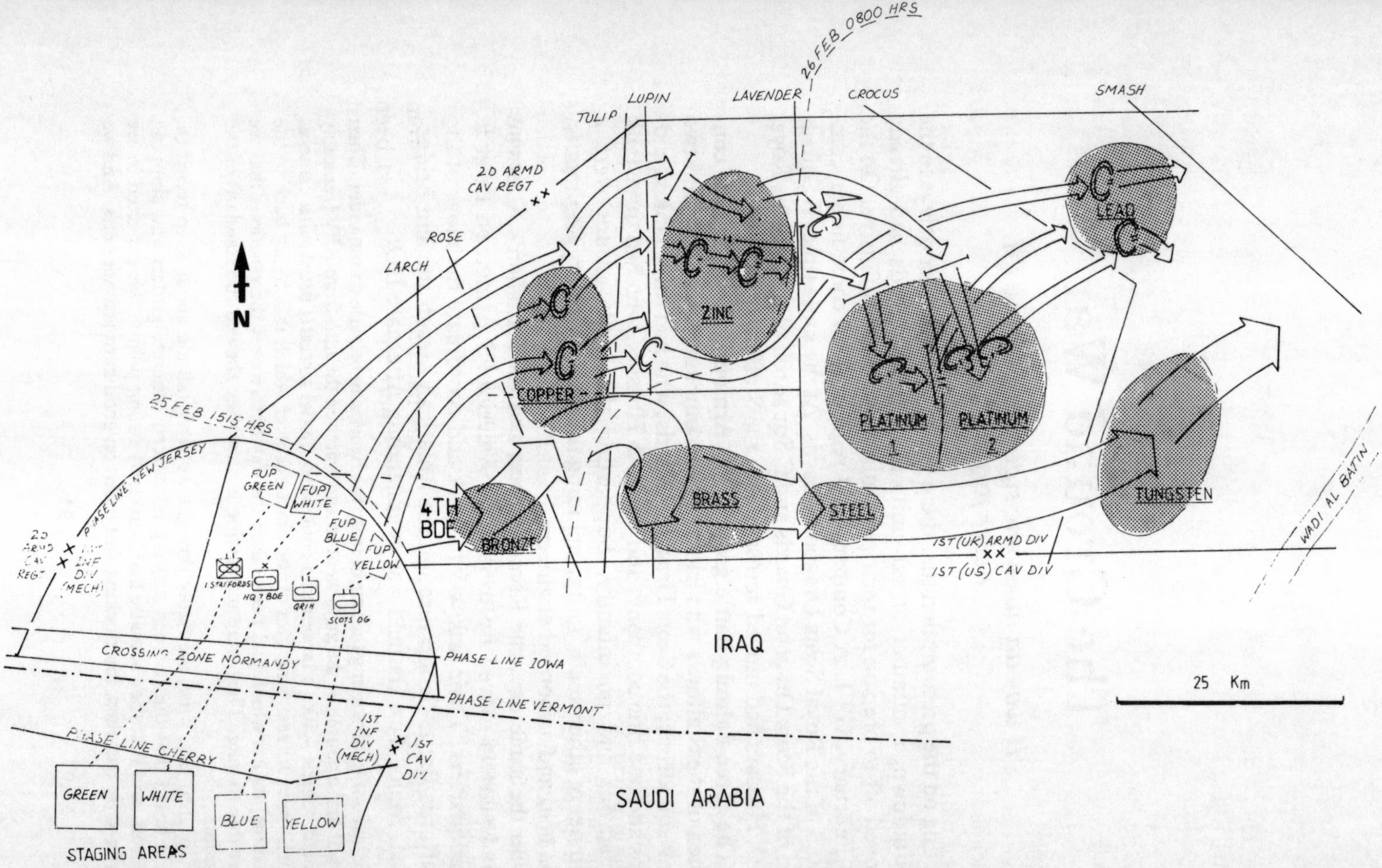

N
26 FEB 0800 HRS
TULIP
LUPIN
LAVENDER
CROCUS
SMASH
2D ARMD CAV REGT
ROSE
LARCH
COPPER
ZINC
LEAD
PLATINUM 1
PLATINUM 2
TUNGSTEN
25 FEB 1515 HRS
PHASE LINE NEW JERSEY
FUP GREEN
FUP WHITE
FUP BLUE
FUP YELLOW
4TH BDE
BRONZE
BRASS
STEEL
1ST (UK) ARMD DIV
1ST (US) CAV DIV
WADI AL BATIN
2D ARMD CAV REGT
1ST INF DIV (MECH)
1 STAFFORDS
HQ 7 BDE
QRIH
SCOTS DG
IRAQ
CROSSING ZONE NORMANDY
PHASE LINE IOWA
PHASE LINE VERMONT
25 Km
PHASE LINE CHERRY
1ST INF DIV (MECH)
1ST CAV DIV
GREEN
WHITE
BLUE
YELLOW
STAGING AREAS
SAUDI ARABIA

7TH ARMOURED BRIGADE

didn't see any of that. We just saw shallow, linear trenches. Small shelters rather than bunkers, built to the rear of them. Really very poor quality stuff.'

The Recce Platoon are well practised in the techniques of route marking, but this operation was on a scale they had not previously encountered. As well as the British 1st Armoured Division, the American 1st Infantry Division plus numerous other supporting units were all to be routed into Iraq through this breach area. This meant an individual route had to be allocated to each major unit, and this in turn was subdivided to allow tracked vehicles to move separately from wheeled ones. All the routes converged upon the cleared lanes through the Iraqi border defences, then fanned out again into the bridgehead as they headed towards the designated forming up points (FUPs) from which the battle groups would break out of the protection of the bridgehead and advance to contact with the opposition.

The Staffords were allocated Route Green, which lead from Lane Charlie, the passage through the minefields, to FUP Green, and it was essential that it was clearly and accurately marked. Colour Sergeant Mark Banks was Second in Command of the Recce Platoon as they started their task on G day:

'We got the go-ahead to move, and the Americans breached the defences, and we then followed through along the first lane that they opened. Then we were held in a control point for about 12 hours. Our job was to do a left turn and come along the breach to where Lane Charlie was. From there our task was to mark the exit from the breach to the FUP. When we got in there, we didn't have a lot of time because they'd already started opening Lane Charlie.

'My job was to stay at the exit and drag everybody onto the route as they came through. That went very well. It was probably only an hour or so after we got there when the first British vehicles started coming through. To actually mark the route, we used orange mine marker poles with cylums on them. Every third or fourth marker, we would drop off a vehicle.'

For the rest of the Battle Group, G day had been frustrating. From early in the morning, reports of the Americans' progress had been coming in. These already indicated resistance in that area was minimal and the operation was progressing ahead of schedule. Battalion Headquarters was told they should be prepared to cross the breach from 1100 hours on G+1. This was a significant advance on the original plan which had envisaged the Battle Group crossing the berms in the early hours of G+2.

Eventually, at 1400 hours, the order was given for the vehicles to move off from Keyes. They were to drive north for about 60 kilometres to a staging area just short of the Saudi/Iraq border. This was a long, slow journey, and the last vehicle did not arrive in the staging area until 2300 hours that night. Private 'Sid' Wain was a Warrior driver:

'It is a pretty comfortable vehicle to drive. The seat's pretty good, but when you're in it for a long period, your backside goes dead. You have to wiggle your toes to get the blood circulating. What you can do with the seat, which is quite good, is to recline it completely and use it as a bed when you stop. It's easy to drive as well. In the cockpit, to your left, there's a dashboard like a car dashboard with all your speedos and mileometer and warning lights. There's a control so that you can open and shut the back door with the hydraulic ram. On the floor, there's a brake, an emergency brake and an accelerator. The gearbox is semi-automatic; you just select the range according to the ground you're crossing and put your foot down. It's very fast, we did over 80 kph cross country out there and there was still some left. You steer it just like a car with a half steering wheel, like an aeroplane control.

'It is a bit hot in the driver's compartment because you're sitting right next to the engine. You're wearing a lot of clothes as well, because you've got your normal desert suit on, then you've got your NBC suit on, plus an anti-flash mask and gloves. On top of that you're wearing a helmet. It's like walking from the cold into a nice centrally heated room where the heat suddenly hits you. You're drinking virtually all the time. With the hatch down it's nearly unbearable. You're just cracking up because of the heat. At one point I remember I was just banging on the hatch. Not for someone to let me out; just to let steam off, trying to cool myself down. It was like sitting next to a 12 bar heater. Sweat was pouring off your skin, stinging in your eyes, and you were drinking all the time.'

The soldiers in the back of the Warrior didn't have to tolerate the same temperatures as the driver, but nor did they share his advantage of being able to see what was happening outside, as Corporal Melvyn Downes explained:

'When the seven blokes in the back have all their kit on, as they did have from when we moved off, it was really cramped, really uncomfortable. But after a few hours the joking started. Someone would say, give us more room, or, who's turn is it to get a brew on? Of course, you couldn't get a brew on while you were moving. You'd hear, oh I've got a sore arse, or, I'm cramped up, when can I get my kit off? Even though we knew it was for real, it still seemed like an exercise. I couldn't believe that people were moaning about things like that when any second we could have gone over a mine, or been shot at.'

The night of 24–25 February was spent in the staging area. At 0630 hours the Commanding Officer was summoned to Brigade Headquarters, where he was told all timings had definitely been advanced, and the Battle Group would be departing early that morning. Then the Brigade Commander, Brigadier Patrick Cordingley, revealed that 7 Brigade would lead the British forces into Iraq.

Until this stage, the Divisional Commander, Major General Rupert Smith, had retained the option of sending either 4 or 7 Brigade through first. If the enemy had put up a stiffer resistance, 4 Brigade would probably have led, for they had an additional infantry battalion and were therefore more suited to the task of punching a hole through a determined defence. On the other hand, if, as was the case, the enemy proved to be weak and lacking a coherent defence, 7 Brigade with its fast-moving, armour heavy grouping was the ideal formation to exploit quickly over the distances involved.

Whatever the tactical realities, the question of who led into Iraq was a matter of pride to all concerned and, having been deployed in the Gulf far longer than 4 Brigade, everyone in 7 Brigade, including Brigadier Patrick Cordingley, was delighted they had been selected:

'It was an interesting mechanism I think, that 4 Brigade had developed. They said that they were going to go through the breach first. It's rather like saying, I'm going to be posted to France or something. If you really want it, if you tell enough people, the theory is that it will happen. Because there was a level of pride involved over who had priority, and because 4 Brigade had not been there that long, it was, I think, a mechanism that they used to gee everybody up.

'My own personal view was, I'd like to go through first as a matter of pride in the Brigade, and priority because we'd been there longer, and all that sort of thing. Good honest competition. I didn't feel too strongly about it, and actually you could argue that if there was a dodgy problem on the other side, whoever went through first would have to deal with it, and actually I didn't mind it being 4 Brigade! Of course, they had more infantry to deal with that sort of thing anyway.'

The Commanding Officer returned from his orders at 7 Brigade, and the word was quickly passed down to the Battle Group that they should be prepared to move by 0900 hours. The vehicles were already lined up in three parallel lanes facing in the direction of the border. There was no need for dispersal, because there was no air or artillery threat to guard against, and a gap of only 10 metres was left between each lane. The soldiers took what might be the last opportunity for a long time to stretch their legs, write a last letter, or check their weapons and equipment.

At 0830 hours, a single shot was heard in the vicinity of the C Company Warriors. A soldier who was checking his rifle had accidentally fired a shot, which had hit Private Shaun Taylor, a member of the Milan section attached to C Company. Corporal Darren Wilson was 'Nobby' Taylor's detachment commander:

'We'd all been sitting there for a few hours, and I'd just left Nobby at the front of the vehicle and sat down in front of my vehicle for orders. Then a shot went off, and I turned round and saw Nobby fall to the ground. I was there virtually before he hit the ground. It's just something you can never describe, ever; the way it happened and our reaction. It was complete and utter shock.

'The strangest thing was that we were so close to going. We had a guy come from the reserve; he was a 548 driver and he was already Milan trained. He joined our detachment and we just got in the vehicles and carried on. Not as if nothing had happened: I mean, we'd all been crying by this stage, we were all shook up and in bits. I can remember sitting in the turret and driving past all the other vehicles thinking, I wonder if they know what's actually happened. Everybody should know, because he was a good guy.

'None of us wanted to talk about it. We all believed that Nobby was going to be OK. We had to believe that to carry on. I think we all had to believe he was going to be fine, and after it was finished we were all going to visit him with a bunch of flowers, grapes, Lucozade, in hospital. We were all saying, when we go and see Nobby, or, wait till we've finished, I'm going to go and tell Nobby this. As if he had sprained his ankle and was sitting on the sideline.

'But in the back of our minds we must have thought, he might be dead. When it had finished, once we'd done all the fighting, and they came up and said, we've got some bad news, it hit us again. That's when it really hit us.'

The Milan Platoon Commander, Captain Tim Sandiford, was further up the line of vehicles when he heard a radio message about the shooting:

'I picked up my rifle and ran over to see what was going on, and when I got there the medics were already there working on young Taylor, who'd been shot through the chest and shoulder. By that stage he was horribly yellow and waxen. Corporal Wilson was holding his head and I was shouting at him, trying to get him to keep talking. There was a stage when it appeared that he was slipping away and wasn't saying anything coherent, he was just murmuring and mumbling back. They then pumped him full of something and he started to come round a bit.

'Having seen that there was nothing I could do there, I then went to find the rest of the section and get them sorted out. It was rather unpleasant because at the time, when you wanted to sit them down and give them a cup of tea and so on, I was actually saying, right, you're now going to do that, you're going to do that. I wouldn't let the lad who'd shot him and another guy who'd been to school with him go round and see him. They were fairly cut up as it was, and they hadn't really seen what state he was in. It was a hard decision to make but I would do it again. I turned up, pushed them about and disappeared again. Had I then known that we wouldn't be moving for another three hours it would have been different.

'Having got the rest of the section back in the wagon, I then went back to Taylor and shouted at him, farewell, I'm off, I'll see you after the war. He responded, as far as I'm concerned, as coherently as he had been till then. So I left with a feeling that he was going to survive and get better. The doctor then came up to me after the helicopter had arrived to casevac [casualty evacuation] him and said, I don't think he's going to make it, which rather knocked me back, but at least I was prepared for it then.'

The doctor at the scene was Captain Richard Gale:

'He had an entry wound just on the left side of his chest which came out just under his collarbone. He was conscious when I got to him, the company medics had already got a drip in. I put a chest drain in and got a litre of fluid off his chest virtually immediately. He was doing quite well while we waited for the helicopter, which took a while to come in.

'Then suddenly he just went off. He had a cardio-respiratory arrest, he stopped breathing and his heart stopped. So I intubated him, then the American medics turned up. They were doing all the usual bullshit of, let's go sir, let's fucking go, and I said, let's just fucking wait shall we; it being quite difficult to intubate somebody in that sort of environment. We effectively put him on the chopper dead although the resuscitation continued.

'I then wandered off for about 20 minutes. I was pretty pissed off about it. Then the sergeant major came up and said, get a grip sir, we've still got a job to do; he was absolutely right, of course, spot on. When we got back from the Gulf it did prey on my mind a bit; but then, we had minimal kit, we're not an intensive care unit. There is no massive technological back-up on the spot and no senior registrar to go to for advice. As the only doctor on the spot, you're it.'

Although he was not directly involved in the incident, it posed a dilemma for the Adjutant, Captain Chris Hughes:

'We were about to go, we'd just been told 30 minutes to go. It then became a bit of a controlled crisis. We were desperately trying to get a helicopter in, and it didn't land in the right place. We could see the bloody thing five kilometres away, and it was a US helicopter. There was an awful lot of vehicles there so it must have been very hard to identify us. In the end we had firefly strobes [a high intensity, hand-held light beacon used to attract helicopters by day or night] going, smoke going, and eventually he saw us. I was constantly on the radio chasing it. Then I became aware that we had 15 minutes to go. And we'd got to go. It was the first time for me that operations were about to override a serious casualty/death. That wouldn't even happen in Northern Ireland; somebody would stay with the guy, you wouldn't just abandon him. And that's what we were about to have to do in my opinion. We were going to have to go. Very difficult.

'As it happens, the helicopter came in then and literally lifted him about two minutes before we were due across the start line. So that sort of dichotomy lifted. Could we have left an ambulance? An ambulance is a big asset to a battle group just about to go to war. I don't know what we would have done.'

The Battle Group eventually rolled out of the staging area at 1000 hours, after a couple of delays imposed by the traffic jams ahead. The route to the breach was 15 kilometres long, and the Operations Officer, Captain Mark Steed found it easy to follow:

'All the routes were quite well marked because the Americans had gone through before. There were pickets with cylums on them and huge great marker boards with letters on them: in our case, a huge great red board with a letter C in it. We simply followed that through the obstacle. It got a little bit unclear at one stage, where the wheeled route crossed the tracked route, but fortunately we all came out in the right order at the other end.'

Major Tim Gatfield had a good view of the Iraqi defences as he passed through with Alternate Headquarters before the main body of the Battle Group:

'The breach itself was only about two strands of wire. The engineers at this stage were beside the track placing TNT on top of the mines that they'd uncovered, and as we went through they stopped the rest of the traffic and blew all the mines, and then we carried on. The minefield was pathetically thin; it can't have been more than 100 metres deep.

'There was some evidence of positions which had been filled in. The American tactic was to fill the trenches in using a tank with a plough fitted to it. The idea was that the Bradleys [the US equivalent of the Warrior] would put down suppressive fire while the plough tanks went along the trench and filled it in, people and all. The trenches that were left were once again pathetic. Just a straight line parallel to the front, no zig-zags, no bends, no real shelters. There were about three destroyed vehicles and that was it. It was really just another bit of desert. Not the big obstacle that we'd expected to see.

'When we got to the FUP, we found it was actually based on an abandoned Iraqi position. That was the first time that I got out and wandered round. I couldn't believe how pathetic they were. They had only two or three inches of overhead protection. They stank; they were full of rancid bedding. There were vast amounts of paperwork, boxes and boxes of records, files on each man and identity cards. A bureaucratic nightmare. The equipment was in an awful state. The ammunition had been left outside and the boxes were wet and half-full of sand. Belts had been left on the guns, and you could see the links were rusting on the gun.'

Once the Battle Group reached the far side of the breach they picked up Route Green, which was manned by the Recce Platoon Scimitars, and followed it for about five kilometres to FUP Green. The FUP lay just inside the edge of the protective American bridgehead, which was marked on the maps by a line codenamed New Jersey. To the north and east of this line lay the Iraqi positions which the Staffords were to take on. Once again, things began to speed up. The Brigade had expected to stay in their FUPs until the early hours of G+2 but, as soon as they were complete and ready to move, the order came to break out.

The Staffords were in the most westerly FUP; to the east of them, in FUPs White, Blue and Yellow, were the brigade supporting troops, the Queens Royal Irish Hussars and the Royal Scots Dragoon Guards respectively. The brigade plan was to have the Irish Hussars Battle Group leading with the Staffords following on the left, and the Scots Dragoon Guards level with the Staffords on the right. The whole Brigade had a frontage of only 10 kilometres, and was constrained by its boundary with 4 Armoured Brigade on the right and the American 2nd Armoured Cavalry Regiment on its left. To cross either of these boundaries without clearance was to risk being engaged by other friendly forces, who would be expecting to see only enemy vehicles in front of themselves.

An additional complicating factor was the deployment in front of the Brigade of medium recce vehicles of the 16/5 Lancers. Their task was to identify and report in detail on the enemy positions directly to the Divisional Commander, to provide him with up to date intelligence.

Because the Brigade exercised no direct control over them, it proved difficult at times to differentiate them from enemy vehicles in the conditions of poor visibility which prevailed for the next four days.

The whole tenor of the Allied advance had been laid down by General Norman Schwarzkopf. It relied upon speed, surprise, and weight of firepower to deliver shocking blows to the Iraqi defences, and to continue to move through them at such a rate that they would never have time to regain the initiative. With the ground troops available to him, Schwarzkopf was able to make a number of coordinated strikes into Iraq and Kuwait on G day, thus confusing the enemy as to which was to be his main point of effort.

To the west of VII (US) Corps, XVIII (US) Corps (which included the French Foreign Legion Division and the American 82nd and 101st Airborne Divisions) was advancing very quickly northwards to cut off the Iraqi line of retreat from Kuwait and Basra. To the east, the pan-Arab forces, known as the Joint Force Command (North), were breaking through along the line of the Wadi Al Batin. Further east again, 1 (US) Marine Corps was punching through the Umm Gudair oil fields heading directly for Kuwait City; and along the coast, another corps-strength Arab force, predominantly Saudi Arabian, was sweeping up from Ra's Al Khafji towards Kuwait City. The option of a marine amphibious landing was still available to the Allies, but, even though it was never used, the threat sufficed to pin down at least six Iraqi divisions along the Kuwaiti coastline.

Within VII (US) Corps, 1 (UK) Armoured Division was to advance north-east for about 100 kilometres into Iraq, destroying a tactical reserve armoured division which had been identified along their path. It was then intended that the Division would establish a counter-penetration position inside Iraq, facing north-east towards the Republican Guard Force divisions which were positioned in Iraq to the north and north-west of Kuwait. Their eventual thrust eastwards, into Kuwait, was not a part of the original master plan.

Moving parallel with the British, but to their north, was the remainder of the Corps. This included the American Army 1st and 3rd Armoured Divisions and 1st Mechanised Infantry Division. They were supported by the American 2nd Armoured Cavalry Regiment. They too were tasked with destroying the Republican Guard.

The long build-up to the ground war, and the allied air supremacy, had resulted in an unprecedented volume of intelligence regarding the deployment and capabilities of the Iraqi units in the path of the Allied advance. Information was collected from numerous sources including satellite imagery, air recce, Special Forces operations; and interrogation of Iraqi deserters and prisoners. Other sources were also used, but these remain classified for obvious reasons. The result was that every Allied unit had an extremely good idea of the location of the main Iraqi positions within their area of operations.

This information was disseminated to the Staffords in the form of traces: large sheets of tracing paper overprinted with the Iraqi positions shown by red symbols, and with a number of reference points marked so it could be placed over a map. The traces were continually updated by 'Intsums'; written or verbal messages relating to the enemy dispositions. In addition to these detailed locations, information was passed down about the type of equipment, particularly tanks, which would be encountered on each position; the estimated effectiveness of the troops; and even the state of their morale.

This constant flow of detailed information kept the Battalion Intelligence Cell busy until the start of the ground war. From G day, events moved so quickly that very little new intelligence of any immediate value at battle group level was available. Their most important task prior to the breakout was to sift through the mass of information, and extract any of particular relevance to the operations which would involve the Staffords.

Because the information about the enemy was so detailed, the 1st Armoured Division plan was formulated as a series of attacks on known objectives along the chosen axis. The objectives were all codenamed with the names of metals. Along the 120 kilometres from the FUP to the Wadi, 7 Brigade had four major objectives to deal with: Copper, Zinc, Platinum and Lead.

The largest of these, objective Platinum, covered an area of some 200 square kilometres. There were other, similar sized, objectives for 4 Brigade to take on to the south. Copper was bisected by the inter-brigade boundary, and each brigade had the responsibility of clearing its half of the objective.

The aim was to clear these objectives of any enemy and continue a high speed advance to the Wadi Al Batin, which formed the western border of Kuwait with Iraq. Once the wadi had been reached, a number of options were open to the Allied commanders. The choice was dependent upon the progress of the remainder of the Allied operation, and, perhaps more importantly, upon the movements of the Republican Guard Force divisions.

At 1525 hours on 25 February, G+1, the Warriors and Challenger tanks of the Staffords Battle Group thundered out of FUP Green, across line New Jersey. They were heading in a north-easterly direction into

Iraq and towards Objective Copper, which lay some 30 kilometres away. As they moved off it began to rain heavily, prompting a number of soldiers to speculate on the capability of the Americans to manipulate the weather as part of the master plan. Lieutenant Colonel Charles Rogers manoeuvred his Warrior between the two tank squadrons leading the battle group:

'In the FUP, the other two battle groups had managed to replen [replenish with fuel] which we didn't because my A1 Echelon who carry the fuel had been routed into a minefield, which had caused some damage to some of my resupply vehicles. Then they had to be rerouted, so we didn't get time to refuel, and it was something I was constantly concerned about that day.

'Anyway, at 3.25 we kicked off. Whack! Off we went at a hell of a rate. And we went for it. We knew where the enemy was in general terms, in these bite-sized chunks which they'd named Copper, Zinc, and so on. Each one was about brigade sized, so we were going for a whole division. The Irish Hussars were out front, with the medium recce in front of them. Unfortunately Warrior and Challenger just go so much faster than medium recce vehicles, and have so much better optics, that we kept bumping into them that afternoon and evening. The tanks had every right to open fire. They could see hot spots [through their TOGS thermal imaging sights] at four kilometres, and it was very difficult to tell whether they were medium recce or the enemy.'

The first hour of the advance was uneventful. Then, shortly after 1700 hours, the Recce Platoon, who were travelling with the Mobile Milan Section on the left (northerly) flank encountered a group of Iraqi soldiers on the ground. Captain Richard Wootton cautiously directed the operation to capture them:

'We'd been moving at a cracking pace and I was thinking, well there's absolutely nothing here. Then the lead squadron reported some enemy on our northern boundary. The CO tasked me to go, and I gave orders over the net for half the platoon to deal with it, and we set off. Half the Mobile Milan followed us as well, and I thought this was pretty good teamwork; they did it without being told, and off we went. In fact the CO gave me a bollocking on the air; he said, you're not moving yet, why not? I said we were fire and manoeuvring, because we were moving off into territory that we didn't know. That is, keeping one vehicle static and observing, covering the other one as it moves forward, and then when it stops, leapfrogging the other past it and so on. But we just couldn't move quickly enough like that, so we all had to move at the same time. That went against the grain.

'Then we had a report that there might be a vehicle there as well, so it was a little more worrying. I kept looking at the satnav as we moved, and we were starting to go outside the boundary into the American area, and all of a sudden you think, I hope the Americans aren't coming up on my flank. Anyway, it turned out to be three Iraqis who claimed to have been captured by the Americans already. Of course we went through all the proper drills for taking prisoners, because we'd heard that some of them had got Claymore mines attached to them and were suicide bombers.

'As we were dealing with them, what should come from our west but three

Apache helicopters, and that was quite frightening. They do look like big wasps and they're quite aggressive. They were about two kilometres away and I was pretty sure that they would see our IFF, Identification Friend or Foe, markers. Those were inverted vees painted on the vehicle and a big luminous panel on the back of the turret.

'Dealing with the prisoners was a time-consuming business, and the Battle Group wanted to press on. We got a message to just leave them there, so we gave them a bit of food. In fact I gave one of them a cigarette because he asked for one. In fact, I was feeling compassionate towards them so I gave them a packet, which I came to regret a couple of days later! They were in a miserable state; they wanted to be taken, but we had to leave them there.'

Shortly afterwards Major Chris Joynson, commanding B Company, came across some more Iraqi stragglers. This group, unlike the Recce Platoon's prisoners, did not contain an English speaker:

'We went out very nervously and searched them; they were the first Iraqis we had seen. It was quickly obvious that they were not going to resist. They were quite convinced that we were going to kill them. Having searched them, I tried to tell them to walk away, go down there, but I couldn't be understood. So I just mimed a marching action to the senior one, while pointing back down the axis. He seemed to take it that I wanted them to do a bit of drill or something, because he got them all together and they went marching off swinging their arms parade square style! Even the Warriors coming up behind us noticed these very smart Iraqis marching back down the axis, which they thought was quite amusing.'

Night came very quickly in the desert, and the cloud and heavy rain which continued to fall turned the night of 25–26 February into an inky blackness. By dusk the Battle Group was nearing the northern edge of Objective Copper and still moving, albeit more slowly. Captain Mark Steed was travelling in the back of the CO's Warrior:

'It was one of the darkest nights that I've ever seen, or couldn't see. We had convoy lights, white lights low on the back of each vehicle, and also a red torch on the back of the turret which worked very well. You could see where the squadrons were deployed; we were at the forward edge of the companies. I think that's what kept us all together. We found the image intensifier sights on the Warriors were virtually useless in those conditions because there was no ambient light at all. The tanks had quite good visibility with their thermal imagers. The drivers were just locked on to the red lamp in front of them.

'Then Major Austin Ramsden, commanding B Squadron, reported a number of heat sources to his front, unidentified at three or four kilometres. We'd been told that the 16/5 Lancers [medium recce] were forward and on our left flank, and our first thought was that maybe they'd strayed in. Austin got progressively closer, still couldn't identify these hot spots, and asked on a number of occasions if he could engage, but the CO said hold for now. He thought it was the 16/5th who'd strayed in, and was very loath to open fire on unidentified heat sources. We were coming up to Copper at this stage, and the Irish and the Scots DG had already reported enemy well forward of Copper, so we knew there were enemy about.

'It went on and on, and it was like one of those thriller films where it's getting more tense and the music's building up by the minute. Then we asked Brigade to get the 16/5th to put up light in case it was them. Then a green Verey light went up. It was them. We were very annoyed that they were within our boundaries and we didn't know about it. The CO wasn't sharp with them. I think he was more relieved that we'd found out that it was them and we hadn't razzed them up because it came very, very close to that.'

By 2200 hours that night, all three Battle Groups in 7 Brigade had passed through Copper without encountering any sort of resistance. It is possible that the positions had been abandoned. The Staffords cleared the northern edge of the objective and then started to move towards Zinc. The Irish Hussars were also well on the way to Zinc.

The most southerly battle group, the Scots Dragoon Guards, were just exiting the eastern edge of Copper when the leading tanks of D Squadron began to pick up indications of an occupied enemy position. They knew a divisional communications site had been spotted in that area some days before and so they prepared to attack. Any assault on dug-in troops ultimately requires the infantry to go and winkle them out. A Company were a part of the battle group, and they were warned to prepare for an attack. For Major Simon Knapper, this was not the start to the war he had hoped for;

'Before the attack, my main concern was that we would have something to do, a little attack, before last light. We just needed something to warm up with. I had always wanted to do the first British armoured infantry assault, and we all wanted A Company to be in first. I just wanted to do one daylight attack to get the guys over the hump of doing it for real. Of course, when it happened at night I thought, bloody hell here we go, but actually I was amazed at how well it worked. I put it down to the four months training and BATUS before that. The training had given me total confidence in the Company. Everyone knew what everyone else was doing, that was the main thing.'

The extent of the position proved to be extremely difficult to define in the darkness. It was decided that, as speed was of the essence, a quick attack would be launched by A Company, supported by a troop of Challengers, onto a system of occupied trenches and bunkers which could be made out through the tanks' night sights. Because the enemy situation was so unclear, Simon Knapper elected to dismount only 1 Platoon and his company headquarters, leaving 2 and 3 Platoons mounted in their Warriors so they were available to move quickly to support the operation if needed. Lieutenant Andy Layton was commanding 1 Platoon that night:

'The feeling of elation was incredible, fear didn't cross my mind. To be honest, I think the commanders have all said the same. You've got so many things on your mind that you just don't get a chance to worry about it. As we moved up into the FUP for this assault, the normal drill was to batten down. But I didn't batten down

DIAGRAM NOT TO SCALE

KEY:

- A Coy Warriors : 0B - Coy Comd; 0C - Second in Comd
- Mortar Fire Controller's Warrior
- Milan Section Warriors
- D Sqn SCOTS DG Challengers with callsign
- FV 432 ambulances
- IRAQI positions

N

① ① ① ② 2 PL ③ 1 PL with 30 ④ 0B with MILAN ⑤ 3 PL with 32

31 30 32 0B MFC 1 PL 3 PL 0C 2 PL MILAN SECT

1200 m

INITIAL FORMATION. RESERVE (2IC WITH 2PL) 600 m FROM FORWARD PLS.

CROSSED START-LINE 2130 Hrs

COY ECH

LAD with ammunition and fuel

25 FEBRUARY (G + 1)

A COY ATTACK ON COPPER

that night because I just couldn't see a thing; I couldn't even see the tail light of the Challenger in front of me.

'Shortly before we got to H Hour everything started to fire, and there was tracer and HESH rounds going off everywhere. I felt very detached from it then. We went in following the tank, and then the tank commander said, I've got a hot spot, I'm heading for it now. And I was screaming at him on the radio, give us a countdown [of the distance to run to the edge of the objective], tell us what you can see! He said 200 metres, dismounted infantry, trench system. Then he said, 100 metres to go. So I said, brake now; then, 50, prepare to debus. Then we stopped and I shouted, debus, debus!

'It takes a while for the commanders to get down out of the turret, and so Dennis Rogers, my platoon sergeant, was the first one out of the back. He crawled forward about 50 metres and then gathered the platoon together as they debussed. We then just kept fire and manoeuvring forward and forward. My guys fired about four magazines each. I was using my runner, Corporal Bailey, to relay information between me and my sections because my radio had gone down and the noise was phenomenal. We still hadn't located any enemy but the guys were all firing to suppress anything that was there. I said to Sergeant Rogers that we had to control the fire, and asked him to get over to the left to make sure they conserved ammunition.

'While this was going on, Simon Knapper was trying to find me in the darkness. He came over and said, get them going! He wanted them to move more quickly. Then he just got up, started yelling at people to get going, and just sprinted forward. It was quite graphic because he's got a load of long scrim [torn-up strips of hessian to break up the outline of the head and shoulders] on his helmet, and he'd got his bayonet fitted, a small radio on and his chest rig; he looked quite wild. At this, my guys just looked around and followed him. There was a road up there and he said, get them across the road, and the whole platoon got up en masse and moved over there. At that stage I said, it's no good, we can't locate them. Simon then said that he'd heard on the radio that there was another contact over to the right, so we mounted up to go and deal with that.'

It is possible that the enemy observed by the tanks on the position, and whose presence had prompted the attack, had withdrawn to the more substantial defences which had now been identified. Meanwhile, the other two platoons were manoeuvring with the tanks of D Squadron to assault the larger position. As Major Simon Knapper described at the beginning of this book, it was a communications site, and there was no time for deliberate orders. It was to be another quick attack without any artillery support, because the guns supporting the Brigade were being held for the attack on Zinc. Light was provided by the Scorpions of the Scots Dragoon Guards recce troop whose 76 millimetre guns were capable of firing a parachute illuminating round. The only other light on the battlefield that night came from tracers and burning vehicles and equipment.

The company moved into assault formation behind the tanks and prepared to bear down upon the trenches. 1 Platoon were slightly delayed when the platoon commander's driver suffered a number of broken fingers, trapped between his hatch and the hull of the Warrior as his platoon commander jumped on it. Dennis Rogers, the platoon sergeant, had to take over driving and, in a well-rehearsed procedure, Corporal Steve Turvey, the senior section commander, assumed the role of platoon sergeant.

This time there was a great deal of return fire from the trenches. Captain Jack Ferguson, the company second in command, watched the Warriors go in:

'There was fire coming back at that stage. I've seen nothing like it before. It's fine when you go to BATUS and watch that magic firepower display when everything is going down, but when you see the tracer coming the other way it's something else again. But even then, crazy as it may seem, I didn't stay battened down. I was so confused about what was happening that I opened the hatch and I was up, trying to take it all in.'

On the objective, as soon as the back door of the Warrior opened, the soldiers inside could see the green Iraqi tracer flying past them. Private Michael Flackett, who later went into an assault with C Company, expressed what many soldiers felt as they looked out for the first time:

'I felt like staying in. I felt like staying in the wagon and locking the door.'

Private Andrew Kelly had only joined A Company three days earlier from the battle casualty pool, as a replacement for a soldier injured in Ray:

'I went round the front of the vehicle, saw all the positions, and just shit myself. I went back round the back of the wagon and then the section 2i/c said, get your fucking arse round the front and give us covering fire. So I went round and started firing, and then we moved on towards the bunkers.'

In C Company, Corporal Melvyn Downes had already briefed his section on what was to happen when they debussed:

'I said to them, I'll be the first man out, and I expect you to follow me out. I said that if they didn't, I'd come back, if I made it back, and I'd shoot whoever stayed behind. I meant it as well. In fact, as soon as I got out, everyone else was out as well. I think, having lived so closely together for five and a half months and worked together, nobody would have done that.'

One of the luckier men that night was Private Mark Eason:

'The LSW gunner got out first, and I just followed him. Then I started firing myself. There wasn't time to think, we just moved forward; it was the training, it was just automatic. I was shooting at the muzzle flashes that I could see. Corporal Heaven then came out of the vehicle, and he was in the middle of us. We moved forward one bound, and then on the second bound a flare went up, I saw a flash go off in front, and I got hit. I thought, oh no! I was just lying there, the whole of my side had gone numb. I thought I'd been shot through the chest. Then after a few seconds I began to realise that I hadn't been wounded. The round had hit my jacket, hit my combination tool and split it, and then it went into the magazine in my pocket and stopped there. I had a fair bruise afterwards, but that was all.'

Three members of 3 Platoon were injured during the attack. The section commander, Corporal 'Angel' Heaven was the most serious casualty, receiving multiple wounds from shrapnel. Andrew Kelly witnessed the incident:

'We all took cover while some grenades were thrown, and then Corporal Heaven was hit. He just laughed at first, then he looked down and blood had started gushing out of his chest. He said, I've been hit, and then he coughed up some blood. Then we could see the blood start to stream out of his arms and legs as well. He was in bits. They gave him morphine, and then the medics came in and took him away.'

The other two casualties were Private Andrew Kelly himself, who had minor shrapnel wounds to his legs, and Private 'Alfie' Roberts who was hit by a large lump of shrapnel in his thigh. Corporal Heaven and Kelly were casevaced that night, but Alfie Roberts stayed with the Company for a further 48 hours before he accepted that he would have to be treated. Major Simon Knapper had nothing but praise for the medics, mostly bandsmen, who dealt with the casualties:

'The casualties were initially loaded into Warriors and brought back to a central position before being transferred into an ambulance. It then headed off into the blackness. How the hell the ambulances ever found where to go and then got back to us without satnav, I don't know. They deserve some credit. I was always really impressed when the ambulances reappeared. They did absolutely brilliantly.'

By all accounts, the attacks that night were exactly what the soldiers had trained for. No attempt was made to clear individual bunkers by going into them; in the darkness that would have been a foolhardy risk. White phosphorous, luchaire and high explosive grenades were posted into every bunker encountered, and all positions were subjected to intense fire from tanks, Warriors and the soldiers themselves as they were assaulted. The Company advanced through the position with their Warriors following them, sometimes embussing to move off to a new objective identified in the area.

Iraqi resistance, which had shown some spirit in the opening minutes of the encounter, rapidly waned. Once the firing had stopped, figures began to appear out of the darkness offering their surrender. The whole action had lasted just over an hour and a half, and the company then moved off, carrying approximately 50 prisoners on the hulls of the Warriors. These were dropped off at a pre-arranged prisoner of war collection point established by A1 Echelon. No count was made of the number of enemy killed in this attack, and there was not time to search the position in daylight as the CO of the Battle Group was pressing the Company and D Squadron, who had supported the attack, to move on and rejoin the rest of the Battle Group, which had continued to advance eastwards towards the southern edge of Zinc. By 2300 hours, A Company had rejoined the Battle Group and were able to pause for a couple of hours before the advance continued.

The Staffords Battle Group had also halted just short of Zinc, and were taking the opportunity to refuel the vehicles. The order to halt had come from Brigade Headquarters, who were planning to unleash a massive artillery fireplan onto Zinc. It was to employ all the available artillery assets; in particular the multiple launch rocket system (MLRS) manned by 39 Heavy Regiment Royal Artillery, and the M109 155 millimetre tracked guns of 40 Field Regiment Royal Artillery. The Ops Officer, Captain Mark Steed, knew the fireplan was coming:

'We sat on the north-west corner of Copper refuelling, and we'd been told that we would probably be there for a couple of hours. There was still this miserable drizzle falling. Then bang on 0100 hours, way over to our right, west of Copper, you could see the MLRS launching. There were a lot of them; it was an awesome sight, something I'll never forget. These fireballs would streak off into the cloud and they would disappear up into the murk with a huge rumble. Then, six or seven kilometres away, you could see them coming down at the other end, huge great flashes and real bubbling fireballs as they hit the floor. Or they'd be carrying sub-munitions. Then you'd see a bright pop in the sky, and the first time you'd think, oh that one's a dud, it's not going off, and then there'd be a brrrrrp. God knows what area it covered, but it was just really bright sparky flashes on the ground and this bandsaw type explosion. They were the most terrifying. You could see why they were called grid square removers. Beyond that again, you could see the dull, HE orange flash of the M109s. It was a massive amount of artillery.'

Impressive though it was, the last 48 hours had been exhausting and extremely stressful. A number of soldiers shared the feelings of Captain Chris Hughes:

'For the first time since we had started moving, I had taken off my radio headset. I knew we had about 45 minutes during the bombardment before we would be moving again. It was the loudest thing I've ever heard, and the earth was shaking, but I was so tired that I didn't bother to go outside to have a look! I partly regret that now because everyone was going, fucking hell, you want to see it out here. But I just wasn't interested at the time.'

By 0500 hours on G+2, 26 February, the Battle Group was moving again. They passed through Zinc at 0530 hours, but found nothing more than abandoned positions and vehicles which had been destroyed by the bombardment or earlier air strikes. The Queens Royal Irish Hussars Battle Group was still leading the Brigade, and the Scots Dragoon Guards with A Company were on the south. They had identified a further Iraqi logistic position short of Zinc and, as Simon Knapper related, they assaulted it at daybreak:

'We were lined up with C Squadron, overlooking this Iraqi supply dump. Before we went in a US psyops [psychological warfare] team was brought up. They used loud hailers and were calling on the Iraqi troops to surrender. You could see them in there around the building and behind a berm with what looked like a BRDM in front of it, but it was howling with wind and it appeared that the message wasn't getting home.

'What we then did, because we felt they did want to surrender, was to do a dry run in. The tanks were trained on every vehicle they could see, and the moment a shot had been fired at us, they would have destroyed the place. So we did a dry run right up onto the position and no rounds were fired at us. We then took prisoners. It was at this point that we realised that actually their resistance overall was crumbling, and after that it got pretty boring really.'

The scene was now set for 7 Brigade to close with the largest enemy position within their area of responsibility, Platinum. This had been divided into two distinct parts by the brigade planners. Platinum I was the western half of the objective, and was believed to be less heavily defended than Platinum II to its east. Brigadier Patrick Cordingley planned to coordinate the movements of his battle groups through this position.

The first phase of the operation called for the Queens Royal Irish Hussars Battle Group to move east from their final position on Zinc to a start line on the western edge of Platinum I. They were then to sweep through Platinum I, always heading directly east, until they reached the boundary with Platinum II where they were to stop. From there, they could give fire support to the Staffords as they implemented the second phase of the plan by driving down through Platinum II from a start line on its northern edge. The whole operation was to be supported by preparatory artillery fire, and strikes by British Lynx helicopters firing TOW anti-tank missiles.

For the Irish Hussars to carry out their task effectively, they could not afford to continue without any integral infantry support. Consequently, C Company was ordered to move from the Staffords and join the Irish Hussars for this operation.

The potential problems of a short notice re-grouping such as this are great. The company must first find its new battle group, then ensure it has the new codes and radio frequencies it needs to be able to communicate with them. It must completely understand the battle group's modus operandi, and be able to slot in with the briefest of instructions. It is a tribute to the level of training attained by the units of 7 Brigade, that C Company had completed the regrouping operation by 0900 hours, less than two hours from the moment when they had been warned they might have to move.

Major John Rochelle, C Company Commander, described the subsequent operation:

'As we moved over to join them, we passed through the area that the artillery barrage had hit the night before. That was the first time that I saw a number of bodies. They didn't appear to be very badly cut about, which surprised me. There were also a lot of the bomblet rounds about which hadn't exploded, so one had to move rather gingerly.

'I met up with the CO of the Irish Hussars, who told me what was going on. We then sat in behind the two tank squadrons which had been engaging Iraqi positions on Platinum I for some time. They started to bring up the psyops team, but they couldn't get there in time before the Staffords mounted a preliminary operation on some troops to our north-east.'

As the Queens Royal Irish Hussars were moving forward towards Platinum I, they had encountered an enemy position to their northern flank, outside the boundary of Platinum. It dominated the ground across which they intended to advance, and the CO was keen that it was neutralised. The Brigade Commander therefore ordered the Staffords Battle Group to take on this task, as they were close by and available.

Lieutenant Colonel Rogers decided it would be susceptible to a company/squadron group attack and, at 0830 hours, called in the squadron leader of C Squadron which was part of the Battle Group, and the company commander of B Company, to brief them personally. They then set off to marry up with their troops, who had been led round to the start line for that operation by the company and squadron second in commands.

At 0920 hours, the tanks of C Squadron crossed the start line for this clearance operation and drove south towards the reported position. Almost immediately they encountered the enemy, who were dug in with their vehicles along the line of a berm. The tanks engaged some abandoned lorries at first, and then spotted a number of T55 tanks and MTLB armoured personnel carriers, all of which were destroyed.

B Company were following behind the tanks, and it seemed as if there would be little for them to do, so comprehensive was the destruction wrought by the Challengers. When the squadron stopped at the far end of the position, the company debussed and began a methodical clearance operation through the trenches, bunkers and few vehicles which had not been destroyed. Sergeant 'Dixie' Oliver, Platoon Sergeant of 6 Platoon, was one of the first on the ground:

'The trenches were very well concealed: they were flush with the ground, and where we had stopped, we were right amongst them. So I told the platoon commander quickly about them, and then I immediately debussed. I went straight out of the back, had a quick look round, and there was a trench just to the right of the wagon. I cleared it with fire; I couldn't get in it because the entrance was too small, but I checked inside and there was nobody there. I could see 5 Platoon about 300 metres to our front, and they were on the ground dealing with prisoners. They were obviously unaware that there were trenches behind them that hadn't been cleared.

'So I went back and reported to the platoon commander, and then we got a section on the ground to sweep through, forward to 5 Platoon, to relieve this danger. The Warriors were to move behind us, covering us with chain gun and Rarden. We shook out and moved forward in extended line. There were loads of fighting holes on the ground which we systematically cleared with fire, although we didn't find anyone in them. Then, on our right, we spotted the enemy in some bunkers. As we swept round to take them on they surrendered, so I ordered the guys to cease firing.

'But there was still an MTLB with a machine gun mounted that no-one had cleared, off to our right. We crawled to the lip of the scrape that the vehicle was in. Then they covered me as I moved forward, lifted the commander's lid, and dropped a white phosphorous grenade in. When it had gone off, we ran round the back and opened the doors, and sprayed automatic fire in.'

The platoon commander of 6 Platoon was Lieutenant Steve Neale:

'While the boys were on the ground dealing with the MTLB, an Iraqi truck came tearing across the position from right to left, in between myself and 4 and 5 Platoons. I remember the Company Second in Command coming up on the radio shouting, stop that vehicle! We swung our gun onto it just as a Milan hit it. It kept rolling forward for a while, and we started to fire the chain gun at it. At the time it was just a target, we had to destroy it. I gave my gunner the word of command, co-ax, go for it. His first burst hit the cab as they were trying to jump out. It was quite strange seeing these men go from being rigid to being completely floppy and hitting the ground like sacks of potatoes.

'At that point we just carried on engaging it. We cut back through the truck, and that was the worst moment of it when, all of a sudden, out of the back of this lorry, blokes started appearing. They hit the ground, so we ignored the truck and started shooting at them on the ground. They were still moving, still posing a threat, so my gunner cut back through them. It wasn't until Sergeant Pulizzi came on the air, check fire, check fire! Then I realised that one of our sections was on the ground, moving up to deal with them. We had been so engrossed, glued to the sights, that I had to punch my gunner to stop him from firing.'

Being close to the lorry, and on the ground, Sergeant Gino Pulizzi quickly realised the Iraqis in the lorry no longer posed a threat:

'I went down to them and started to administer first aid. They were in a right mess. There were a couple of dead, and one had his leg blown off; it was a mess. We gave them morphine and bandaged them up, but mainly we had to reassure them. For some reason, they thought we were going to bayonet them. They were really terrified, but my first instinct was not to harm them, it was to get them out of there because they were wounded, they were in a bad way. So I got the ambulance and we casevaced them.

'These were the first dead and injured that I'd seen. It was hard to get myself going. My hands were covered in blood. I know I was shaking; I started shaking when I first saw the casualty with his leg shot off. I thought that what I had to do was to get the blokes working. I had to keep them busy. Once we'd finished doing it, got them casevaced, and mounted up again, that's when it hit me. We were all a bit shaken, but I was pleased with the way the platoon had handled themselves and just got on with the job.

'It changed my view of the Iraqi soldiers. When we first went in, I must admit that I was going to give them a right hard time whether they were fighting or were prisoners. But I saw old men, people with no shoes on. They were starving, had no water, and were just wearing tatters. And I realised then that he probably did have a hard core of troops, but these weren't them. They were just blokes with a uniform thrown on their back.

'After that incident, when we had prisoners, I made sure we sat them down, gave them a cup of tea and something to eat. We knew that they just didn't want to be there. If Saddam had looked after his troops, they might have put up a better fight, but these just didn't want to know. On that position, one of the other platoon sergeants found a number of officers actually shot in the back by their own blokes.'

The wounded Iraqis were treated by the B Company medics and by Captain Richard Gale, the Battalion Senior Medical officer:

'The worst casualty was the Iraqi who had been hit in the right leg by a chain gun. The medic had already got a drip into him, and I basically amputated his leg with a pair of plaster shears, which was the only instrument I had with me which could do the job. I passed it to the medic who was helping me, who said, well, you don't get cas sim [casualty simulation – theatrical type make-up used to make exercise casualties look realistic] like this in Germany, do you sir? There was only morphine available for anaesthesia. The leg was put in the grave with one of the other Iraqis who had been killed, but the Iraqis who were there got very upset by this. They wanted it buried separately, so we did.'

With the objective cleared by 1100 hours, B Company was urgently required back with the rest of the Staffords Battle Group to prepare for the main assault on Platinum II. C Squadron had already returned. Because a large number of prisoners had been rounded up, someone was needed to look after them. The Battle Group Alternate Headquarters, which was not involved in the main assault, was sent forward to guard them until they could be taken away by the prisoner of war organisation following behind 7 Brigade. This successful preliminary operation had cleared the way for the Brigade attack on Platinum, and the Queens Royal Irish Hussars Battle Group with C Company prepared to advance to carry out the first phase against Platinum I.

Ferozeshah Day parade

Sergeant 'Tank' Stalker – Mentioned in Despatches

Brigadier Cordingley addresses the Battalion prior to G Day

After a hard day's training. . . .

Dark skies in Kuwait

Christmas in a Warrior

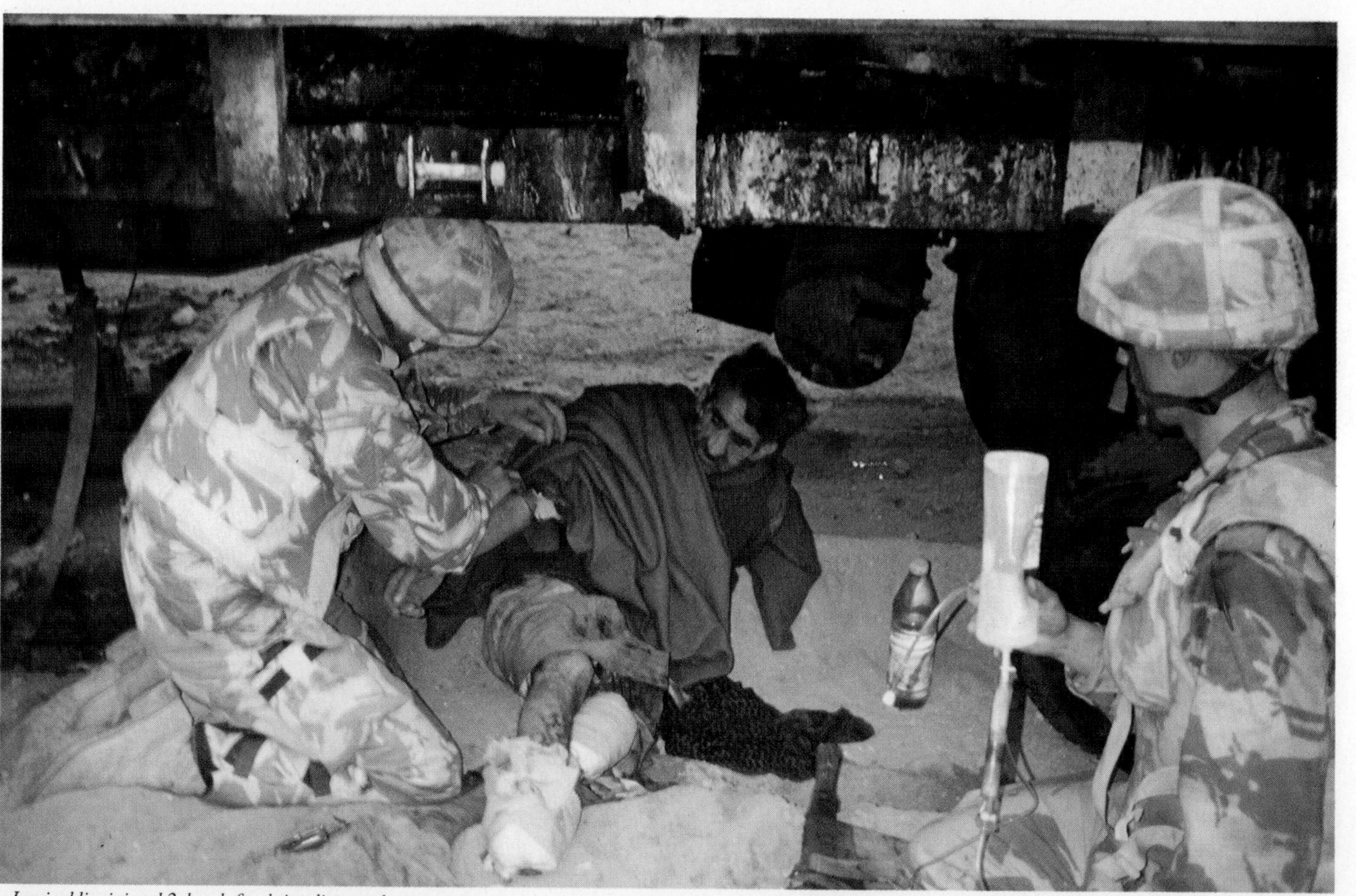

Iraqi soldier injured 2 days before being discovered

Flights home

Welcome home

7

Victory

'Talk about giving sudden orders. I said, right, move now, and that was it.'

C Company led the Queens Royal Irish Hussars Battle Group into the attack on Platinum I. Normally, tanks would lead any advance into enemy-held territory, but on this occasion C Company was ordered to clear and secure an area on the edge of the objective from which the tanks could launch their armoured thrust. This was the start line of the attack. Major John Rochelle was not entirely happy with the plan:

'Once the B Company preliminary op had taken place, I was then tasked to move forward to secure the start line for the attack on Platinum I; which slightly disconcerted me, because we were effectively going into an area that, as far as we knew, hadn't been cleared. But it appeared to be clear, so we said, OK, and moved forward fairly carefully. When we got there, we told the Irish Hussars that it was clear. As they started to move forward, the Army Air Corps also came up to start looking for, and engaging the targets in depth towards Platinum II.

'At that stage a sandstorm came down and it really was horrendous. If it hadn't been for the satnav that we had, we wouldn't have been able to do very much. It only went up to about 12 or 15 feet, so the helicopters could see over the top of it, but we couldn't. There was literally a wall of sand being blown towards us.

'Once the Irish Hussars had started their advance, we were then tasked over to join their A Squadron to clear an area that they had been looking at. We picked up an intimate support troop of tanks and drove in to assault it. We stopped in the middle of the position and could see that it was a fairly large defensive position, but it turned out to be abandoned. There were a number of vehicles there, but that was about it. Two platoons dismounted and had a look around, but we soon realised that it wasn't worthwhile continuing, so we got back in and drove on. We then continued to the end of that position, where the Irish Hussars established a firebase to support the Staffords' attack onto Platinum II.'

By 1240 hours, the Irish Hussars' clearance of Platinum I was complete, and the Staffords were given permission to start their operation into Platinum II. At the same time, the Scots Dragoon Guards Battle Group was ordered to move north-eastwards from its holding position

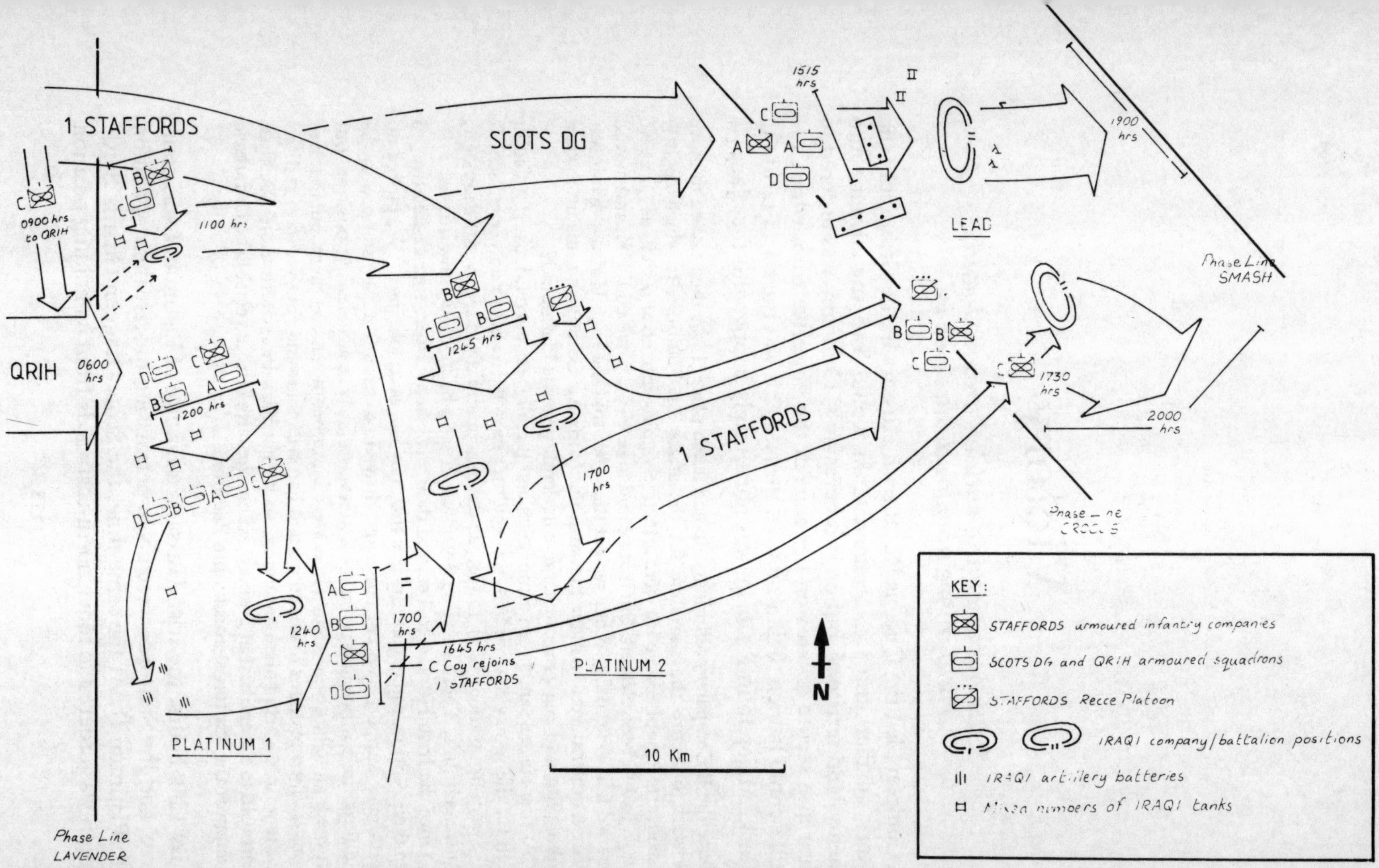

1 STAFFORDS

SCOTS DG

QRIH

0900 hrs to QRIH

0600 hrs

1100 hrs

1200 hrs

1245 hrs

1240 hrs

1700 hrs

1645 hrs C Coy rejoins 1 STAFFORDS

1515 hrs

1730 hrs

1900 hrs

2000 hrs

PLATINUM 1

PLATINUM 2

LEAD

Phase Line LAVENDER

Phase Line CROCUS

Phase Line SMASH

10 Km

N

KEY:

STAFFORDS armoured infantry companies

SCOTS DG and QRIH armoured squadrons

STAFFORDS Recce Platoon

IRAQI company/battalion positions

IRAQI artillery batteries

Mixed numbers of IRAQI tanks

26 FEBRUARY (G + 2)
7 ARMD BDE ATTACKS ON PLATINUM AND LEAD

in the south-east of Zinc, skirting the northern edge of Platinum to take up a position on the western edge of objective Lead. This would enable the Brigade to continue straight on with an assault into Lead if the enemy on Platinum were to capitulate with little or no resistance.

As the Staffords prepared to cross their start line at their H Hour of 1245 hours, the Royal Artillery battery commander, Major Julian Lyme-Perkis, coordinated a number of different fireplans onto enemy positions which had already been identified. While this was going on, the recce group, which comprised the Recce Platoon and the Mobile Milan Section, were making best speed to move into a position to protect the vulnerable eastern flank of the Battle Group as it advanced south. The Second in Command of the Recce Platoon, Colour Sergeant Mark Banks, recalled an unexpected encounter as they moved:

'We suddenly came across a position with a couple of ACRVs, a couple of T55s, a BMP, and some soft-skinned vehicles. We were coming up behind them, and we could see the position was still manned. There were still people in the tanks, and this was when the Mobile Milan Section came into their own.

'Corporal 'Bonnie' Tyler fired his Rarden at a T55, and that alerted them to the fact that we were behind them. They started to batten down in the T55, but one of the Mobile Milan vehicles which was right in front of me fired at the T55. He hit it right up the backside, caught it with a cracking shot. It lifted the whole of the back end of the tank off the ground. The guy in the commander's cupola must have shot at least 40 feet straight up into the air, still holding onto the hatch which had separated because of the impact. They then fired another 15 missiles, and hit with every one of them.'

The commander of the Mobile Milan MCT that fired was Corporal Darren Fern:

'I first saw a BMP which was out of view of the rest of the recce group. It had moved from its scrape, and it looked as if it was going to engage us. I was screaming at Morris in the back, take that vehicle out! But he was having problems locating it through his sights. It was getting a bit dangerous, so I got in the back and I hit the BMP. It just obliterated it. The turret came off and the doors and hatches blew open from the pressure of the round. At this point, I switched straight away to my right hand missile and fired at the T55. As the missile was flying, I saw the tank commander's hatch open, and he came out waving a piece of white cloth. But it was too late then, and the missile hit the turret at the rear. He came flying out and then the turret lifted off, and then all the ammunition blew up.

'There are two sides to the way I felt about that engagement. At that point, I was rather pleased with myself. I'd been in the Platoon all these years, fired on ranges, and now I had actually done it for real. That was, like, the ultimate. But then, later on in the conflict where we were burying their dead, and we saw the damage that the Milan and other anti-tank rounds had done, it hit us all; it made us all feel pretty sick. You were thinking, that could have been me, so there was this mixed feeling. I've put it in the back of my mind now, and I'd like to try and just forget about it. I don't feel any guilt; they did something wrong, and we basically showed them the right way of doing things.'

The Battle Group assaulted into Platinum II with the two tank squadrons leading, and B Company following up centrally behind them. It rapidly became clear that there would not be much resistance on the position. The Commanding Officer's Tactical Headquarters moved well forwards, just behind the tanks, and the Ops Officer, Captain Mark Steed, had a clear view of the enemy defences as they rolled through them:

'I remember this incredible scene. The further south we got, the more scrapes and the more vehicles there were. I could see the Challengers engaging hull-down T55s, and you could see the good strikes from HESH. One or two were burning, and then there would be all these secondary explosions as the ammunition went up, and that was quite spectacular. They weren't firing back at all.

'The most amazing sight was in the centre of the biggest part of the position. All these Iraqis were just loafing around with their hands in their pockets, wandering around aimlessly, like little Lowry figures. Then one of the tanks would fire a round which would go literally 20 feet above them on its way to destroy a T55 in a scrape, and all they'd do would be to scamper on for about 50 or 60 yards, still with their hands in their pockets, and then carry on their sauntering again.

'Then, as we got near the end of the position, we had a call on the radio from the engineers. They were working to our rear, destroying all the kit the tanks hadn't engaged with explosive charges. They had just blown up one vehicle, and were sitting back admiring their handiwork, when two T55s appeared out of the murk coming towards them and firing main armament and co-ax at them.

'So they all leapt into their wagon and closed the door, and then realised that the first man they'd pushed in was the driver! So they had to undo the door, all get out again so the driver could get round to his hatch, and then all pile in again before they could escape. So we had this frantic call from them saying that there were two T55s running rampant in the rear area, and could somebody help them please. One of the squadrons was told by the CO to send back a troop of tanks to go and sort them out, and two Challengers then went screaming back that way.'

The recce group, having pushed on after their earlier engagement, were now moving parallel to the Battle Group down the eastern edge of Platinum II. The Commanding Officer was keen for them to catch up with remainder of the Battle Group, which was by now some kilometres further south. Mark Banks recalled an encounter with the enemy which lent added impetus to their movement:

'We were moving along through a sandstorm which kept lifting and then dropping again, so visibility was changing from minute to minute. The next thing I saw was the Samson recovery vehicle come flying past us. I've never seen a Samson go into turbo power like it! The cause was two T55s which had come up behind it, and it was really lucky for us that there was a sandstorm blowing, because we managed to outrun them and lose ourselves in it.'

Corporal Steve Elliot was driving the Samson at the time:

'We'd been following along with the recce group, and suddenly, the next thing I knew, the commander was shouting down the intercom, get your foot down, we've got T55s behind us! So of course, I dropped two cogs and flew past recce; they didn't know what was happening. They call me the fastest Samson driver in the west, now.'

While the advance continued, the Battle Group Alternate Headquarters continued to guard the prisoners captured in the B Company/C Squadron preliminary operation. It was becoming increasingly clear to them that they were stationary in a very vulnerable position, with little protection beyond the Rarden cannon of the sole Warrior in the headquarters. To complicate the situation further, a violent sandstorm was blowing all around them, and the Scots Dragoon Guards Battle Group was due to pass very close by them en route for their new position overlooking objective Lead. The battle group radio log records the following message at 1340 hours:

'From callsign 0C [Alternate Headquarters] to callsign 0 [Battle Group Main Headquarters] – Large friendly callsigns are moving 500 metres to my south, ensure they know my position. The reply from 0 was – They know.'

The Adjutant, Captain Chris Hughes was manning callsign 0:

'There weren't enough people readily available to take on our prisoners, and Alternate HQ had been stuck there for some hours. Then we had this call from them saying, tell Brigade that we're here because there are tanks coming towards us. I said to him, they know; but I then got on to Simon North, the watchkeeper, and said, look, just do remind them again that Alternate's there. They came back and acknowledged that they did know, and that the Scots DG and the Irish knew as well.'

Sergeant Major Baz Barrett was with Alternate Headquarters in his 432, which was parked next to Major Tim Gatfield's Warrior:

'It was literally a couple of minutes after that message was sent that I heard machine gun fire coming down very close by. I said to Sweeney, my driver, for fuck's sake, Sweeney, are they firing at us? What's happening? Have a look through your periscope and see if you can see anything. We could still hear all this machine gun fire but he couldn't locate its source.

'Then there was a massive shock, as if the front of our vehicle had been hit. There was a sprinkling of shrapnel on the armour outside. I thought we'd been hit near the driver's compartment, and my immediate reaction was to grab hold of Sweeney to see if he was alright. So I checked him, and he was alright, and there was no obvious damage to the vehicle.

'Then I thought we'd better get out if the vehicle was the target, so we got out and took cover outside. I could see other people from the headquarters taking cover and scurrying around. There was a lot of screaming and shouting going on. There was a guy lying on the floor next to his vehicle, screaming. I remember shouting to somebody to grab hold of the guy and help him out, and then I ran back into my vehicle to get on to the radio to try to make them stop. I felt that it was almost certainly friendly fire, even at that stage.'

The Warrior had been hit by a 120 millimetre HESH round fired by an unidentified British Challenger. The HESH round is designed to defeat a modern tank by detonating on the external armour, thus sending a shock wave through the steel into the crew compartment. When the shock wave reaches the inner layer of armour, under normal conditions, a scab of metal will fly off and hurtle around the inside of the vehicle, destroying everything in its path. Fortunately for the crew of callsign 0C, the round impacted on one of the Chobham armour plates to the rear of the hull, and had dissipated its energy on that, so there was no more than a dent in the actual hull of the Warrior, and no lethal damage inside.

Captain Tom Wagstaff was manning the radio inside the vehicle when the round struck home:

'Suddenly I felt a bang. The lights went out in the back of the Warrior and we were knocked off the seats. I thought, Christ, what's happening. It all happened so quickly. We then leapt out of the Warrior to get away from it, because my immediate thought was, he's going to follow this with a second round. He's hit us once, he'll hit us again. We got about 100 metres away from the Warrior and just hit the deck.

'I then looked back, and I could see a Challenger about six or seven hundred metres away. The conditions that day were pretty hazy because of the sandstorm. We lay on the ground and just prayed; my arse was going, sixpence half a crown. I really didn't know what was going to happen. Then I made my way back to the Warrior to get on the radio, but because it had been hit the comms were knackered. At the same time I saw one of our watchkeepers, Captain Toby Tennant, who had been hit, and was screaming, my legs, my legs!'

Toby Tennant's memory of the incident is remarkably clear:

'I was poking my nose out of the back door and round the side, to try to identify who was shooting the machine gun at us. I couldn't see anything at first, but then I saw a flash through the sandstorm in the distance. It just didn't register what it was. Now I think it must have been the muzzle flash, because about half a second later there was a loud concussion and I ended up on the floor. I don't know how long I lay there stunned before I came to.

'I looked down and my left leg was stuck out at a very strange angle, and I thought, why the fuck has this happened to me? It wasn't hurting at all then, but it was clear there was something wrong. I yelled out, my legs! Come and give me a hand! Corporal Scaif tried to drag me out of the way of the vehicle alone, but I weighed too much. So he called Corporal 'Arthur' Lowe over, and then they just dragged me out of the way while I held my leg vaguely straight. I was talking to them and saying, I'm bleeding, because I wasn't sure if they knew that I was bleeding. I couldn't see any blood but I could feel it all trickling down to my bum inside my trouser legs.

'I was talking to them all the time and saying things like, go on, put some direct pressure on there. It's still bleeding, time to put some direct pressure on the groin. So they were sticking their fists into my groin to stop everything bleeding. Then they got me bandaged up. Morphine went in bloody quickly. A drip went in pretty quickly and they squirted a litre into me before you could say Jack Robinson. They got another drip in, and that was well on its way by the time the medics arrived; that probably saved my life actually.

'Eventually John Miller, the doctor, arrived. I said, hi John, we've got a bit of a problem here. He said, alright Toby, we'll sort you out. He checked me out and then said, right, I'm going to put you out for a while to straighten your leg. Anyway, he gave me a cocktail that gave me the effect of a general anaesthetic and erased my memory of that period. The only thing I do remember is talking to Corporal Duvall about sheep farming, because I was obviously quite high. Then they straightened my leg and apparently I screamed in his face. The poor fellow told me later that it was his worst nightmare. After that, they put me into a wheeled ambulance and off I went down the casualty chain.'

As Toby Tennant was being treated, a Challenger tank pulled up beside the headquarters. Major Tim Gatfield was the senior officer on the ground:

'We were all clustered round Toby, very concerned, and very worried about him. An officer of the Scots DG came up at this stage, and I thought it was him who had fired. I gripped him by the throat and said, you bastard. I was about to swing one. He was saying, it wasn't me, it wasn't me, I don't know who it was. I saw it happen and I came over. I calmed down then and went off to send a sitrep on the radio. But I was still very upset.'

Baz Barrett had been trying to reassure and occupy the soldiers on the scene:

'Then it was a matter of getting around, finding out exactly what had happened, and trying to sort people out, because some people were shocked and one guy was in total shock. Everyone couldn't believe that we had been shot at by our own people. I remember that, very soon after the shooting, a tank arrived on the position. A couple of the soldiers actually picked up their weapons and were going to blow this bloke away for firing at them. Sweeney got hold of these guys and dragged them away and said, come on, sort yourselves out, don't be stupid.'

Brigade Headquarters was immediately aware of what had happened. Regular reports were sent to them by the Staffords, and Brigadier Patrick Cordingley monitored the incident on the radio in his tank:

'When a thing like that happens the first reaction is to try and stop anybody else firing, if indeed it is your side firing, and I think we must assume it probably was. When you pass a battle group across the back of the other two, you're taking a calculated risk. Manoeuvre warfare is a risky business. You can blame anybody any way you like, but I'd like any blame for any of these things to be put onto me. I was the man who gave the orders to manoeuvre people round each other. When something like that happens, you do feel immensely sad, but you can't allow that to stop you doing what you were doing.'

This whole sorry incident occurred in the middle of the Staffords assault onto Platinum II and, clearly, the advance was not going to be halted as a result. The Battle Group Main Headquarters coordinated the evacuation of Toby Tennant, and the recovery and subsequent replacement of the damaged Warrior, while at the same time monitoring the ongoing operation.

By 1730 hours, Platinum II was declared clear of resistance, and most of the surrendering Iraqis had been rounded up and grouped together. There were more than 300 of them in the Staffords' area alone, and the speed of the 7 Brigade advance meant that the prisoner of war handling organisation was some way behind the leading battle groups. A policy decision was taken to leave most of the prisoners to fend for themselves. Only officers of the rank of colonel and above were transported to a central collecting point for special handling.

Even before the end of the Platinum II operation, orders were being given over the radio for the next phase of the unremitting advance. The Staffords were to move north-east to Lead, where they were to secure the southern edge of what was to become a Brigade leaguer. The Scots Dragoon Guards had already cleared Lead of what little enemy remained after the medium recce units had passed through earlier in the day. C Company was to rejoin the Battle Group, and further orders would follow that night detailing subsequent operations. Lead had been the last objective earmarked for 7 Brigade, as nobody had expected they would advance at such a speed. At Corps and Divisional Headquarters, frantic planning was taking place to identify likely targets for a continuing advance by the 1st Armoured Division.

On the ground, the move to the new positions on Lead seemed relatively straightforward. Satellite navigation meant that even in the sandstorm and gathering dusk, the sub units could move accurately along a designated route to their final positions. C Company set off from their holding position on Platinum I across Platinum II to marry up with the Staffords on Lead, but as Major John Rochelle, the company commander, explained, they came across some unexpected resistance:

'We were moving along with two platoons up, company headquarters in the middle and the other platoon in reserve, about two or three kilometres away from the place we were headed for. It was about half past five in the afternoon. We then saw what I took to be a long berm. Behind it there were lots of people moving about, carrying weapons. There were also a couple of small buildings in the area. It was a surprise because we thought the area was clear. It was billiard table flat, absolutely no cover at all, an expanse of desert with this berm and, as it transpired, the berm was actually a banked up road.

'I called the Company to a halt and looked through the binoculars and the Raven sight, and I could see they were Iraqis. They were not attempting to surrender, but they were not trying to fire at us either; they probably hadn't seen us. So I told the platoons that we were going to open fire over the top of this berm to try and persuade these chaps to surrender. We did that for about a minute, called a halt, nothing happened. So we fired again, this time into the top of the berm and into the buildings and called a halt again. This time they started to surrender, lots of them, and they started to come forward. So I gave the order for the platoons to dismount and get these people to come forward to them. Then another lot appeared over to the right, to the south of the berm, and I ordered 9 Platoon to swing round and deal with them'

Lieutenant Andy Nye was commanding 9 Platoon:

'There were loads of prisoners coming up to us, and we went firm and the sections dismounted to take the prisoners. I thought that I really wasn't doing an awfully good job in that particular position, and so I would move to the right. So I said on the net, I'm moving to the right to cover our flank, and got the go-ahead from John. As we were starting to move the vehicles, from behind a white flag somebody fired an RPG 7 at us. I was getting ready to get out at this stage, so I just grabbed a headset and screamed out, contact wait out! Which is the cry which theoretically focuses everybody's attention on the fact that somebody is under fire, and clears the net of radio traffic.

'Then I debussed and ran forward to Callsign 32 [one of the section Warriors], which was still smouldering because it had been hit by the RPG which had sent white phosphorous all over the top. The first person I spoke to was Guardsman Chant, who said, he's dead, Ted's dead, boss! I was thinking, you sick bastard, that's not funny, that's not funny at all. It took a few seconds for it to sink in that what he meant was, Ted's been killed. Then I thought, that's not part of the training, it's not part of the plan; what have I done. I felt, then, massive guilt. Why didn't I just sit in reserve and just stay there rather than move up to deal with those prisoners?

'Then 32 put some fire down and some fire came back at them. We joined in with some of the other guys. Unfortunately, 31, in its haste to avoid the missile, which it did, went from going forward rather fast to going backwards even faster and snapped the gear linkage. If that wasn't enough, the main armament had a misfire, a dangerous situation for it to be in, and it had a jam on the co-ax. They had got no way of fighting the vehicle. They had no way of defending themselves. I was told afterwards that Grainger, the driver, cool as a cucumber slacked his seat off, unharnessed himself, turned over and started undoing all the bolts to repair the gear linkage. All this while the vehicle was being fired at.

'We continued to advance, and we'd probably gone about 100 metres when we came across the RPG launcher, which got everybody's blood up. Then we had a contact with about a section's worth of Iraqis in that area. It resulted in a brief but fierce firefight. I can remember distinctly the soldiers with me just hammering that area with small arms fire. They had cleared the stoppage in the co-ax of 31 by then, and it absolutely pasted the area. We didn't see any movement after that.

'I went to look at Moult's body. A very, very optimistic move on my part. I didn't really want to believe that he was dead, and I went there to make myself 100% sure, which I regret doing. I don't regret checking, but I regret seeing him. It was a pretty disturbing thing to see. We'd seen lots of bodies, but when it's somebody that you know and you've worked with that well, it's different. We'd discussed things; not as private soldier to officer, yes sir, no sir. We'd discussed our wedding plans, how are you going to do it boss? What sort of things are you going to have at your wedding? There was a really empty, horrible feeling. A sense of loss isn't really the right way to describe it.

'We didn't get a replacement for him, and I didn't want one; that would have been a nightmare. I didn't want his close muckers thinking, he's replacing Ted and he's not as good, or he's not as clever, or he's not as much fun. I was very happy not to have a BCR. I didn't need one. If we'd gone into battle again, then 32 would have been the section which would have gone out and severely damaged anybody's sense of having a nice day.'

Private Carl Moult, 'Ted' to his colleagues, had been killed instantly by the impact of the RPG 7, a shoulder launched anti-tank rocket. His body was taken back by ambulance down the casualty chain, the company commander refusing to bury him in Iraq.

By now it was almost dark and there were still signs of resistance in the area. One of the buildings in the area of the road contained some Iraqis who would not surrender. Corporal Melvyn Downes observed the operation to deal with them:

'A section of 8 Platoon led by Sergeant Stalker advanced up to the building with an English-speaking Iraqi to tell them to surrender. They were just expecting them to come out and surrender, but when they got close to it the Iraqis started chucking grenades out at them. The section got down and filled the place full of lead. We were watching the whole thing from about 400 metres away. They were taking this building apart, firing luchaires and grenades into it.

'Then two Warriors drove up and they were firing HE into the building. There was so much that it reminded me of a cowboy film, where you see a shack absolutely riddled with rounds for about 10 minutes. After that you wouldn't expect anybody to still be alive. In fact, there was one man dead inside and another hobbled out, injured.'

C Company spent another hour gathering in nearly 300 prisoners, and ensuring that the area was clear, before they felt it was safe to continue with their interrupted move to meet up with the Battle Group. The other company and squadrons had made it to Lead without incident, but the Commanding Officer, with his Tactical Headquarters, had encountered some resistance on the way there, as he recounted:

'We went over a rise in the ground and came under fire, which was a bit distressing. It was small arms and the odd anti-tank round. The small arms fire was bouncing off the Warrior but luckily the RPGs didn't hit us, and this caused me to go into personal action. I then crushed my finger in the hurry to get down through the hatch and into the turret!

'There were lots of enemy in front of us at a distance of about 500 to 1000 metres, mostly running, obviously some were firing, and there were some vehicles there as well. So we took on the vehicles, and I was terribly proud that we got six hits with six shots. Unfortunately most of them were bulldozers, which was a bit of a challenge!

'Everybody started firing then, the BC [battery commander] started, and then a missile disappeared off to the left and hit something; and I started to get this

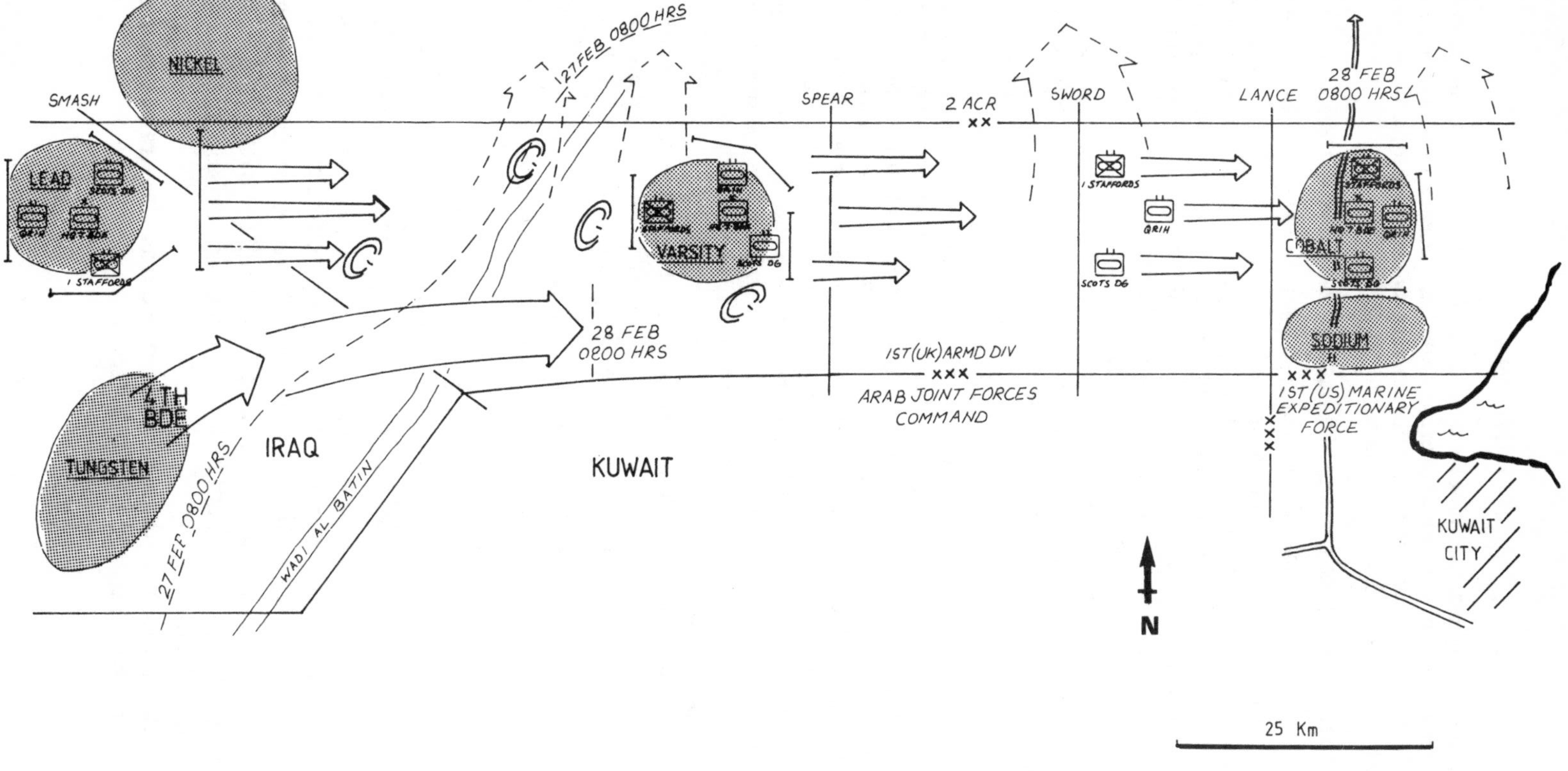

7TH ARMOURED BRIGADE
G + 2 TO G + 4

uncomfortable feeling that things were getting a bit out of control, and probably more dangerous for my own side than anybody else. The enemy had stopped firing at us by this stage. Most of them were running. So we stopped, and they really started to come in to us just as it started to get dark.'

Captain Mark Steed was in the back of the CO's Warrior:

'The CO said he could see a couple of white flags about 500 metres forward of the vehicle, and somebody had better get out and investigate it. So Chris Hughes and I straight away thought, right, this is where we're getting out. We whipped on our bayonets, I grabbed Corporal Berry and said, you come as well, and we jumped out.

'It was horrible, because it was a murky night and you could just make out this landscape. It was like something that you see on the field firing ranges when you're waiting for the targets to pop up. There were these abandoned bulldozers and a lot of open ground. You got out the front and thought, well actually this is getting a bit serious. The other two got out first and I said, give me a call when you're down. So they gave me a shout, I ran round the side, very conscious of all this tracer lighting up the sky on our right from C Company. All we could hear was these Warriors, ticking over behind us. You still feel quite naked even though they're there.

'We manoeuvred forward in bounds, covering each other, and then looked behind us and the Warrior looked an awfully long way away. We thought, dare we go any further? But then we heard somebody shouting very faintly in the distance. Through our sights we could just make out one chap waving a white flag. After a while he came forward and came up to me. I could see from about 30 yards away that he still had his rifle slung across him, so I shouted to the other two, he's still got his weapon. Apparently in the Warriors they could see through their night sights lots of shadowy figures running around in the area that he'd come from, but we couldn't see that on the ground. It's probably just as well, because I'm sure we wouldn't have stayed out there!

'We managed to get him in, and he was very frightened, this chap. He had eyes like saucers, shouting at the top of his voice. We grabbed him and got his weapon off him and laid him on the floor, and then we heard more shouts from behind. So we got him to call the others in. They were all terrified too. More and more kept coming in after that and within the hour, between the three of us, we had 83 prisoners to look after. Then some of the provost lads appeared and took them over so that we could continue on.'

By 2100 hours on the night of 26 February, the Battle Group was in position on the southern boundary of Lead, prepared to counter any Iraqi penetration of the Brigade position for as long as they were there. Even before all the vehicles had arrived, at 2000 hours, the Adjutant had warned everyone over the radio to be prepared for rapid subsequent operations, details to follow. This was the result of the 7 Brigade warning order which had been passed down to all the battle groups, but no further information could be given at that time because the plan was still being formulated.

Brigadier Patrick Cordingley remembered it as a frustrating night for the staff of the 7 Brigade Headquarters:

'We then had a situation where the orders got changed three times during the course of the night. We were going for Basra, we were going north-east, we were going stright into Kuwait. Those were the three options.

'This was the Divisional plan, but in each option, 7 Brigade appeared to be in the vanguard. We were ahead of 4 Brigade by now, who were preparing to deal with Tungsten. So you had this situation where we had to chop and change throughout the night. And of course every time you get something you pass it on immediately, and then people start to make plans. So it was an immensely disturbed night for everyone until eventually it became clear that we were going to move due east.'

The onward movement of 1 (UK) Armoured Division, and therefore that of 7 Armoured Brigade, was inextricably linked with the political and strategic dictates of the war. In addition, commanders at all levels were acutely aware of the problems of keeping the lines of communication open, so the fighting units could be resupplied as necessary. The further the armour moved into Kuwait and possibly Iraq, away from the secure bases in Saudi Arabia, the more difficult it would become to guarantee the integrity of the route along which the combat supplies would have to travel.

Nonetheless, most of the Staffords would have preferred to have continued the advance up the Wadi al Batin that night. The probable result of such a move would have been an encounter battle with one or more of the Republican Guard Force divisions, which were known to be stationed to the north-east, inside Kuwait. The orders for such an operation were actually issued during that night, but were quickly revoked, and by the early hours of 27 February, G+3, the Brigade had been tasked to advance eastwards into Kuwait at 0800 hours that morning. The Brigade's objective was codenamed Varsity, and was situated some 30 kilometres inside Kuwait, 50 kilometres from the Brigade's hasty defensive position on Lead.

During the night, the Battle Group took the opportunity to refuel all the vehicles and to replenish with ammunition as necessary. The A1 Echelon, which delivered combat supplies to the fighting vehicles, had been moving throughout the day in their wheeled lorries and Land Rovers to keep up with the fast moving armoured formations. Now they moved amongst the Warriors and Challengers, using no lights and keeping noise to an absolute minimum as they distributed cases of Rarden and tank ammunition and pumped diesel into the half-empty fuel tanks of all the vehicles. Once this operation was complete, and while the fighting troops snatched a few hours sleep, the echelon vehicles drove back to the Brigade Administration Area, where they restocked themselves in preparation for the next opportunity to replenish the Battle Group.

27 February was to be an uneventful day for the Staffords. Their task was to advance into Kuwait as far as objective Varsity, which was believed to contain an enemy position of approximately brigade strength. The whole Brigade was to move, as it had done from the time of the breakout, but this time the Scots Dragoon Guards were leading with the Irish Hussars to their north and the Staffords to their south. Once again, the axis of the advance was directly due east. To the south of 7 Brigade, 4 Brigade was holding firm in the area of objective Tungsten. Lieutenant Colonel Charles Rogers stationed his tactical headquarters, as normal, just behind the leading tank squadrons:

'We started off, forming up around six o'clock, and we crossed the start line by 0800 hours. We headed east across the Iraq/Kuwait border, and towards what was deemed to be an independent brigade on Varsity. This was still very much an advance to contact; it was not an administrative move cross-country. There was no action at all on the way there or through the objective itself. This was over a distance of 50 to 60 kilometres.

'We got there by lunchtime to find nothing much. A lot of kit lying around, the odd prisoner sitting around, but by then we were really bored to tears with the bloody prisoners. We sat there from after lunch, all night, on this next objective. Things were so fluid that they weren't quite sure where to go next. The great problem at that level is de-confliction of boundaries to ensure that we didn't start shooting each other up. We certainly put up all the flags we had: Union Jacks, regimental flags, you name it. We had heard by then that the Irish Hussars had had a recce vehicle taken out by an American Abrahams tank in the north, and everyone was very aware of that particular danger.'

The drive into Kuwait, across a landscape which bore clear witness to the ferocity and intensity of the Allied air strikes, created a powerful impression upon those soldiers who could see it. Those who travelled in the back of the Warriors had their first opportunity to walk over a deserted Iraqi position in daylight once the Battle Group had organised its defences on Varsity. Sergeant Gino Pulizzi had expected the battlefield to look different:

'I had expected to have to fight for every inch of ground, trench to trench. I didn't expect it to look so empty. We saw an MTLB out on its own, and it looked so out of place. I thought we'd see all these mega trenches, but the trenches we saw were little four man trenches just dug into the sand with no revetting to strengthen them. They were full of pots and pans and blankets just thrown in.

'It smelt different. There was that smell that is peculiarly Arab, and then you could smell the cordite and explosives mixed in with it. You could see where the planes had bombed them; there were black craters everywhere. But there again, there weren't as many craters as I thought I'd see. I thought it would be like the moon, but there was just the odd crater here and there with the Allied propaganda leaflets floating around among them.'

Corporal Melvyn Downes was also surprised by what he saw:

'It just looked like some kind of scrapyard, like the ones we've got at home. But once we had looked at it we realised that if they had stayed where they were and put up a fight, the war would have gone on for a lot longer. We had been led to believe that they would be in trenches with no overhead protection, which had been a boost to morale. When we saw what the bunkers were actually like we were amazed. You couldn't see a lot of them until you were on top of them, and when you went inside some of them were living a life of luxury. They had double bunk beds, even TVs in some of them. They had TV aerials sticking out of them. We thought to ourselves, bloody hell, there's them living like this, and we've been living like shit for the last few months!

'There's no way we could have bypassed some of those positions in Kuwait if they had chosen to stay and fight. It would have been necessary to clear each bunker; it would have been a wicked fight.'

The Iraqi positions were not littered with bodies, as many of the Staffords had expected. Nonetheless, there was still evidence of the massive destructive power of the Allied assaults on most of the positions, as Lieutenant Steve Neale explained:

'It was quite surprising to see the look on the faces of some of the young soldiers when they actually realised, these are dead people. A lot of them hadn't seen them before. I had only experienced cadavers at university, which are quite different. It was a total look of horror on their faces until they were gripped by their section commanders. That was one of the lasting impressions which will stick in my mind. It took a lot of motivation from the section commanders to get themselves going as well as their sections.'

Brigadier Patrick Cordingley's overriding memory of Varsity was the atmosphere:

'When we stopped there, for the first time I remember thinking, I wonder why it's so dark? Then suddenly I said, I wonder if this is the oil wells burning? Of course it was the beginning of going into that awful, oppressive time in Kuwait.'

The pause on Varsity gave the soldiers the chance to eat a decent hot meal for the first time in the last 48 hours. As Lance Sergeant Andrew Dillon explained, however, they had not been totally without food during that period:

'We ate quite well, actually. We stuck as far as possible to the normal meals, breakfast, lunch and dinner. We had the BVs going virtually all the time. We had loads of brews, whenever it was possible to do it. As soon as the vehicle stopped it would be passed round. It was just to keep yourself going, just to keep the morale up slightly by getting something warm inside you. As far as food goes, we would eat on the move if necessary; just heat a tin up and crack it open and pass it round.'

Once C Company had prepared their hasty defensive positions on Varsity, the Company Commander held a service of remembrance in the field for Private Ted Moult. At this stage the soldiers did not know that Private Sean Taylor had also died of his wounds. Major John Rochelle conducted the service:

'I gathered together Private Moult's platoon, and anybody else who wanted to come along, and we held a service. It was a very moving occasion for me and, I think perhaps, for most people. We didn't know where the Padre was and, quite honestly, it wasn't the time or the place to get him up. The advice that one is given in the Army administrative handbook is that where there is a lull in the battle, you must make the time to say goodbye properly to your fallen comrades. That was the first opportunity that we had to do that.

'All that I did, was read the burial service from the field service prayer book, and added a couple of readings. I think that was enough to lay people's minds to rest in terms of saying farewell to their fallen comrade. I certainly felt better for it, and I think particularly the guys in the Platoon understood why we were doing that at that particular time.'

Private Paul Lister, one of the soldiers from the Prince of Wales's Own Regiment attached to the Staffords, was serving with C Company. Despite being from another regiment, he and his comrades had forged close ties with the other soldiers in the Company:

'When Ted had been killed, the OC held this remembrance service for him on this patch of ground. He read this poem and he got quite emotional. I remember looking round, and there was a good spirit there. People were coming up and saying, are you alright? People seemed dazed and washed out. Honestly, I'm glad it was a short war, because I don't think we could have gone on at that pace much longer.'

Most of the soldiers who attended the service felt that it was a good idea. Lieutenant Andy Nye was one of them:

'I can remember having mixed feelings about it at first, but I was chuffed to bits that John was going to do it. When it actually happened it was excellent, it was exactly what we needed. Up until then the phenomenal sense of humour of the soldiers had kept them going. Sometimes I didn't know whether to laugh or cry, I really didn't. But you still had people who were very, very affected; especially the blokes in Ted's section.

'John did half the service, and I did the other bit. It was just a reading and a few words, but it was good. A lot of people came even though there was no compulsion. Tears were shed and people felt generally pretty gloomy, but we did, definitely feel better after the service. There was a sense of being purged. People had, together, said what everybody felt, and everybody had a lump in their throat or shed a tear. It was a case of, war is like this, these things happen, it is very sad and it's not taking anything away from the loss that we feel.

'I can remember in the middle of it, John choked. Because he was speaking it came from him, but everybody was feeling like that. They didn't look up or think, Christ, the boss feels like that; everybody just knew. Nobody had to say anything, everybody knew exactly how he felt. It was such a big gap. It wasn't as if Ted was a massive personality, but by that stage everybody in the platoon was a personality, even if they were very quiet. They were all integral to the working of the unit, and with his absence there was just that feeling that we are not as we were.'

While the soldiers attempted to get some rest, the Commanding Officer was summoned to 7 Brigade Headquarters to discuss subsequent operations with Brigadier Patrick Cordingley. He was told to be prepared to advance at first light the following day with the remainder of the Brigade.

The task was to strike north-east, deep into Kuwait, towards a position codenamed Denver. This was located near the coast and well to the north of Kuwait City. It was envisaged that the 1st (US) Infantry Division would move parallel to 7 Brigade on its northern flank towards similar objectives in that part of Kuwait. It was known that the Iraqi Republican Guard Force divisions, in particular the notorious Medina and Hamerabi Divisions, were still largely intact, and the expectation of most of the soldiers was that they would now encounter the cream of Saddam's forces.

In fact, once again plans were changed at short notice. Lieutenant General Sir Peter de la Billière explained why:

'The Division's task was to prevent the Republican Guard forces in the north attacking the flanks of the American main thrust that was designed to swing north-eastwards. So they had to draw down those Republican Guards, leaving the Americans free to break through. We had, however, moved ahead very much more quickly than expected and we didn't really get attacked by those Republican Guards. Indeed, the Americans did get diverted and started attacking them. So you had a position where the Americans were to the north, and we were in the Wadi Ala Batin area.

'The plan was then for us to head up the line of the wadi and to destroy the enemy positions to the north. Had we done that, we'd have been right in front of those American forces with all the possibility of both air and artillery, particularly artillery, overshooting their immediate battle, and us and the Americans getting entwined in a very unfortunate blue on blue attack. So although that's what they were told to do, once it became apparent that the Americans were going to be almost in competition for that task, quite rightly we were told, forget that, you've now got another task; which is to push on towards the coast, picking up any enemy that are in the way. And that's what running a war is all about.'

The Iraqi capitulation was becoming increasingly apparent to those directing the Allied offensive. The previous day, Saddam Hussein had announced his plan to withdraw from Kuwait. This gesture was of limited significance, as the Allies by that stage were on the point of entering Kuwait City. Most of southern Kuwait had been reoccupied by Arab and American ground troops, and, to the north of 7 Brigade, VII (US) Corps was pushing deep into northern Kuwait. Its vulnerable western flank was protected by the French and American troops of XVIII (US) Corps, which had consolidated their positions around the Baghdad/Basra highway in the area of An Nasiriyah. As the night of 27 February drew on, the message was passed down from the Joint Force Headquarters to all units that a temporary ceasefire would come into force at 0800 hours the following morning. This resulted in another rapid change of plan for 7 Brigade.

The Commanding Officer was forced to abandon the orders he had given the previous night for the advance to Denver, and issue fresh orders to take the Battle Group to their new objective, Cobalt:

'We were really going for it now. Talk about giving sudden orders. I said, right, move now, and that was it! But they knew the formation that we needed to go in; all you had to do was give way-points to put into the navigation aid. They knew all the drills, so it took less than five minutes to change the orders for the entire Battle Group.'

Sergeant Dave Donnelly was one of those on the receiving end of this change of orders:

'Over the last 36 hours or so, we'd had about three false messages, rumours really, that it was over. Then they'd say, no, we're going on again. So I said to the guys in the wagon, don't count your chickens before they're hatched, but we're going for a ceasefire this time. The cut-off time was eight o'clock. We had to get to the Kuwait/Basra road by then. It was about six in the morning at this stage.

'It was Wacky Races! We went flat out. No word of a lie, we were dodging bar mines as we drove. They were laid on the surface and we just snaked through them. We'd come up to an abandoned Iraqi position and the tanks would say, beware, there are mines here. So you'd really be straining your eyes looking for them. At one time I'd stopped and then Sergeant Lane said to me on the radio, if you look five metres to your left there's a bar mine. I looked down and there was this bloody thing right by my tracks!'

The Ops Officer, Captain Mark Steed, was able to survey the scene from the turret of the Commanding Officer's Warrior:

'We paused momentarily on our start line and then shot straight on. We couldn't afford to waste any time; it was a case of, if you're not there you'll have to catch up, the race goes on without you. And it really was a horse race, with Colonel Arthur Denaro, the CO of the Irish Hussars, in the lead, whipping everybody on.

'We came across a few abandoned positions, and then we started to come across a lot of dug-in armour; T55s that had obviously been attacked from the air or had just been abandoned. There was this real air of a mad dash to get away; short notice evacuation by the Iraqis. Stuff left with the engines still ticking over. A lot of it looked alright, some had been damaged by the air strikes, but it looked as if they'd just decided to leg it and abandon the equipment. It was still raining and very dark at this stage, even though it was only mid-morning. We found out shortly afterwards that this was the result of the fires from the oil wells in Kuwait that Saddam Hussein had torched. All this abandoned stuff would just appear out of the gloom like the Marie Celeste.'

As Sergeant Major Nigel Whitehouse found, it was not just equipment which littered the positions through which the Battle Group passed:

'Lieutenant Banton came up on the air and said, I'm driving through a position now where there are lots of human remains. I was following along behind, and we drove through it and there were. It looked like an infantry company's position where they had obviously come under air attack, thought it was over, and all got out to go back to their secondary position; and while they were all out in the open, in came another attack which cut them to pieces. There were arms, legs, torsos, heads, bits of torso all over the place. Probably about 150 men.

'But even that didn't look horrifying, because it had obviously happened a while before we got there. It had congealed and dried and it just looked like lumps of meat. You knew what it was, but it wasn't an horrific sight because it wasn't still fresh. It was unpleasant, I mean: you thought, bloody hell, they were caught out badly, but that was it and then on you went again.

'The drivers did try to avoid the remains. We were driving in the tank tracks anyway because of the mines, so if anything was going to go bang at least a Challenger would take it. Anybody with any common decency would avoid them, and in fact we recorded the position so that someone could go back and give them a proper burial later.'

Everyone who took part in that final, frantic dash to objective Cobalt on 28 February, G+4, compared it with a race of one sort or another. It was in fact a race against the clock. In theory, the Allied advance was to cease at 0800 hours, and with 7 Brigade positioned on the Kuwait/Basra highway by that time, any further escape northwards by Iraqi troops would be halted. Major Simon Knapper, commanding A Company, was still attached to the Scots Dragoon Guards Battle Group:

'We set off in the normal formation. The Scots DG had this wonderful 'flying wedge' formation which was a vee formed by the three tank squadrons with us, the infantry, travelling in the middle. We were going as fast as the Battle Group could travel, which was about 35 kph, which is pretty fast for an armoured battle group moving cross country. Even then, the Warriors were still only on half throttle. We didn't stop for anything; the aim was to reach the road, and not to waste time picking up prisoners.

'I was near the front with the CO and, when we hit a quarry area about 5 kilometres from the main road, we continued on while the rest of the Battle Group shook themselves out and checked out routes through it. It was a totally black sky, early morning, very dark and very misty, and then suddenly in front of us were these massive pylons. As we got closer to them, logically heading for the gap between the two pylons, there were all the wires hanging down touching the ground. So we crossed them near the pylon legs and then I remember thinking, we must be near the road now.

'There were abandoned vehicles and wrecks littered all over the place. We'd already crossed this line of tarmac but I'd thought, this can't be it. Then I crossed another line of tarmac, and suddenly realised this was the dual carriageway and this was it. We knew that we were heading for the main Kuwait City/Basra highway, which was a motorway, and suddenly we had passed this blackened, tatty strip of tarmac with wrecked vehicles all over it; it just didn't look like my mental picture of a motorway.

'We then drove down it to our blocking position where the Company was going to come in, in and out of all the destroyed vehicles and craters. I gave the grid to the Company, who had just reformed this side of the quarry, and they came down to us going flat out. There were Warriors doing 75 kph down there. It was a brilliant sight to watch them as they came out of the quarry, and then swept down towards the road.'

In less than 100 hours, the Staffords had driven 290 kilometres through three different countries. They had been involved in action against a numerically superior enemy who'd had many months in which to prepare his defensive positions and strategy. Stafford soldiers fought in every major engagement that was undertaken by 7 Armoured Brigade, for the loss of two men killed and a handful wounded in action. They took part in more fighting than any other British infantry battalion in the Gulf.

Such a result would not have been possible without the enormous contribution of every part of the Allied forces, from the airmen who inflicted such devastation on the ground positions in support of the attacks, and the artillery groups which provided an intensity and concentration of firepower never before seen in battle, to the most unsung storeman who humped cases of bottled water in the rear area. Ultimately though, it was the soldier who had to step out of the back of his Warrior onto ground that he had not yet seen, with the only certainty being that in front of him he would encounter the enemy.

As the Staffords began to prepare defensive positions astride the Basra/Kuwait highway, it gradually dawned on them that this really was the end of what their opponent had promised them would be the mother of all battles.

8

Consolidation in Kuwait

'You sometimes couldn't tell how many you had buried because there were so many parts of bodies around.'

As the Staffords started to consolidate their positions on the highway, word had already reached their families in Fallingbostel and England that a ceasefire had come into effect. For the last five days, the relatives had received scant news of the progress of the Staffords. Media coverage of the ground war had concentrated largely on the activities of 4 Brigade, because the majority of journalists had been attached to 4 Brigade units on G-1 in the expectation that 4 Brigade would lead the advance into Iraq. No mail had been sent out from the Staffords since the start of the offensive, and the soldiers had not received any, priority having been given to moving combat supplies forward to the battle groups.

This dearth of information did not, however, prevent the families in Fallingbostel remaining comparatively well informed. What little hard news there was in the days leading up to, and during, the ground war was supplemented by rumour and informed speculation. Sue Layton realised that G day was approaching when the flow of letters from her husband began to diminish:

'Andrew's letters started to decrease about two weeks before the start of the ground attack. That was a sign to me, because Andrew's always been a good letter writer: he's always phoned when he has said he is going to, he's always turned up when he has said he's going to, he's that type of person.'

The Commanding Officer's wife, Gay Rogers, had an unexpected hint that the offensive was not far off:

'The hierarchy in the Army really was superb during the Gulf War. They were much, much more considerate of families than I think they have ever been in any other situation. Charles Guthrie [the Commander of the 1st British Corps, based in Germany] rang me once a week; Peter Inge, the Commander in Chief, rang a couple of times.

The best call of all was from Peter de la Billière. His man management is fantastic. He rang on 10 February, when people's morale was at a very low ebb. The air war had been going on since 17 January. We had no idea when the ground war was going to happen, and we didn't know where our men were; people were beginning to be quite unhappy. Then I suddenly got this phone call at nine o' clock on Sunday morning.

'This voice said, you don't know who I am, but my name's Peter de la Billière. So I stood to attention and said, of course I know who you are! We chatted, and he said he'd been with the Staffords the day before, and what a fantastic job they were doing and so on, which was great. Then he said to me, I can't say very much over the phone, Gay, but we can see a light at the end of the tunnel. I said to him, we can't. Then he said, I can promise you we can see a light at the end of the tunnel. Be assured there is a light at the end of the tunnel.

'We actually had a wives' lunch that day, and I think we must have had about 150 wives there. I went on the PA system of the disco and I told them about it, and you could feel the atmosphere change instantly. He knew the boys would be going in very soon, and he obviously was very sure, even then, that it would be very quick when they did go in.'

Ellie Banks was in Newcastle staying with her aunt when the offensive was launched:

'Somehow I knew that they were going to go in that day. I was restless all night, because I just knew, deep down, that they were going in. I got up that morning and my aunt said, they've gone in. I said, I knew it. We were supposed to stop there till about tea-time, but I just wanted to get on the way to Germany more than anything. I wanted to get home in case anything did happen because they had that as the contact phone number. I felt so alone and out of it, it was terrible. I just wanted to get back. For the first time in my life, I wanted to get back to Fallingbostel!'

Despite her initial worries for her husband's safety, Ellie Banks felt a degree of sympathy towards the Iraqi soldiers when the first television pictures of them surrendering were broadcast in Germany:

'When I first saw them on the television coming out of their trenches, looking awful, I felt sorry for them. But it was more anger towards Saddam Hussein than anything. I thought, how could he let them sit there like that, hungry and wet? It was him, I think, more than anything else, that made me feel bitter. I still think that they should have gone into Iraq and got him. We said we should have gone over there; when he saw us coming he'd run a mile!'

For the wives and parents of the soldiers in the Gulf, the period of the ground war was undoubtedly a time of great stress and emotion. Some of the children, too, were affected by the lack of information. Neil Loftus was a teacher at Shackleton school in Fallingbostel:

'We would tend to wait for the children to bring the subject up rather than talk to them specifically about it. Then we'd talk about it as a small group. Some wanted to talk about it, but then there were also some who were totally oblivious to what was going on. Once the war began, the behaviour of certain children at home got bad enough for the parents to come in. One lady asked me to have a word with her two sons, just like a fatherly sort of figure. So I had a chat with them, just to help out mum while dad was away. It mostly showed itself in little things, though: behaviour at home, naughtiness in the playground, that sort of thing. I think generally though, they were really very good; it was hard to believe that their dads were away fighting a war.'

News of the end of the war was broadcast on all the English language radio and television stations in Germany. Lorraine Mortimer switched on satellite television news on 28 February, as she did every morning when she woke up:

'I got up really early that morning, and I just caught the very end of the news because Sky News repeats itself about every 15 minutes. I thought, did I hear ceasefire? So I rang the information centre up, this was about six o' clock in the morning, and I said to the bloke, is there a ceasefire? Is it true? He said, where did you hear that? And I started to go down; it was just the way he was talking. So I said, I've just heard it on the news that there's a ceasefire. He said, what's your name? I said, Lorraine Mortimer. And he said, well Mrs Mortimer, it's true. I said, oh my God! If that man had been in front of me, I would have kissed him. So I slammed the phone down and I rang my friend and said, Kelly, Kelly, Kelly, it's all over!'

For Gay Rogers, the news of the ceasefire brought added worries:

'That was the only day I broke down. I didn't and wouldn't and couldn't believe that it was true. I said I would never believe it until Charles rang me and told me that it was all over. I was very, very frightened that they would all relax, and then step on mines and things like that. That was the worst day of the whole campaign. It was a dreadful day for me, and I think it was a bad day for quite a lot of people. We knew by then we had lost one soldier, and I went into the Families Office that morning and discovered we had lost another.'

On the previous day, the unenviable task of informing John and Marjorie Moult, the parents of Carl Moult, that their son had been killed had been undertaken by the Regimental Secretary, Major Mac McLean. Marjorie Moult had always expected her son to return safely from the Gulf:

'I saw these two people outside and I said to John, there are two fellows at the door. I said, leave it a minute, they're probably canvassing, as you do. Anyway, I said to John, they're not going away, they're looking at the bedroom window. So John went round to the front and came in with them. Major Mac just told us about Carl, that he had been killed by enemy action in the Gulf. He didn't tell us a lot on that first visit. He couldn't, because they didn't have all the details. It was terrible. We didn't expect that, not from our lad. In his letters he'd say, I'm OK mum, don't worry, I'll be back.

'He had a lot of friends. We knew that then, but since the others got back from the Gulf there have been so many of his friends who've been round to see us. And they come to see his grave now. You can see his mates sitting on the seat and they're crying. When the lads from his section come to see us, they always go down to the cemetery. John says they lie there talking to him. His mates have missed him. He's a lad that anyone would miss. The Army have been very good to us. We can't fault them. They've even offered us a holiday in America. Anything we needed, we only had to ask. We honestly feel as if we're part of the family now, the Regiment.'

Another UK-based Stafford officer, Major Mick Ore, was required to pass on the news of Private Shaun Taylor's death to his parents. Shaun's mother, Kathleen, was alone at their home in Stourbridge:

'Dennis was at work, and I'd just gone over the road to my friends. Then I saw this man and woman stood at the door. I said, they're Jehova's Witnesses, aren't they? They didn't go, and they stood there looking up and down the street; and I said, I hope they haven't come about my poll tax. I hadn't paid the last two months' payments. So I said, I'd better go and see what they want.

'I crossed the road and this bloke was stood there with a folder, and I thought, oh Lord, it is the poll tax. I hope they don't take my new three piece suite! That's really what I thought. He said, Mrs Taylor, and I said yes. Is Mr Taylor about? I said, no, he's at work. So he said, can I have a word with you. I opened the back gate and took him in, and it just never occurred to me at all that it was Shaun. The guy just stood there and he said, you've got a son, Shaun, in the Army? And I said yes. And he said, well I'm sorry Mrs Taylor, but he was killed in action this morning. He was shot.

'I just went a bit mad. I jumped up off the chair, and he tried to grab me, and I said get off, and pushed him out of the way. I think I kicked him as well, but I'm not sure. I ran off round to my friend's house, banged the door open and ran round screaming, he's dead, he's dead! And that was how I was told.'

Shaun's father, Dennis, was at work:

'We'd just sat down and were having a cup of tea, and Joe, the chap I'd bought the business from, came up. But as soon as he walked in through the door, I knew. I don't know what it was, but I just knew. I said to myself in my head, don't let this be. And then he just stood by the door and he cried and said, Shaun's been killed. I was just numb, there was no reaction at all. We're Christians, and my first reaction was, God, what have you done? What's happened here? I just couldn't believe it.

'When I got home and went into the house, all our pastors were here, and all our friends. Then our daughters Karen and Belinda were fetched. They'd already seen their sister, Debbie, die at home. That had knocked them for six, and now to have this as well. I just went outside on my mate's patio, and it hit me then. I broke down completely then. All the comforting in the world won't help you when you're feeling like that.

'I had a big problem with my faith then. I've only been a Christian for three years. My first concern was, where was Shaun? I thought, my son wasn't a Christian when he went out there. I was asking God where he was. We know now that he's in heaven. My faith had hit rock bottom then, but since then, His support and the support of the church has really kept us going.'

News of the fatalities had reached Fallingbostel soon after the families were informed. Carla Hughes was moved by the response of the wives in the garrison:

'I was driving to the NAAFI the morning that we found out that the soldiers had died, and I noticed one little bunch of flowers underneath the Battalion sign on the main road through the camp. Then there were two bunches, and then I put some flowers with them. I don't know why I put the flowers there, and still I don't know why. I'm not a sentimental person and it's not something I would normally do, but once I saw some flowers there it became very important that I also put some flowers there.

'And then it just grew and grew. In the end three of us went down with buckets and baby baths and put them all in water. For the most part they were just bunches of flowers, not formal tributes, although we did have company wreaths done later; but at that time they were just from the individual wives. As a Stafford, it was very important to me to see that other people had also done that. Not only Staffords had come. A few of them were signed but mostly they said things like, from two Scots wives, or something similar.

'Although I didn't know either of the lads who had died, it was a shared grief really. I think a lot of people were very grateful for the flowers. I'd seen something similar at the Liverpool stadium after the disaster there, and at the time I had thought, what a strange thing to do. I hadn't ever conceived that I might have wanted to take flowers to the stadium, but I'm sure that if I had been involved then I would have done. It was very comforting that other people were bothering to do it now.'

In Kuwait, the remaining daylight hours of 28 February were spent organising hasty defensive positions centred on the Basra/Kuwait City highway. There was no certainty that the ceasefire would hold, and the Brigade wanted to be prepared for any eventuality. As the soldiers walked round their positions, they witnessed at first hand the devastation which was to be shown on television screens around the world during the following days. Sergeant Major Nigel Whitehouse was in the south with A Company:

'It was worse than the scenes they showed on television. Further down the road going towards Kuwait there was a line of bodies which had all been shot through the back of the head. They were Iraqis, and we think that they were conscripts who had been executed by the Republican Guard. They hadn't even had the common decency to bury them. Then as you walked up the road there were bodies in the vehicles where the air raids had shot them to pieces. They had been trying to get out of Kuwait in whatever type of vehicle they could lay their hands on.'

As the situation became more stable, the Staffords took the opportunity to make a more detailed search of their locations. Gold Sergeant Andrew Harding, one of the Grenadier Guardsmen attached to the Battalion, led a patrol around his platoon's area:

'We were near an abandoned Iraqi comcen [communications centre], and we were tasked to clear anything that the Iraqis left in the desert. So where there was a tank hulk, we had to make sure there were no bodies in it. Any ammunition, grenades, and things like that were collected in. Any lorries, Land Rovers and things like that were collected together. We dragged artillery pieces and tanks into another area. Generally we just started to clear up the areas. It was just one big area cleaning fatigue really.'

As well as the destruction on the ground all around them, there was an omnipresent reminder of the vandalism wrought on Kuwait by the retreating Iraqis. Captain Jack Ferguson described it:

'There was one particular day where the wind just stopped. So the great clouds from the burning Kuwaiti oil wells in the south, and the other ones from the northern oilfields came together, and you had this huge, black sky overhead. It was the middle of the day, but the sun was like a little light shining through it. It was horrible. It was like something out of a horror movie. There were purples and blacks in the sky, and it was full of it. It really was strange: there was just an eerie feeling throughout the area. It was something you had to see, it was incredible.'

Most of the soldiers felt the numbers of corpses they encountered on the highway did not have as great an impact on them as they might have expected. There were some sights, though, which could not fail to make a lasting impression, as Lieutenant Nick Todd described:

'The killing looked very indiscriminate. There were bodies all over the place. Someone in the Company found a family of mother and father and two daughters who had just been shot through the back of the head, which was rather upsetting. We sent out a burial party for them straight away.'

Some of the dead had been lying in the desert for a considerable time, and for reasons of hygiene, burial parties were formed within every company to deal with them. Sergeant 'Dixie' Oliver took one of these parties out:

'We found three dead soldiers who had been cluster bombed. One was a major, one a captain, and the other was a sergeant. They'd been looting; their bag of loot was still beside them. The soldiers, and even myself, realised at that stage that this is how you end up as a soldier, and was it worth it. It really hit us then. It brought us down to earth a bit, thinking, this could be me.

'Some of the guys were quite disturbed because these Iraqis were a mess. Having said that, to me, they just looked like mannequins, they didn't look real. I just buried them with the dignity they deserved. They were buried as soldiers, not as enemy, not as Iraqis; they were buried as soldiers. They weren't abused or kicked or robbed because they were Iraqis. They were dead soldiers and treated as such. We didn't say a prayer over the grave, because we weren't sure of their religion. What we did was, we just gave them a moment's silence. We just stood there and observed a soldier's respect, which I thought was the right thing to do.'

Captain Jack Ferguson was responsible for the documentation of the dead Iraqis:

'Where we could, we noted what details there were. It was very hard because they didn't wear dog tags. In most cases it was just a case of recording: estimated three bodies buried at, and then a 10 figure grid reference. You sometimes couldn't tell how many you had buried because there were so many parts of bodies around. We gathered in lots of documents. We got lots of Kuwaiti passports and ID cards in a great big bag which one of the boys brought in, which we subsequently returned to the authorities. The personal documents from the bodies, wallets and so on, were all centralised. Then they went back down the line to Brigade and Division.'

Not all the Iraqis in the Staffords' area were dead, though. A number appeared from bunkers to offer their surrender, and a very few wounded soldiers had managed to survive until they were discovered by clearance patrols. Colour Sergeant Mark Banks was on such a patrol in his Scimitar when they found a wounded Iraqi:

'We came across an Iraqi Land Rover and a civvie ambulance. There were three dead bodies lying around the Land Rover, riddled with shrapnel wounds. There was a guy lying by the ambulance, covered in blankets, but we didn't see this guy at first. I called in another vehicle and we got a burial party together and started digging holes to bury these people. We walked over to where this other guy was lying, although at this stage we thought it was just a pile of blankets, and then a hand moved from underneath the blankets.

'This soldier, we later discovered, had been lying there for two days. We got all the blankets off him, and then spent nearly two hours trying to put an intravenous drip into him, but he'd gone into traumatic shock, so we couldn't get a needle into his veins at all. His chin had been taken off and he had half of the back of his head missing. How he survived, lying there for two days, is beyond me. We gave him sips of water because he was asking for it, and we spent a long time trying to sort this guy out.

'We couldn't get communications with the Battle Group because the coastal cliffs were screening our transmissions. So we sorted out this guy as well as we could, and then we took the stretcher out of the ambulance and strapped it to the front of my vehicle. Then we put this guy on the stretcher. I had one of the vehicle gunners sitting on the decks of my vehicle, giving him first aid as we drove back. It took us three hours to get back to the Battle Group. When we got to the Basra road we met one of our ambulances, so we stopped and cross-loaded this guy. As we took him off the Scimitar, he asked for a cigarette! It was very satisfying to know, that after he'd been lying there for two days, he had now recovered enough to want a cigarette.'

Those Iraqis who were not wounded or dead were rounded up and moved to a central prisoner of war cage, which was hastily constructed near the Battle Group position. The Regimental Sergeant Major, Steve Huyton, had been responsible for prisoner handling in the Battle Group throughout the operation:

'During the advance, we ended up with so many prisoners that we couldn't just disarm them and leave them to roam the desert, because if they reorganised themselves and took people by surprise, you don't know what might have happened. So we kept them in a holding area, and waited for the prisoner of war handling group to come up.

'There was one incident which I thought was very interesting. They were all sitting there with their shamaghs over their heads. We stood them up at times and made them walk about. Their heads were down and they were dawdling about, they didn't want to do anything. When they sat down, they slept where they were.

'This Iraqi brigadier came over to me and said, may I talk to the soldiers? I said, yes, you may. Well, he went amongst them, and he really rifted them. I looked at him and I thought, yeah, I bet you could be a right bugger if you wanted to be. He was dragging these shamaghs off their heads and telling them, sit up! Get a bit of pride about you. You could tell that was what he was saying, because these guys were straightening themselves up and tying up their boots. He had one who wouldn't move, and he grabbed hold of him and gave him a real talking to and then got a senior NCO over and said, deal with him.

'And after about ten minutes he had got them all sorted out. He said, may I stand them up? I said yes, and backed off all my troops. So he stood them up and walked them round, and then he sat them down again, a bit more verbal to them, and then he walked away again. You could see that, regardless of them being defeated, he still had a bit of pride in himself. That was good to see, and it was good for our soldiers to see it.'

By the end of the ground war, the most common feeling towards the enemy prisoners was one of pity. Private Paul Garrett summed it up:

'The thing was, you knew they were enemy, but you felt sorry for them. Some of them wouldn't have boots on their feet, so some people were giving them boots so at least they could walk. We were feeding them, giving them water, generally just helping them out. Yet they were still the enemy. It was strange.'

Private Danny Nokes discovered the Iraqi prisoners appreciated more than just cups of tea and boots:

'We caught two prisoners, and the inside of our wagon was just full of porn, pictures which had been sent out to us. It was nothing obscene, just tits and bums. When these two prisoners got in, once they saw the pictures they were loving it. They had big smiles on their faces, and were pointing at them and chattering to each other.'

Corporal Darren Wilson did not feel quite the same, however:

'To this day, I don't know why, but I didn't feel any pity for them whatsoever. No matter how bad a state they were in, even if they had no boots and no clothes and they were starving, I couldn't feel that. They could have been running around in loin cloths and throwing spears, but they were still there to kill me, my crew, my friends. Even now when people say, they were a bunch of vagabonds, they were rubbish and no good, I can't look back and say, yeah, I suppose I should feel sorry for them. I can't do that. I don't know why, I just can't.'

It is perhaps understandable that some of the soldiers who served with C Company could not muster up quite the same degree of sympathy for the enemy soldiers as other members of the Battalion. C Company had suffered the loss of the both of the Staffords who were killed during the ground war, Privates Taylor and Moult.

It was only when the war was over that the Battalion learned of Private 'Nobby' Taylor's death. Captain Tim Sandiford noted in his diary:

'Our worst fears were confirmed the night after the ceasefire. It all remained businesslike. I went and told the crew of [callsign] 33A straightaway, then 32 and the Mobile Section, and then 31 and his close friends personally the next morning. I had obviously thought about young Taylor, and to a degree was surprised that I didn't feel more whilst informing everyone, etc; but we asked [Padre] John Tee to come and have a small service for Nobby, and as soon as we started, I cried and couldn't stop. An hour later I felt much better, and realised what a weight it had lifted. Although not religious, I found great comfort in the fact that he had received communion 24 hours before the accident and hence that the Padre knew that he was in a better place.'

Arrangements had been made for the bodies of the two soldiers to be flown back to England, and bearer parties to escort them onto the aeroplane at Al Jubail airport were chosen from amongst their friends in the Battalion. Private Stuart Burton was a member of the party:

'I felt a bit better when we put them both on the plane. For me, it didn't really sink in until then, until we saw the coffins. We couldn't all get back in time for the funeral, so this was the next best thing. When we got there, someone noticed that there weren't any flowers on the coffins, so they dashed off into the town and bought some and we put them on the coffins; that made everyone feel a bit better as well. We'd done it properly.'

As February moved into March, the Battalion began to wonder when they might get out of Kuwait and back to England and Germany. In fact, although no dates had been set, the arrangements for flying out the Brigade were already in hand, and now a decision had to be taken on what order the units would fly back in, as Brigadier Patrick Cordingley explained:

'There was the rather painful business of balloting which regiment or battalion would go home first. I think the poor old Staffords came out fourth. They wanted to go home as formed units, and that seemed the best way of deciding it. As far as a date went, when you looked at what the soldier wanted at that stage, he wanted to know when he was going home. He had been there damn nearly six months, and he had come out on a promise from all and sundry that he was going for six months and no more.

'It was something I spent an enormous amount of time discussing with senior generals. Even if it was bad news, it was better to have it than weak promises. You cannot tell a soldier under these circumstances that the ceasefire wasn't when he stopped fighting, because that's when he reckons his ceasefire has come because he has ceased firing.'

On 6 March the Prime Minister, John Major, flew out to meet and talk to all the British units involved in the operation. He did not visit the Staffords personally, but a number of soldiers were transported to a central location to hear him speak. Sergeant Major 'Sammy' Salt thought he should have answered the question that was on everybody's lips:

'I don't think his visit went down well, because he didn't give us an answer as to when we would be going home. This was the Prime Minister, and he was with his troops. Storming Norman had got his troops moving back already. Well, that was fine, because some of his boys had been there a long time. But John Major could not give us an answer.

'The guys didn't want to hear, well done, you've done a good job boys. What they wanted to hear was a date for going home. If he'd said 5 September they wouldn't have minded, because they would at least have known they had a definite date. But he couldn't give it to us, and it really peeved the guys. They all came back and said, I wish we hadn't gone, because it didn't cheer them up at all.'

While they waited in Kuwait, there was time to speculate on what might have happened had they pursued the Iraqi forces northwards into Iraq instead of pulling up short where they did. Opinions differed at the time, although subsequently most felt they had left their task unfinished. The debate as to the legitimacy of a pursuit into Iraq in the context of the UN resolutions was not necessarily the primary consideration of the soldiers. Captain Jack Ferguson was forthright in his views:

'I believed then, and I still believe, that we should have continued. We should have gone all the way. We should have gone at least to Basra. My one wish was to piss in the Euphrates, and I never even got to see the damned thing!'

Sergeant Gino Pulizzi also felt they should have continued the rout:

'At the start of it, the feeling was going through my mind that if I don't see any action, then how can I go back and say that I took part? That wasn't important in the end because we did get stuck in, but a lot of us still felt that we should have carried on into Iraq. We did feel cheated. We thought, why stop now? And, of course, the most annoying thing is that he's still in power now. We were ready to go all the way and we should have done.'

Sergeant 'Dixie' Oliver felt the Battalion was certainly capable of carrying on, despite the fact that the advance to Cobalt had been almost continuous, with very little in the way of rest:

'We did have a brief rest period, where we managed to get two or three hours sleep and we refuelled the wagons. We were well fed and well trained. The commanders certainly were the ones who lost out on sleep, but at least at platoon level we could have gone on. People like the CO must have been under a lot of pressure, and I think it would have been very difficult at that level and at company commander level without a proper rest first. It would be a very difficult decision because the commanders are always stretched. From what I heard, we had the equipment and logistic back-up to keep going. There were a lot of arguments for going on. I wish we had gone to Basra as a show of strength and just to nip it in the bud, but if we had done, I don't think we should have stayed there. We had achieved our aim and I was proud to be a part of it.'

Captain Mark Steed agreed with 'Dixie' Oliver about the element of fatigue:

'We probably couldn't have gone on straightaway because everybody was actually absolutely knackered; I know I was. I think everybody was quite drained by then. I must admit that when I heard the Americans were still fighting in the north, I wondered, are we going beyond the UN resolutions here doing this? Have we not done enough? In hindsight, we didn't do enough, we could have done a lot more, because Hussein's still there. But at the time it seemed as if it was enough.'

In Fallingbostel the Duchess of York, wife of the Colonel in Chief of the Regiment, paid a visit to the wives and families. Her stopping points in the garrison were well attended, and the schoolchildren were given time off to line her route. The headmaster of Shackleton school, Mike Bennet, organised the children:

'We were asked if all the children would like to go and watch, which meant we had to get hold of some more flags for them. So we took them down there. I was told it would all be organised when we got there, but they weren't. It was a good job I organised them, or else there would have been a long line of children from two schools and nobody on the other side of the road. Then the secondary school was stood down that day, and some of their louts were there, and of course they weren't in control of them. They were shouting, come this way and let me take your picture, things you wouldn't expect your own children to do. I was bouncing up and down the line making sure mine stood up straight.'

The visit certainly boosted the spirits of the families, many of whom felt that Fallingbostel had been rather overlooked by VIP visitors in the preceding five months, but their overriding concern now was to see their husbands back safe and well.

At last the flight dates were announced. A small advance party was to return on 11 March, and the remainder would fly back between 19 and 24 March. Fiona Foster, the wife of Captain Nick Foster, saw her husband rather sooner than she had expected:

'Ten days after the ground war had finished, Daniel, our son, fell down some concrete steps and ended up in hospital for a week, which precipitated Nick's early return from the Gulf. I actually saw Nick for the first time in the hospital. Seeing him walk down the corridor was a very, very strange experience, because obviously by then I was very upset about Daniel, I'd had a very difficult night, and I was very tired. So seeing Nick again was just the biggest relief out.

'Obviously it wasn't quite the home-coming that I'd anticipated; we spent our first night together in separate villages, let alone separate houses! I was just relieved to have them both alive. I had a sort of post-trauma period when I got very tired and very shaky. The end of the war and Daniel's accident happened in such close succession that I don't think I'd ever really relaxed in between, so by the time Nick got home, I just sort of keeled over after that.'

Preparations in the Gulf for the move back involved transporting all the men and vehicles from their location north of Kuwait City back down the coast into Saudi Arabia and to the port of Al Jubail. Enough drivers and commanders were left with the Warriors and supporting vehicles for their drive down the single usable carriageway of the highway, and the remaining men were then flown by Hercules from a makeshift desert airstrip in Kuwait to Al Jubail. On arrival, they were bussed into Camp 4 to await their flights.

The last few days were intensely dull for everyone not involved in the implementation of the complex move plan to Germany. The advance party had already returned to Germany on 11 March as planned, but the remainder had over a week to wait before they were due to leave. Personal equipment was loaded onto civilian ISO containers which would return to Germany by sea, and the soldiers were left with just hand baggage containing the bare essentials.

The Warriors were parked up in a large holding area, and were cleaned and prepared for their sea move. Those which had classified cryptographic communications equipment fitted had their doors and hatches welded shut for security reasons.

Warnings were issued that no captured weapons or equipment were to be taken back to Germany, and an amnesty was declared to enable such souvenirs to be handed in without fear of recrimination. Many of the men took advantage of this, but some did attempt to evade boarding checks at the airport. One soldier from another unit, who caused a metal detector to alarm as he walked through it, was found to have an Iraqi AKM assault rifle taped to his body!

Eventually, according to the schedule, on 19 March, the first batch of soldiers left Camp 4 for the last time, and were driven to Al Jubail international airport to catch their flight home.

9

Homecoming

'... she opened her arms and said, Daddy! That was it, I was in tears.'

The flights, which all returned to Germany, were made in chartered jumbo jets of British Airways and KLM. All the usual facilities were laid on by the airlines, and in particular, alcoholic drinks were available; the first that many of the Staffords had seen for over five months. Major Chris Joynson enjoyed his flight home:

'The air hostesses on the British Airways flight which brought us back were magnificent. They realised we'd been without alcohol for some time and they gave us anything that we could possibly ask for. There were all sorts of proposals of marriage! One of the girls was called Laura, and all the boys were singing, tell Laura I love her. They came out at the other end wearing our desert kit. One of the boys had got one of their aprons on. It was extraordinary. I think they enjoyed it as well. The boys were well behaved: they got oiled, but they were well behaved. It was really a very jovial party in the plane.

'We arrived back at Hanover where the Colonel of the Regiment greeted people as they came off the aircraft. We realised we'd got one or two drunk people on the plane, so once we had found out which side of the plane the Colonel of the Regiment was going to greet people on, the drunken ones were pushed off to the far side and got away from there and put on the coaches.'

On the Commanding Officer's flight, it was apparent that inebriation was setting in amongst some soldiers within a few hours of take off. He did not want to appear heavy handed, but at the same time was loath to step off the aircraft at Hanover leading a group of drunkards to a reception with their families. To moderate the potential problem, he managed to persuade the flight crew to broadcast an announcement that the aeroplane was now over-flying Cypriot airspace and, because it was past the local closing time, service of all alcoholic drinks would have to cease until the aircraft was clear of the area! This had the desired effect, and by the time drinks were once again made available, most of the passengers were sound asleep.

Lieutenant Nick Todd found the film which was shown on his flight stirred the emotions of his travelling companions:

'We got into the airport, and the RAF there said, smokers on the right, non-smokers on the left, and on the far left there are some nice chairs for the officers. At which point a big moan went up from all the boys; it was a case of, here we go, they're officers again. That was the first time we had been segregated or been given any of the privilege of rank for five months, and it felt quite alien, not sitting together with your gunner or your radio op.

'Then on the plane all the officers were put in first class, which caused some more chuntering. It soon settled down, though, and once everyone had their first can of beer, which they gave us before take off, no-one said a word. The funniest thing about the flight back was that they showed the film 'Ghost' with Patrick Swayzee. The end of the film is a bit of a tear-jerker, and after the noise and the hullabaloo that had been going on throughout the flight up to that point, it suddenly went quiet. I walked back down the aisle to talk to two of the platoon commanders who were smoking, so they couldn't sit up in First Class, and there were all these battle-tested guys sitting there looking at the screen, and there were quite a few tears in evidence.'

Only the members of the advance party, who had arrived back in Germany on 11 March, were met at the airport by their families in the full glare of the international media circus. For the remainder, their reunion had to wait until an hour or so after they had landed, during which time they were cleared through customs and taken by bus from Hanover airport up to St Barbaras Barracks in Fallingbostel. The families were informed of each flight manifest in advance, so they knew when their husband or father was coming home, and arrangements were made for them to meet on the battalion square.

The Regimental Band returned on one of the first flights, and were then on hand to play in each new plane-load of soldiers as they arrived. Nearly every house and every road in Fallingbostel had been decorated for the homecoming, and the buses drove in through streets lined with balloons, Union Jacks, and yellow ribbons. As they entered the camp area, a collection of floral tributes in memory of Privates Taylor and Moult lay at the foot of the regimental signboard, a poignant reminder of their loss.

The single soldiers had no relatives waiting to meet them. No arrangements had been made for UK-based families to fly out to Fallingbostel for their return, and, as Lieutenant Steven Neale explained, it was not the sort of welcome many of them had expected:

'It was pretty much of an anti-climax. I think by that stage all we wanted to do was to get to bed, and the free alcohol from British Airways didn't help in that respect. We got off the coaches and a can of beer was thrust in our hands, but then we just took our kit over to our bunks and crashed out. We found the following week a bit of a drag, because we had to spend it in camp sorting out kit. We couldn't understand why we couldn't just bang the weapons in the armoury and bugger off home.'

For the families in Fallingbostel it was a different matter. They had been waiting a long time for this day, and as Ellie Banks found, the emotion of the occasion was difficult to contain:

'When they got off that bus, it was the most incredible feeling. It was like a blind date in a way; my stomach was churning, I felt nervous, it was terrible really, you just couldn't help yourself. The atmosphere on the square was electric. I watched them all come in. Mark had gone off to Zimbabwe when Gemma was ten months old, and she didn't recognise him when he came home, and this had stuck in his head. He had said on the phone, do you think Gemma will recognise me? I said, of course she will. When he got off I said to her, there he is, look Gemma. And I bombed up to him and said, I'm alright, then she opened her arms and said, Daddy! That was it, I was in tears.'

Vicki Lane, who had married her husband Robert five days before he departed for the Gulf, was also extremely apprehensive:

'I was so nervous. I didn't know what I was going to say to him when he got back. I stayed up the night before; I never went to bed once. I was ready at eight o'clock that morning. I even took him a beer up. He'd said on the phone, I want a beer when I get off that coach. It did feel strange, because I hadn't really felt married while he was away. When he got in that first day back he said, now we can start our married life. It was weird hearing him say that, I wanted to say, what are you on about?'

Many of the married soldiers found the readjustment to domestic life somewhat disconcerting. The changes Lorraine Mortimer noticed in her husband, Richard, were fairly typical of those commented on by other wives:

'They all came back different to what they were when they went away. In my case, my husband's harder, he's not as soft as he used to be; I can't get him round my little finger any more, which as far as I'm concerned is bad! They're more selfish, I find: they think of themselves more than anything. Generally, if they want to do something, they'll do it.

'The first couple of weeks it was like a honeymoon again. It was all hunky dory, we were all on holiday. When we came back from the holiday, that's when we realised there was something wrong; but you couldn't put your finger on it. My husband said to me the other day that he misses the lads. They had, like a relationship going, and he misses being with them. And I suppose some of the men will want to go out. Normally Richard is really quiet, but we went to this one particular do where there were some lads from the Greenjackets who were attached to Richard's lot, and they were hugging each other, and I couldn't believe that. I thought, bloody hell, what's the matter with him? But he says he misses the relationship they had, the friendship. He misses talking to them and having a laugh with them.'

Jessie Rennie, the SSAFA (Soldiers, Sailors & Air Force Association;

a charitable support organisation for service families) social worker in Fallingbostel, saw the emphasis of her work shift when the Battalion returned:

'The child-care side of my work decreased dramatically. People with whom I was involved in a fairly concentrated way were able to switch off. Hubby was home, everything was going to be fine. Marital problems, on the other hand, have been a very important part of my workload since they got back. I know Relate is very well booked up for appointments, and the bulk of my work now is marital related.

'I think the problem is that the wives have been independent, and they have realised they can cope. Especially where the marriage was a bit rocky, and they might have considered leaving in the past but thought they couldn't possibly cope on their own, and now they know they can. They were in charge of finances, they were doing things they wouldn't normally have to do. Some of them have gained confidence. Also, in some cases the wives have got into a routine with the children and their lives, and there is almost a resentment that this routine has changed. It's all part of the adjusting process. For some of them it may take some months.

'There were plans for a lot of work to be done with the families before the men came back. Talking with the wives and preparing them. It was all going to be based on the lessons they had learnt after the Falklands. It happened, but in my view we didn't do enough. That was partly because it finished so quickly, so I can't be too critical. There was an element of people saying, well come on now, there'll be a few problems, but, stiff upper lip and all that. This is the Army, this is their job. We did meet with the Staffords, who had been keen to have our support. It wasn't going to resolve everything, but it was preparing them for it. We couldn't say, your husband will be this or that. What we were saying was, you may find you'll have absolutely no problems; on the other hand, you may find you'll resent your husband coming back, that's normal. There were so many options, but we just wanted them to be prepared for it.'

Most of the soldiers were aware of the changes in their outlook and personality brought on by their experiences in the Gulf. For the majority of them, these changes were transient and they soon readapted to their pre-war way of life. Private Colin McDonald, a keen boxer, found he was less tolerant of people during his leave in England:

'Everyone kept saying, you've changed. It's made you more aggressive. I didn't give a monkey's on that leave; if someone wanted to be hard with me, I hit him. I have changed; I reckon everyone's changed.'

Corporal Christopher Cassell thought any change in the soldiers was being overstated:

'I think the public in England got an impression of us lot all going to war, having this big, horrendous battle over there, and then, because of all the publicity about battle shock after Vietnam, a lot of people were thinking that was how we were going to come back. I only live in a small village. There are people there I haven't spoken to for years who wrote to me. I even got a postcard from Singapore from people I'd never heard of. And they all said, I hope you're coping alright and so on.

'When I went home it was a case of, are you feeling alright? You're not shaking or anything like that? They expect you to come back like a broken man who can't cope with life anymore. As if you had really changed in some fundamental way. And it wasn't like that.'

There were, however, some psychiatric casualties of the war. Captain Richard Gale, one of the Battalion medical officers, encountered them as patients on his return to Germany:

'I don't really think psychiatric is the right word. There are some stress-related problems. They range from not sleeping, to not being able to talk to the girlfriend because she doesn't understand me. There are those who think the Battalion's changed, when the Battalion is the same but they've changed. Then there are those with impotence problems, and the others who have been involved in minor thefts, totally out of character. I'm sure there are more, but most of them will cope, either by talking to their mates or by working it out themselves. I have had very little need to make any formal psychiatric referrals. Most of it can be sorted out with a bit of counselling from the community psychiatric nurse.'

Within the Staffords, the soldiers were informed that counselling was available on a voluntary basis. Lieutenant Andy Nye felt this form of support should have gone further:

'I've been very surprised that they've left it up to the individual soldiers to seek any help. I don't feel that there has been enough counselling since we've been back. On leave, I would wake up, bolt upright, sweating like a pig and feeling as if I'd had a really nasty night out. All I could remember was saying, I must tell him. I've got to tell Ted to get down. Which is perfectly understandable; you don't have to be a psychologist to work it out. But when I interviewed my platoon after leave, I said, I'm interviewing you to get things off your chest, and also to find out what your leave was like; but if I tell you about my leave first, then you'll know what I'm talking about.

'And I told them about waking up at five o'clock in the morning because I couldn't get out of the routine of getting up for stand-to at the beginning of leave. I spent all my time with Liesl, my fiancee, and a number of times I woke up with Liesl in floods of tears because of the things I was saying in my sleep.

'A lot of the guys had similar stories. Waking up, sleeplessness, bad dreams, and not being able to cope with a lot of strange people. There were those who went to the cinema and had to leave after 15 minutes because they couldn't handle that many people in a confined space. Because of all this, I am surprised that they haven't had a professional in to say, I don't care whether or not you think you need help, but you're going to talk to me. It does definitely help if you can talk to someone who understands.'

The physical casualties of the war had their recoveries to consider while the remainder of the Battalion was on leave. Corporal 'Angel' Heaven had healed up remarkably well from the shrapnel wounds he suffered during A Company's night attack, and was back in Falling-bostel when the main body returned. For Captain Toby Tennant, however, the process was proving to be a long haul:

'I was sent back from the Gulf once they had stabilised my condition, and I arrived back in England and was taken to RAF Wroughton on 3 March. Until I got back here, I'd had no contact with my family. My parents were away skiing when I actually got injured, but they came home as soon as they heard I had been injured. They were there to meet me when I got back to Wroughton, but I wasn't very well then. I had a pretty high temperature because of the infection in my legs; I must have got a lot of dirt and crap from Iraq in the wounds. My legs used to stink: I'd lift the sheet up and feel really quite ill. The smell of rotting flesh is quite horrendous. I felt sorry for the nurses who had to change those gunky sheets all the time.

'I was in Wroughton as an in-patient for 85 days. I think the whole healing process is going to take over a year. I'm happy to be alive, but I would like to know who did it, because whoever it was has messed me up good and proper. My legs were probably the best part of my body, because I could run quite fast and play sports, and they are really wrecked now. There is nothing I could do about it now, but I would like to know. I would like to talk to the guy. I don't think I would be angry if I met him now, I would just really like to talk to him.

'The shrapnel went into my left leg halfway between the ankle and knee, and shattered the tibia and fibula. The speed of it blew all the bone fragments out of the side. There is also quite a lot of muscle and nerve damage which will probably never fully recover. The right leg was hit by a bit of shrapnel which took out quite a lot of the muscle which lifts the foot up, so I've now got permanent foot drop; I've lost that muscle completely, it will never grow back. That's the problem leg.

'They took out my fibula on the right leg to allow room to push all the remaining muscles round. The idea is that they will take a tendon from the back which is working, lift it over the ankle joint, and attach it onto the tendons at the front so that hopefully I will be able to lift it again. If that doesn't work, they will probably have to fuse the ankle joint permanently.'

The war did have happier consequences for some soldiers. Private Stuart Burton, like a number of his colleagues, replied to one of the unsolicited letters sent to the Battalion by well-wishers;

'I wrote to a girl who had sent us a Christmas card, and she passed my letter on to a friend of hers who lived in Poole. The next thing I knew, I got a letter off her with a photo. I kept writing to her for the rest of the time we were out there, but I didn't meet her until I went back to England on leave. Anyway, I ended up marrying her at the end of May.'

As the garrison returned to its peacetime routine, there was time for the units who had fought with each other to reflect on their newly formed relationship. Having been little more than neighbouring units before the conflict, they had now shared an intense and unique experience. Major Simon Knapper had spent the entire land battle attached, with his company, to the Scots Dragoon Guards:

'We were very proud to be attached to the Scots DG. We had worked with them in BATUS, and actually knew their way of doing things better than we knew the Staffords. I think that they enjoyed having us along and they looked after us very well. We played up the 'England's infantry' bit to counter the 'Scotland's cavalry' tag, but there was no rivalry.

'The principle that we worked on was that we were always there when they needed us, but never in the way. They understood how we worked, and our strange ways and different needs. Despite our detachment from the Staffords, I don't think we suffered an identity crisis, quite the opposite in fact. We knew that if the Staffords really needed us for an attack we would have been called back, and would have been equally proud to have gone in with the Battalion.'

The Second in Command of the Scots Dragoon Guards, Major Mark Auchinleck, had always been impressed with the Staffords:

'As regards their professional ability, I first saw the Staffords on Soltau and then in BATUS, and I thought then that they were a bloody fine battalion. I would be absolutely happy to work with them again if anything like this were to crop up once more. I know those are the feelings of Colonel John, the Commanding officer, too. Watching the last attack go in at BATUS, he said, I've never seen anything so ferocious. I have no doubt at all, having seen them in BATUS and then on the ranges in Saudi Arabia, that had we come up against any more serious resistance, they'd have come up trumps then too.'

Captain Tom Wagstaff, one of the Prince of Wales's Own Regiment of Yorkshire officers who had served with the Staffords, had enjoyed being with the Battle Group:

'I think once it had finished and the "glory" side of things was starting to take effect, which it did, our reaction was to get away from the Staffords as quickly as possible, because we didn't want to get snowed under with all their jubilation. It was their battalion, and we wanted to get home to our battalion. But now time has gone past and we can look back on it, I think the Staffords did an excellent job. There was no animosity towards us within the Battle Group. When it came to flying back, for example, they let us go back first. They were very gracious.

'As far as I'm concerned, the point is that any county line regiment could have done what they did, but the fact of the matter was they were picked, they were the first to do everything, and they did it bloody well. I hope this doesn't sound too eulogistic, because of course there were occasions when tempers rose and you'd do the odd bit of slagging down: our regiment wouldn't do it that way, and all the rest of it. That happened with both the officers and the soldiers.

'But at the end of the day, everybody just pulled together and got on with the job in hand. The real sense of pride was in the fact that it wasn't the Paras, it wasn't the gladiators, the so-called elite units; it was a county infantry regiment who came from Germany with no experience of desert warfare, trained themselves up, and then did the business magnificently.'

As the research for this book was being carried out in June 1991, just over two months after the Battalion had returned from the Gulf, an atmosphere of foreboding, very real and almost tangible, hung over the barracks. The Secretary of State for Defence, Tom King, had announced that the proposed British Army cuts, embodied in the consultative document 'Options For Change', were to be implemented.

Everyone knew the infantry was going to suffer the proportionally greatest cut, and the futures of many old and famous regiments hung in the balance. Most of the Staffords did believe, however, that their regiment would escape the knife. This was not because of their recent involvement in Operation GRANBY, but because it was known that the most important criterion in deciding which regiments should go was their ability to recruit in a shrinking national employment market. The Staffords had always been a well recruited battalion; the influx of soldiers from other regiments at the outset of the campaign was due to the increase in establishment numbers, and not because of any innate shortage of manpower.

It was therefore a cruel and unexpected blow when, in the following month, it was announced that the Staffords were to amalgamate with the Cheshire Regiment. A vociferous and well-supported campaign was launched immediately, with the aim of communicating the feelings of all those who supported the Regiment (over 90,000 by the time their petition was presented to the Speaker of the House of Commons) that the proposed amalgamation was unjust and illogical. Sadly for all those involved, at the time of writing there has been no sign that the Government intends to alter its plans. If there is no last minute reprieve, the amalgamation will take place in 1993, and the Staffordshire Regiment in its present form will cease to exist.

The opinions of two different observers appropriately sum up the Staffords, and their role in the Gulf war. Firstly, General Sir Peter de la Billière, the overall commander in the Gulf:

'The Staffords were an outstanding example of the British infantry in action. I think there were probably many battalions which could have done just as well as them, but the point is they did do as well as they did, and they did it in war. It is a great credit to them, and their training and leadership, and the people that made up the Battalion that they achieved what they did achieve. You've only got to look at the gallantry awards to see how well the Staffords did compared with most other formations out there.

'They had a lot of new ground to break. They had this equipment out there that was in question as to its survivability. A great deal of initiative and trials and imagination was required, and they had all of that, and they were determined to make this equipment work. At the end of the day it worked so well, the number of pieces of equipment that got through to the end was almost 100% when at one stage we were talking, over the distance they were covering, of only 30% getting through because of attrition and breakdowns. So I think that is a great credit to their professionalism.

'Then, of course, they absorbed all these other regiments and showed us that, important as the county system is, it isn't the be all and end all of winning a war. We're basically and fundamentally British, and we're all British Army. And if we've got a challenge to face up to, and we're thrown together with men from other regiments, given the right leadership, which existed in the Staffords, then that will, far from being a problem, prove to be an enhancement. The regimental traditions and pride of each regiment will really be self-generating in terms of standards and pride.'

As a professionaly disinterested spectator, Kate Adie had this to say:

'Having visited the Staffords on a number of occasions, I must say, I was absolutely fascinated. I don't think anybody ever really sees the infantry at work. People see tank exercises on television. They might go to an open day somewhere and see helicopters flying. They see ships at sea, and they also see drama series which involve aircraft and ships, but not so much the army. Going to see Rambo films is a load of rubbish because it has got nothing to do with the real thing at all.

'To actually see what the infantry does is very rare. And it's quite amazing. It's raw battle; it's medieval, and I couldn't believe it when I first saw it. To see what the poor bloody infantry still does is an eye-opener.

'If the ground war had become a lengthy affair, the idea was that we might have transferred to Warriors. Then there would be this moment when they shout, out! We weren't at all keen. We looked at what the Staffords had trained to do. To sit in this huge, lumbering, sweaty, smelly, thing. Enclosed, with everything you have. Sitting on the ammunition with pots and pans above you, rifles, helmets, medical gear, gas masks, spades. Everything is with you in this monster; like an armadillo's interior, and it smells like it. And then, you realise, when it stops; that's when the real work starts. People just have to get out and start primitive warfare; where, by this time, you may see your enemy, face to face. It's something very few people will ever appreciate.'

Appendix

Awards for Gallantry and Meritorious Service

MILITARY CROSS
Major S J Knapper, MBE
Major J M Rochelle
MENTIONED IN DESPATCHES
Major C J Joynson
Private S P Savage
Sergeant M C Stalker
Captain M Steed
Captain R G Wootton
OBE
Lieutenant Colonel C T Rogers
BEM
Staff Sergeant A L Flower, REME
Lance Sergeant D A Ibbotson, Grenadier Guards
Sergeant I H Robinson
Corporal C B Sawrey
Mrs J Huyton
COMMANDER IN CHIEF'S COMMENDATION
Captain P E Smith
COMMANDER BRITISH FORCES MIDDLE EAST COMMENDATION
Corporal A J Hinton
USA COMMENDATION MEDAL FOR MERITORIOUS CONDUCT
Private J K Grainger

A Brief History of the Staffordshire Regiment (The Prince of Wales's)

The Regiment traces its origins back to 25 March 1705, when Colonel Luke Lillingston raised a regiment at the Kings Head public house in Lichfield, Staffordshire. The pub still exists in Lichfield and is decorated with Regimental memorabilia. In 1707, Lillingston's Regiment, as it was then known, was sent to Antigua in the West Indies where it remained until 1764, regularly in action against the French and Spanish. During this period, in 1751, it was redesignated the 38th Regiment of Foot.

In 1758, the 38th was joined in the West Indies by the 64th of Foot. Both regiments then fought in the American War of Independence and in 1782, to encourage recruiting, they were given territorial titles; the 38th became the 1st Staffordshire, the 64th became the 2nd Staffordshire, and both regiments began to wear the Stafford Knot emblem.

In 1793, the 80th Regiment of Foot was raised and assumed the title of The Staffordshire Volunteers. During the Peninsular War, the 80th was posted to India, taking part in a number of minor campaigns. Two battalions of the 38th fought with Sir John Moore's Army in Spain, and the 1st Battalion were among the first troops to enter France during the latter stages of the war.

At the end of the Peninsular War it was realised that the British Army couldn't cope with the increasing commitments of the Empire, and a number of new regiments were raised. The 98th of Foot was the fourth and final regiment of foot from which the present day Staffordshire Regiment evolved.

The Cardwell Reforms of 1870 eventually did away with the tradition of numbering British infantry regiments, and in 1881 the 38th and 80th amalgamated to become the 1st and 2nd Battalions The South Staffordshire Regiment; while the 64th and 98th became the 1st and 2nd

Battalions The Prince of Wales's (North Staffordshire) Regiment, later changed to The North Staffordshire Regiment (The Prince of Wales's) in 1920.

During the Great War of 1914–1918 there was a massive expansion in the size of the army, and a total of 35 battalions wore the badge of the North or South Staffords. Over 10,000 men lost their lives in action with these battalions. Seven Victoria Crosses were won by Staffords during this war, to add to the one won during the Indian Mutiny of 1857 and the two won in the Zulu War in 1879. From 1919 to 1939 various Stafford battalions were engaged around the world in India, Palestine, Greece and Ireland.

The Second World War of 1939–1945 again saw an increase in the numbers of Stafford badged battalions; this time 17 were raised. A further three Victoria Crosses were won by Stafford soldiers, two of them during the Battle of Arnhem. The 2nd South Staffords gained the unique distinction of being the only British battalion to gain two Victoria Crosses in one battle in the course of the war.

After the war the regiments shrank to one regular battalion apiece, but they continued to serve around the world in Hong Kong, Egypt, Cyprus, Palestine and Korea. In 1958 both regiments were posted to Germany, where they amalgamated to form the Staffordshire Regiment at Minden on 31 January 1959. After amalgamation the Regiment was involved in the suppression of the Ugandan mutiny, followed by a tour as the final British regiment to be based in the Persian Gulf. Since 1969 the 1st Battalion has spent regular tours of duty in Northern Ireland, and has adapted to the changing role of the modern infanteer.

In January 1987 the 1st Battalion was posted to Fallingbostel in West Germany, and in 1988 it became the second battalion of the British Army to convert to the armoured infantry role equipped with the Warrior fighting vehicle. After the Gulf War in 1990–1991, the 1st Battalion returned to Chester in England in December 1991 to prepare for a six month emergency tour in Northern Ireland in 1992. Amalgamation with the Cheshire Regiment is due to take place in 1993.

Chronological Outline of Events

1990	
24 May–2 July	Battle Group training at BATUS.
2 August	Iraqi invasion of Kuwait.
8 August	Prime Minister announces British Forces will be sent to the Gulf.
28 August	Iraq declares Kuwait its 19th Province.
6 September	Prime Minister pledges more troops to the Gulf.
9 September	Helsinki Summit. Bush and Gorbachev demand Iraqi withdrawal.
14 September	7 Armoured Brigade committed to Operation GRANBY.
11 October	Staffords advance party arrive at Al Jubail.
20 October	Main body starts to arrive at Al Jubail.
9 November	US President announces additional 150,000 troops for the Gulf.
16 November	7 Armoured Brigade declared operationally effective.
22 November	Defence Secretary announces 4 Armoured Brigade and supporting troops will be sent to the Gulf.
27 November	UN Security Council authorises use of force against Iraq.
28 November	John Major succeeds Margaret Thatcher as Prime Minister.
29 November	UN authorises 'the use of all necessary means to drive Iraq from Kuwait'.

6 December	Iraq announces release of all hostages.
1991	
2 January	US President sets deadline for Iraqi withdrawal.
9 January	Peace talks between US Secretary of State Baker and Iraqi Foreign Minister Aziz fail.
17 January	Operation DESERT STORM commences with massive air and Cruise missile strikes.
19 January	Staffords move to Concentration Area Keyes.
29 January	Iraqi incursion to Khafji.
15 February	Saddam Hussein announces withdrawal from Kuwait but shortly afterwards links this to unacceptable conditions.
16 February	Staffords complete in Forward Assembly Area Ray.
18 February	Soviet peace initiative. President Gorbachev meets with Iraqi Foreign Minister Aziz.
20 February	Saddam Hussein rejects Soviet peace initiative.
21 February	Troops are told G day is 24 February.
24 February	G day.
24–28 February	Operation DESERT SABRE, the liberation of Kuwait.
11 March	Advance party returns to Fallingbostel.
19–24 March	Main body returns to Fallingbostel.

Glossary

A1 Echelon	The grouping of vehicles and personnel which delivers combat supplies to F Echelon.
A2 Echelon	The grouping of vehicles and personnel which provides logistic support to A1 and F Echelons.
BCR	Battle Casualty Replacement.
Berm	Iraqi obstacle created by forming a wall of sand.
Cam	Camouflage.
Chagul	A water container which straps to the side of a vehicle and is designed to keep the water cool.
Chobham	Type of armour fitted to Challengers and Warriors during Operation GRANBY. Classified composition but enhances protection.
CO	Commanding Officer – of the Battalion.
Compo	Composite rations – issued in one, four or 10 man boxes, it provides each soldier with 24 hours of high calorie food and beverages.
Dhobi	Laundry.
Endex	End of the training exercise – a peacetime phrase.
F Echelon	The fighting troops.
FIBUA	Fighting in Built-Up Areas, ie. urban environments.
FUP	Forming Up Position, ie. prior to an assault or advance.
G Day	The day the Ground War started – 24 February 1991.
Gallery	Range used for basic zeroing and application shoots with rifle and light machine guns.
GKN	GKN Sankey – the defence firm which manufactures Warrior.

GRANBY	The codename for the British involvement in the Gulf War.
HE	High Explosive.
HESH	High Explosive Squash Head – a round fired by the Challenger gun.
H Hour	The time at which an operation commences.
LAW 94	Shoulder fired, hand-held light anti-tank rocket.
Mess tin	Tin pot with a handle used to cook rations in.
Milan	Medium range wire guided anti-tank missile.
MLRS	Multiple Launch Rocket System.
MTLB	Iraqi armoured personnel carrier.
NAAFI	Navy Army and Air Force Institute – colloquially, the supermarket run by the Institute.
Naiad	Automatic nerve agent detection and alarm equipment.
NBC	Nuclear, Biological and Chemical warfare.
No-duff	Not an exercise message but relating to a real incident.
OC	Officer Commanding, ie. superior officer.
PR	Public Relations.
QMSI	Quartermaster-Sergeant Instructor – a Warrant Officer Class II with a particular skill, normally from a corps.
Rarden	30 millimetre cannon fitted to Warrior and Scimitar.
REME	Royal Electrical and Mechanical Engineers – The Army's mechanics.
RSM	Regimental Sergeant Major – the senior Warrant Officer in the Battalion.
Sappers	Royal Engineers.
Satnav	Satellite navigation.
Scimitar	Lightly armoured reconnaissance vehicle.
Shamagh	Arab head-dress, used to protect the individual from the sun and dust.
Sitrep	Situation report.
T72	Soviet-designed main battle tank – the most modern tank in the Iraqi inventory.
TOGS	Thermal Observation Gunnery System – the thermal imaging sights fitted to Challenger tanks.
UKLF	United Kingdom Land Forces.
Warrior	Infantry armoured fighting vehicle.

Index